30088

GLOBAL YOUTH MINISTRY

REACHING ADOLESCENTS AROUND THE WORLD

GLOBAL YOUTH MINISTRY

REACHING ADOLESCENTS AROUND THE WORLD

TERRY LINHART AND DAVID LIVERMORE

YOUTH
SPECIALTIES

A

ACADEMIC

ZONDERVAN.com/
AUTHORTRACKER
follow your favorite authors

ZONDERVAN

Global Youth Ministry: Reaching Adolescents Around the World
Copyright © 2011 by Terence Linhart and David Livermore

YS Youth Specialties is a trademark of YOUTHWORKS!, INCORPORATED and is registered with the United States Patent and Trademark Office.

This title is also available as a Zondervan ebook. Visit www.zondervan.com/ebooks.

Requests for information should be addressed to:

Zondervan, *Grand Rapids, Michigan* 49530

Library of Congress Cataloging-in-Publication Data

    Global youth ministry : reaching adolescents around the world / Terry Linhart and David Livermore, editors.
       p. cm.
    ISBN 978-0-310-67037-7
    1. Church work with youth. I. Linhart, Terry, 1964- Livermore, David A., 1967- III. Title: Reaching adolescents around the world.
    BV4447.G555 2011
    259'.23 — dc22   2010051059

Cover design: SharpSeven Design
Interior design: David Conn

Printed in the United States of America

11 12 13 14 15 16 17 18 /DCI/ 20 19 18 17 16 15 14 13 12 11 10 9 8 7 6 5 4 3 2 1

BIOGRAPHIES

Malan Nel, D.D., is full-time director of the Centre for Contextual Ministry, Faculty of Theology, University of Pretoria, an ecumenical Centre offering continuing theological training for pastors from a wide range of denominations and other Christian groups. An author of more than 30 books, Malan is involved with many congregations in South Africa and preaches almost weekly somewhere in the country. He also served for many years (until 2008) as program coordinator for the Centre for Ministry Development (Excelsus) of the Dutch Reformed Church. For more information, visit his Web site: www.malannel.co.za.

CHAPTER AUTHORS

Jonny Baker works for the Church Mission Society developing and supporting mission in the emerging culture in the United Kingdom, catalysing, connecting, networking, and training mission and pioneer leaders. He lectures in mission and culture for the Centre for Youth Ministry. He's authored *Curating Worship* and *Alternative Worship*, and he's also contributed to *Mass Culture* and *The Rite Stuff* by Pete Ward. He runs proost.co.uk, is a London Independent Photographer, and blogs at jonnybaker.blogs.com.

Beth Baleke is assistant coordinator for children's (and youth) ministry for Scripture Union Africa. She was awarded a Billy Graham Scholarship to Wheaton College where she earned an MA in Communication. Her BA (Education) comes from Makerere University in Kampala, Uganda. She was a high school teacher and then director of media at Global Outreach Ministries before becoming a children's worker and then Uganda national director for Scripture Union. She is single with a 10-year-old adopted daughter.

Kenda Creasy Dean, Ph.D., is an ordained elder in the Baltimore-Washington Annual Conference (United Methodist) and professor of youth, church, and culture at Princeton Theological Seminary where she works closely with the Institute for Youth Ministry. Her most recent book is *Almost Christian: What the Faith of Our Teenagers Is Telling the American Church* (Oxford, 2010).

Anne De Jesus-Ardina (EdD candidate) is director of youth studies at the Alliance Graduate School, Philippines, where she graduated with a Masters in Youth Ministry. She is wife to Dr. Moises Ardina, Jr. and mother to Mikhael Adrian. Since 1985 she has been involved in youth ministry as a youth director, board member, adviser, and consultant to various youth organizations. Anne is also a freelance writer and conducts seminars/workshops around Asia.

Irena Dragaš was born in communist Yugoslavia, raised in a Christian home, lived through the war for Croatia's independence, college educated in the United States, returned to Croatia, and has been a part of the YFCC team since 1997. (And she is in love with the Adriatic Sea and a few other things and people.)

Rev. Jacob G. Isaac, M.Div., is founder and CEO of Kerygma, an urban youth ministry reaching out to Indian youth. He's also a trained behavior analyst, emotional intelligence coach, and D.Min. student at Bakke Graduate University in Seattle, Washington. He represents South Asia in the WEA Youth Commission and serves as the secretary of the Evangelical Fellowship of India Youth Commission. He is married to Sheela, and they have three daughters: Rebecca, Jerusha, and Deborah.

Dr. Nuwoe-James Kiamu, Ph.D., serves as president of the United Liberia Inland Church (ULIC), the Board of Governance of the Association of Evangelicals of Liberia (AEL), and Evangelical Theological Seminary of Liberia (ETSEL). He, his wife Eleanor, and four of their five children live in Monrovia, Liberia.

Dr. Lucas Leys, D.Miss., is international director of the Hispanic Division of Youth Specialties and vice president of publishing at Vida Publishers. He received his Ph.D. from Fuller Theological Seminary, where he graduated with honors, and he speaks to thousands of leaders and youth at conferences, conventions, universities, churches, seminaries, and schools. Lucas has authored more than 15 books and has been general editor for the G3 Bible. Lucas and his wife, Valeria, have two children.

Dr. Paul McQuillan is coordinator of research for Brisbane Catholic Education (63,000 students), an honorary fellow with Australian Catholic University and academic associate with Charles Sturt University and the Viktor Frankl Institute of Logotheraphy. His research interests include religious experience, youth ministry, and the logotherapy of Viktor Frankl.

Søren Oestergaard, Ph.D., is the director of Centre for Youth Studies and Christian Education in Copenhagen, Denmark, and has served as assistant professor in youth ministry at the School for Leadership and Theology in Oslo, Norway. You can reach him at soren@cur.nu.

Roz Stirling is director of youth and children's ministry for the Presbyterian Church in Ireland, a position she's held since January 1992. Since her own teenage and young adult years, she's passionately sought to communicate the wonder of Christian faith to teens through the Youth Bible class in her church, as a high school teacher, and in her work with InterVarsity Christian Fellowship and the Belfast YMCA. In 2000 she wrote Volume 3 of *Breakfast with God* (Zondervan), a snappy devotional for teens who don't read books.

Rev. Mark Tittley is a youth pastor at His People Christian Church in Johannesburg, South Africa. He has an honors degree in theology and passionately resources leaders for ministry through his Web site at http://www.ymresourcer.com. He's married to Debbie and has three children: Keegan, Ashley, and Drew Nguvu.

CONTRIBUTING AUTHORS

Aaron Arnold is executive director of youthHOPE (www.youthhope.com), a ministry focused on holistic youth development in 13 countries. Aaron has spent most of his 17 years in youth ministry in Chile, where he's conducted extensive research on Chilean youth culture and the church.

Edward Buri, M.Div., is youth pastor at St. Andrews Presbyterian Church in Nairobi, Kenya. He's author of *Love: The Christian Signature*. After graduating with a bachelor of commerce degree from the University of Nairobi, he earned his M.Div. and M.A. from Princeton Theological Seminary. Buri authors an electronic devotional, *The Weekly Faith Booster,* and is a director of Wima Consultants, inculcating integrity and values in Africa. He is an adjunct lecturer at Daystar University in Kenya and the Presbyterian University of East Africa.

Russ Cline directs the Leader Mundial Global Leadership Summit, a ministry of Extreme Response International that gathers leaders from around the world to focus on training, resources, community and coaching (www.leadermundial.com). After 16 years in Ecuador as leaders of Youth World, Russ and his wife Gina have relocated to California. They have three kids: Rheanna, Riley, and Raylin (and a dog named Raz).

Calenthia S. Dowdy, Ph.D., is associate professor of youth ministry and anthropology at Eastern University in St. David's, Pennsylvania. Her research interests include urban ministry and global youth culture with a particular focus on Brazilian shantytowns. Calenthia has also served as youth pastor and community center director in U.S. cities.

Mel Ellenwood is executive vice president of Josiah Venture, an organization focused on equipping young leaders throughout Eastern Europe to fulfill Christ's commission through the local church. He and his wife, Amy, have three children and live in the Czech Republic.

Judy Foo, M.Div., has been the director (Go Centre) of Youth With a Mission in Singapore since 2007. She also has served as a youth worker in a Methodist church in Singapore for 13 years and is involved in training and leading teams on Asian short-term missions. She received her M.Div. from Trinity Theological College in 1995.

Bill Hodgson is national director of Campus Crusade for Christ Australia. A youth ministry veteran of 30 years, he spent his first 20 as founder of Youth Ministries, Australia, training and coaching youth pastors for effectiveness in government schools. He and his wife, Faye, have four married children and two grandchildren. You can reach him at bill.hodgson@ccca.org.au.

Dr. Young Woon Lee, Ph.D., teaches Christian Education at Torch Trinity Graduate School in Seoul, Korea. Dr. Lee served as associate secretary of the Korean World Mission Council of the Billy Graham Center in Wheaton College. In addition, he served at various Korean-American churches as an educational pastor. Dr. Lee has taught Christian education at Seoul Theological University in addition to many local churches and denominations in Korea. He's the founder and director of KEM (Korea Educational Ministries, www.ceducational.com) and is married with two children.

Yoshito Noguchi graduated from Trinity Evangelical Divinity School with an M.Div. in 2002. He has been serving at Grace Mission in Osaka, Japan, as a youth pastor since 2003. He and his wife, Ami, have two kids.

Bert Roebben, Ph.D., is professor of religious education at the Faculty of Humanities and Theology of Dortmund University (Germany) (www.seekingsense.be). He taught previously at the Universities of Leuven (Belgium) and Tilburg (the Netherlands). He serves as chair of the International Association for the Study of Youth Ministry (www.iasym.net).

Astrid Sandsmark is assistant professor in practical theology at the Det Teologiske Menighetsfakultet (MF Norwegian School of Theology) in Oslo and responsible for the bachelor degree program

Youth, Culture and Faith. Before that, Astrid was a youth deacon in Oppegård, Norway, for 10 years.

Junior Zapata lives with his wife and two daughters in Guatemala City, Guatemala. He leads America Latina Schools and Ministries, a Christian school with more than 5,000 students that also includes broad services to the church and general community. One of Latin America's most recognized speakers and authors, his latest book, *Agorafobia* (Zondervan, 2009), is a bestseller.

CONTENTS

FOREWORD

MALAN NEL

Throughout my life as a pastor, and later as a full-time educator, I have been in resistance to what Sarah Little in 1968 called the "future church heresy." Youth are not the future church; they are an integral part of the faith community already. Whenever they are not treated and ministered to as part of the current church, the current church puts its own future in jeopardy. Youth do represent, however, *part of* the future church.

In the adult world that created many of the current culturally influenced churches, it is tough to transform or reform to a Christlike church. Such a transformation is often called deep change (Quinn 1996)—change in identity, purpose, culture, and operational procedures (Osmer 2008). And it is not cheap.

But my experience is that it is far less expensive to hire youth workers to sustain the 'separateness' of youth in their own programs, leaving the adult culture to choke to death, even to extinction. Any such church indeed faces extinction. Many churches are in this sense already on the endangered list and unfortunately not worth preserving. Dan Dick (2007) found that of the 717 churches he researched, half are what he calls 'decaying' (a word he apologises for) since it describes the bodily state after death.

This may be the picture of half the churches around the world.

On the other hand, treating youth and ministering to them as integral to the body already is very challenging. I understand why some churches opt for the cheap way out, sustaining both the self-ishness of (some) adults by keeping youth separate and catering to their needs and desires as if they will never become adults with children of their own (which happens all too soon). In more than one sense, an irreversible separation of generations is a fact. Our calling, therefore, is to facilitate a reconciliation of generations because we have (for far too long already) participated in separating them—and we have in many cases perfected the separation and are already reaping its fruits.

When I was asked to write a foreword to this volume, the invitation stated: "We don't see it as an academic research section, but rather as a pastoral (epistle?) letter from one who has the world in his view and is writing to the upcoming 'Timothys' (representing both men and women) who will be entering the world of global youth ministry. So, share your heart, the passion that Christ has given you for what you're doing at the Centre, and challenge us all to match your own fervour and diligence."

I was thrilled and honoured. To think that someone believes I can do that! When one has devoted one's life to ministry to, with, and through youth—and can still invest in the lives of the many people who serve the coming Kingdom—it is indeed a blessing beyond comprehension.

I could not start but with the first few paragraphs in this essay. This is the core issue in my understanding of what we do in youth ministry. I do, however, believe that this penny drops as difficultly and slowly (if it drops at all) as the one of understanding the missional nature (i.e., identity) of the faith community—the church.

I remember a day when a former Masters student of mine (who is now ministering in Northern Ireland) picked me up at the Belfast Airport. Even before we got to the car, he asked: "Prof, why did it take me eight years for the penny to drop?"

"Which penny?" I asked.

"That the church is either missional or it is no church at all," he replied.

"Be thankful that it dropped after only eight years," I answered. "I know many pastors and members for whom it never dropped."

The same is true for understanding that youth are an integral part of the body of Christ, and that they should be respected, treated, and ministered to as such.

How did we lose sight of this biblical truth regarding the church and youth? Where did we lose the plot? Was the Industrial Revolution the turning point? Were we caught up in the temptation to begin to minister to youth (in the YMCA in the beginning) as if they didn't have parents only because they were no longer living with their parents? And how did we miss the many wake-up calls like Lausanne 1 where it was stated so loudly and clearly that child evangelism can never bypass the parents? In the same way, youth ministry can never bypass the parents. Youth ministry should be home-centred and church-supported rather than church-centred and home-supported—to borrow a phrase from Ben Freudenburg (1998).

One may ask why this should be. The answer is that God is in the life-giving business, and so are we—parents (or any kind of father or mother) are primarily responsible for giving life. And where life is, God is at work (Psalm 127). The very fact that a person is alive is a sign of God at work. The one difference is that we in the faith community confess that life is a gift of God; many other human beings (breathing because of the same gift of life-giving breath you and I breathe with) do not confess that yet.

Youth is an integral part of this reality: They are alive and are as such gifts of God. But their faith or performance does not make them important and alive—God does. And we know that. They may not even know, love, or serve the Giver of Life yet—but it doesn't matter, because they already matter to God.

Both this book and youth ministry are about people who live by what we know. We represent a life-giving God in the lives of youth to whom God and God alone gave life as a gift.

We Christians love God and the life he has given us in Christ. We live because of God and our 'createdness' via our parents. What we got back through Christ and through the Spirit were our originally planned and purposed lives. Through Christ we can now live the lives God wanted us to receive, and live them to the full. Do children then become important only when they are old enough? If so, when is that? Youth are important because they are. There is no "PG-13" here. The very fact of them being alive is the ultimate reason for their importance.

It is for these reasons (and many more) that the scope of this volume is so important. *Global Youth Ministry* represents viewpoints from all over the world of youth ministry. And those viewpoints raise important questions: *How do we show respect to youth, and how do we minister to them wherever we are?* Maybe even more important: *What can we learn from one another as we show respect toward and minister to, with, and through youth?* Learning from each other is an important discipleship principle. Young adults are not only young in the business of being adults; they are also enveloped in their initial spiritual journeys—and they each need partners for this journey. This journey is difficult wherever you might find yourself on the planet, but some regions have it tougher, whether because of financial hardships, political turmoil, or human rights abuses, to name a few land mines.

This book will help us learn how to give *lebenshilfe* to youth with whom we have partnered for the journey. And in doing so, may they (and us working with them) discover that the joy is in the journey as much as it is in the destination. My prayer is that every page of this volume will contribute, in its own way, to the encouragement and empowerment of the rest of us to invest our lives in making life livable and worthwhile. May we contribute to a fuller understanding and experience of Jesus' words, "I have come that you may have life and life everlasting" (John 10:10b). It takes a deep understanding of grace to confess that "in life and in death Christ is my gain" as Paul does in Philippians 1:21.

Finally, a word of deep appreciation to the editors for taking the initiative of putting this volume together—may it become a handbook for many who are researching youth ministry around the world.

REFERENCES

Dick, D.R. 2007. *Vital Signs. A Pathway to Congregational Wholeness.* Nashville, TN: Discipleship Resources.

Little, S. 1968. *Youth, World and Church.* Richmond, VI: John Knox.

Osmer, R.R. 2008. *Practical Theology. An Introduction.* Grand Rapids, MI: Eerdmans.

Quinn, R. 1996. *Deep Change: Discovering the Leader Within.* San Francisco, CA: Jossey-Bass.

ACKNOWLEDGMENTS

We dedicate this book to the thousands of Christian youth workers scattered across the globe who diligently care for and minister to the youth of the world: *We hope the voices in this book not only represent your passion and commitment, but also encourage others to join you in global youth ministry.*

This book would not have been possible without the sharpening influence of our colleagues in the International Association for the Study of Youth Ministry (http://www.iasym.org) and the Association of Youth Ministry Educators (http://www.aymeducators.org).

We are honored to have Dr. Malan Nel of the University of Pretoria write the Foreword. Few deserve the first words of the first book on global youth ministry more than he does. He models for all a passion for excellence in youth ministry and academic study mixed with a Christlike gracious and collaborative spirit. He has served as a kind mentor to so many in the field of international youth ministry.

This book is about the authors of the various chapters and their selfless sacrifice to contribute and represent many others. To those we were unable to include, may the voices of those herein be your echo.

Thanks to those who helped guide us at various junctures along the way: Dr. James Hampton, Dr. Kenda Creasy Dean, Mark Oestreicher,

Mitchell Kim, Graeme Thompson, David Rock, Robert Brandt, Aaron Arnold, and Mindi Godfrey. Thanks also to the staff of J-Life Ministries in South Africa for providing a wonderful setting for writing, editing, and learning.

This book would not have been possible without the administrative assistance of Melissa Diaz and Renee Kaufman. Mark Root (Bowen Library at Bethel College) once again proved his research and bibliographical prowess for yet another publication. Thanks to Melisa Peebles for her gifted writing and editorial review and to Adrienne Searer for her research assistance. Thanks to Tony Wiltse and Courtney Chapman for their helping with various aspects of the project. We extend special gratitude to Kent Eby, assistant professor of Intercultural Studies at Bethel College (Indiana), for his expert review.

We are most grateful to Jay Howver for believing in the vision of what this book could be and his commitment to global youth ministry. Dave Urbanski edits with grace and skill and makes everything better—for that we are so grateful. Thanks to Roni Meek and Jesse Hillman who helped us navigate the logistical aspects of the book process. Thanks to Laura Gross and Janie Wilkerson for proofreading every jot and tittle and making sure of accuracy.

To Kelly and Linda, thanks for being our constant voices of reason and faithful partners in life. And thanks to the youth in our own homes: Lauren, Jayson, Sean, Emily, and Grace.

INTRODUCTION

The growth of Christian youth ministry around the world has been nothing short of phenomenal. In regions where strategic ministry to youth barely existed 15 years ago, you'll now discover well-organized ministries with established histories of effectiveness. Where no youth ministry existed five years ago, a fledgling group of adults works to establish a regular presence among the young people in a community.

A quick Internet search will reveal a growing number of international conferences and regional summits on youth ministry, often coordinated by dynamic cross-national support networks. The conferences draw together youth ministry leaders from various countries for training, encouragement, spiritual renewal, and the sharing of effective strategies. In addition, numerous Web sites facilitate ongoing support and communication necessary for global youth workers who are often quite isolated from other like-minded youth workers.

The latest result of this global growth is that many universities and seminaries now offer courses related to cross-cultural and international youth ministry—and more college- and seminary-level students study global youth ministry.

WHY THIS BOOK?

This book attempts to provide a single reference in regard to the research and perspectives shaping international youth ministry. This text includes various theoretical and theological directions for youth ministry, champions what's happening globally in local contexts, and seeks to meet the growing need for a college-level textbook about international youth ministry. Most of all, we hope the book helps propel global youth ministry toward an effective and transformative future and becomes a helpful resource for those interested in global youth ministry.

We set out from the very beginning to coordinate a widely representative book that features a broad cross section of voices with significant influence in their particular regions. One of the many reasons for this is because "ninety-seven percent of the world's formally trained youth workers live and work in the United States, ministering to less than 3% of the world's youth population." That statistic was an informed estimate made back in 1992 by global youth ministry leader Randy Smith of Youth Ministry International.[1] At the time, it was an accurate assessment and used as a mantra to encourage North American youth leaders to invest in ministry overseas. However, the remarkable and exponential growth of youth ministry around the world over the last 19 years has caused many to wonder if this stat has changed.

In the last decade, a surge in formal youth ministry initiatives suggests that Smith's estimate has indeed changed. Certainly the need for theological education and practical training remains, and the needs are still many. However, we're encouraged by the level of support and education that now exists in all of the regions of the world. And Western youth workers can learn much from their brothers and sisters in Christ in other contexts.

Most of all, this book is a chorus of youth ministry leaders from around the globe, the ones who lead and shape youth ministry in their particular contexts—not just experts who study from afar. What each writes about is important to successful youth ministry in his or her part of the world. While there will be contrasting views among the authors, it's all part of the breathtaking medley that truly is *global* youth ministry.

We constructed a list of prominent leaders in youth ministry around the world—non-North American authors who are influential beyond their country's borders with recognized track records of shaping youth ministry through leadership and published writing. (Any North American included in these pages had to have done extensive research in a different part of the world or spent significant time in a non-North American context, shaping the practice and growth of youth ministry in that region.)

Two exceptional events happened in the construction of this book. First, each author on our list agreed to contribute to the text, an amazing response from such in-demand leaders. However, the second—and perhaps most treasured—feature of the book's development has been the level of servanthood, collaboration, and shared passion for Christian youth ministry that each author has demonstrated. They each exhibited a graciousness and selfless commitment that truly reflected Christ's love and grace. We are hopeful that you'll experience the authors' passion for global youth ministry both through the text and between the lines.

In this book you'll encounter a wide range of views and experiences, some scholarly and some quite practical. The authors come from a variety of Christian traditions, which their writing reflects. This diversity gives a mixture that accurately reflects *global* youth ministry. Attend most any truly "international" youth ministry conference and you'll encounter a similar range of perspectives. You'll find scholars concerned with the theological and theoretical, as well as practitioners working to develop the practical and local expressions of those youth ministry concerns. Each is vital for future success in this growingly pluralistic world. Christian youth ministry connects to state churches and free churches, Protestants and Catholics, mainline and community churches, schools and youth centers, Pentecostals and Evangelicals, mission agencies and community centers, and other collective expressions. If you desire to step into the global arena, then developing wisdom through listening to—

and learning from—a wide range of learned, experienced people is a necessary step.

HOW THE BOOK IS CONSTRUCTED

We wanted to provide an influential text for a wide range of audiences, while championing a global ideal in an educational setting. As such, this book serves as a textbook for classroom use but is not designed to merely impress other academics, leaving others lost in esoteric language and historical terms. This book is designed, simply, for one who wants to learn more about global youth ministry from global leaders who know it well.

We grouped the authors together by region to provide a helpful range of perspectives and maintain some consistency. The regions are not labeled and in no particular order within the book. We begin with a chapter on youth ministry in the UK from Jonny Baker then "travel" all around the globe before ending in North America with a chapter by Kenda Creasy Dean. We then close the book with a series of short essays that focus on getting involved in global youth ministry.

For educators, the book will best serve as a companion text connected to a particular discipline. It can also serve as a primary text in classes or training venues focused on global youth ministry. Each chapter is relatively short and features discussion questions that can be used in a variety of training or educational settings. Assignments can focus on chapters or on regions, and the various case studies will help bring some of the topics to life for readers.

Our hope and prayer is that this book is just a beginning, a launching point for readers to explore this vast subject and take the next step on their journey as they seek where God may have them invest in global youth.

CHAPTER ONE

THE YOUTH
OF THE WORLD

TERRY LINHART AND DAVID LIVERMORE

You've moved to New Delhi to join a team of missionaries from around the world. Your team just met with a small group of Indian pastors to assess the needs of the church in northern India. The pastors are unified in their agreement that one of the primary ways they need help from your team is in reaching their youth. More and more, they see their youth getting drawn into the MTV/Bollywood culture and away from their families and the church. The most outspoken Indian pastor has just returned from nine months' study leave in the United States where he observed the huge enterprise of youth ministry in local churches. He attended a church near Atlanta where the youth group was essentially a "church within a church." They have their own pastor, their own worship service, their own small groups, and so on. He's convinced that kind of segmented ministry is what the Indian church needs, especially in New Delhi. He asks your team how you can help the Indian church develop a youth ministry like this.

Some of the other Indian pastors are not so sure this is what's needed. They fear this kind of approach to ministering to youth will further fragment the youth from the older generations. They also believe youth just need instruction to flee the evils of modern culture and be challenged to commit to church. What do you think? How will you—together with the missionary team and pastors—discern what's best for Indian youth and ultimately for the Indian church? Describe what you consider to be the most important issues. What's your advice?

What images come to mind when you think of the youth of the world? Do you envision children playing on a dusty road somewhere in rural Africa? Maybe you think of an advertisement photo that depicts a racially diverse group of teens, posing and smiling toward the camera. Perhaps you recall a photo you took of a specific child or teenager while on a short-term mission trip. The media provides us plenty of cross-cultural images which will quickly shape our view of that culture if we allow them to. It's easy to find headlines and topics related to global youth, and it's even easier to develop stereotypes that may not accurately reflect reality. The greater (and natural, but damaging) temptation is to push forward in global youth ministry without studying culture, context, and church, while at the same time ignoring contributions from other disciplines that sharpen our knowledge and understanding.

It's a given that global youth workers desire to be effective in their ministries—to be faithful to God's call, passionately pursue change in their communities through teenagers, and participate in God's mission to the world.[1]

But our effectiveness gets a bit trickier because our own cultural upbringing often gets in the way. We don't like some of the steps required for effective global youth ministry as we confront cultural moorings and worldviews, because global youth ministry requires a humble posture of perpetual learning, engaging new ideas, and evaluating present practices. It's easier to keep doing what's familiar and what's always "worked" in our own contexts—even if it clearly isn't working anymore.

THE GROWTH OF GLOBAL YOUTH MINISTRY

The youth of the world present one of the greatest challenges and opportunities for the church today. With the same determination that the Western church displayed in response to the burgeoning youth culture after World War II, a similar international church-led movement has developed with the youth of the world in mind.

The growth of global youth ministry stemmed from three world-wide developments: (1) the phenomenal growth of cross-cultural short-term mission trips exposed millions to the world's needs, particularly those of children and youth; (2) international work became more palatable due to increased comforts and sanitation, affordability of travel, and the emergence of English as a global language; and (3) globalization has brought the children and youth of the world to our television screens, whether in the form of marketed consumerism or news headlines that show the faces of kids in need.

Half of the world's population is under the age of 25, a percentage that will grow before it gets smaller. In some countries, more than 70 percent of the population is younger than 25, and 90 percent of those live in developing countries.[2] By the year 2025, 23 percent of the world will be considered "youth," one of the largest generations in history.[3] Despite its size, it's not an economically powerful group. More than half the youth of the world survive on less than $2 a day.[4] Yet, the potential for such a large demographic seems unlimited, and this generation will define much of the future for every region of the world. So it's no wonder that corporations, church and mission groups, colleges and seminaries, service agencies, parents, and governments increasingly focus on children, youth, and the concerns of adolescents.

A review of the literature on global youth shows that the definition of *youth* differs from region to region. Youth pastors in North America[5] attend the graduation parties of their 18-year-olds as their last official youth ministry contact with those teens, while youth workers in India include people up to the age of 35 as members since the government of India protects them under the "Youth Policy Act."[6] Some cultures don't even have a word in their language that means "adolescence"; rather they employ a variety of terms that refer to young people, an acknowledgement of the difficulty for a single term to represent such a diverse group among its citizens.

Not all scholars view the circumstances facing the youth of the world in the same way. Some focus on the impact of external, globalizing forces and how global youth culture eclipses the local. They also focus on adolescents' similarities and describe a collective youth culture emerging around the world.[7] Others disagree, citing the concept of an emerging global youth culture as a Western idea (or ideal), noting that adolescence differs markedly in various cultures. The emergence of adolescence, however, hasn't been just a Western phenomenon as Klaus Hurrelmann summarized in his research on adolescence in 31 countries: "In all countries, adolescence has become a difficult and sensitive phase in the life course."[8] Still, it's easy to argue that this adolescent period has been a product of Western culture and spread through globalization, which has resulted in both positive and negative effects. According to the United Nations: "Globalization offers clear economic opportunities and benefits, but comes with substantial social costs that often appear to affect young people disproportionately, given their tenuous transitional status within an uncertain and rapidly evolving global context."[9]

Often these differences develop within various academic disciplines—sociology, anthropology, developmental psychology, theology, and even education. As you read literature regarding global youth, discerning the "discipline" from which each author writes will help you understand his or her perspective—and develop your own knowledge base.

No matter the discipline, as the world economy develops and becomes increasingly interconnected—fueled by multinational companies whose wealth dwarfs that of many countries—the youth of the world have become its champions, beneficiaries . . . and victims. How global connectedness affects the local church (for example, culture, faith, and lifestyle) has become a focus of youth ministry leaders around the world.[10]

Some carry the effects of globalization and immigration further, noting the potential for adverse effects on the religious beliefs of children and youth, particularly as cohesive local religious communities lose their ability to influence local culture in significant ways.[11] Yet if churches and Christian ministries adopt reactive stances to global and local shifts, they also may lose their transformational influence in the local culture.[12]

The imperative is, therefore, that at the intersection of church and culture, youth workers will stand alongside youth as they navigate the various currents, thereby assisting in the faith development of young people. The problem is that the intersection changes its location continuously, and traffic is never still. In fact, global youth workers will have to navigate numerous intersections along their journeys.

INTERSECTIONS FOR GLOBAL YOUTH WORKERS
The Message of Global Youth Ministry

While there is a theological and biblical core to Christian youth ministry, the way we communicate the message presents a challenge for global youth workers. You'll see a range of emphases in this book. Do we work to protect young people from the world (and keep them "good"), or should global youth ministry do something more? What does it mean for youth to have faith, and how should they demonstrate their commitment to Christ? Should culture have a role in shaping those expressions? How should we present the gospel message and develop young people's theological understandings?

> What words do you use to describe the message of your ministry? What words *should* we use— *Gospel, the Christian story, God's love, kingdom of God, God's Word,* any others? How can a cultural context affect our word choices?

Christian youth ministry centers on the biblical message concerning the life, death, and resurrection of Jesus Christ. Therefore, it should purpose to help young people build their faith in Jesus Christ.[13] But at the same time, that message is communicated to— and then interpreted by—listeners through culturally influenced filters. Some of the best models and methods in one culture may be ineffective or, worse yet, offensive in another; materials and methods that challenge and captivate in one culture don't translate well and may even miss the mark in communicating cross-culturally. In fact, we often aren't aware of our cultural moorings until we see them from another's perspective.

To unwind this problem, leaders ought to learn from their host cultures by asking exact questions of their friends in these new cultures and observing a variety of experiences within them. The ability to differentiate among people, ministries, regions, and even dialects in a culture are important indicators of a growing knowledge base. With each "brushstroke" of learning that you acquire, you'll paint a clearer image of the cultural issues. And that takes a significant amount of humility and time.

Global Youth Ministry Is a Theological Enterprise

One of the central—and often busier (to new practitioners)—intersections in global youth ministry crosses theological knowledge with youth ministry practice. In many parts of the world, ministry flows out of a stated connection to historical and practical theology, and the conversation among youth workers uses theological vocabulary. The theological conversation is wide-ranging, a diversity that forces global youth workers to develop their theological knowledge base and their ability to use this knowledge in order to think, act, and respond faithfully. Therefore, if your ministerial training and interests have focused on methodology, the push to articulate theologically may be challenging, as well as surprising.

Cross-cultural ministry requires an ability to address issues with a theological sensitivity—a balance between historic disciplines of theology and practical theology. Though many in the West likely champion the latter, the former remains crucial to navigating this crowded intersection. One way to ramp up theological knowledge is to read theological books written by scholars from the desired cultural perspective in which you want to minister. And then you may find yourself successfully discussing issues related to ancestral worship with church leaders in Swaziland or China, developing a way to communicate a theology to deal with materialism in Asia or Brazil, or conducting a knowledgeable conversation on the role and function of various Christian sacraments in Eastern Europe or Thailand.

Global Systemic Issues' Influence on Local Youth Cultures

One of the more important discoveries we can make about new cultures comes from listening for and learning where external forces intersect with indigenous (in other words, internal) cultural values. It's crucial to listen to those within the culture share how their cultural world has changed due to globalizing influences. As you read this book, you'll see that the West has tremendous influence in various cultures—and the responses to that vary. To what extent have youth adopted new cultural practices that came from outside their culture? How has the globalized world intersected with the local culture, and how has this influenced church life and faith practices?

In many regions, *economics* places demands on young people, including participation in the general workforce at younger ages and oftentimes away from home. *Health care*, or lack of it, affects the developmental viability of the youth in a particular region. *Schools and education* shape how youth think and what they think. The role of— and transition to—*marriage* is a significant cultural component that often shapes how one interacts with the institutional church. Finally, *access to technology* and the ability to use it fluidly is one of the most dominant factors for young people. Generally speaking, those with access to technology are better educated, healthier, and face a more affluent future than those who cannot participate in the global world. Of course, this view is laden with assumptions shaped by our Western perspectives; but as globalization influences the world, these are realities that scholars are concerned with and will study.

Nowhere on earth can this tension be seen more clearly than in Africa. Historically, the people of Africa have had to endure strong influences (and that's putting it mildly) from Easternization (Islamic, Arabic), Westernization (Christianity, literacy), and globalization (external, technological, economic).[14] If you travel for any length of time in Africa, you'll observe the competing forces at play. And the exogenous influences often look more appealing to youth than the indigenous ones.

The temptation for global youth workers is to participate in the exogenous, to perpetuate a trivialization of the local, and, in the process, demean and alienate others and miss potentially rich opportunities to participate in the communities in significant ways. The wise youth worker, however, will find ways to harness aspects of global and local in order to realize effective ways to connect them to Scripture, the gospel, and the ongoing work of the church.

Globalization and the Economic Divide

The economic perils of the world—particularly that of widespread unemployment—intersect with a growing population to create a global traffic jam. While the rich can avoid the perils of that crossroads, the gap continues to widen as many countries note their shrinking "middle class" with larger percentages of the population falling into adverse economic and employment situations. Global youth ministry leaders need to recognize how significant economics are.

Arguably this significant divider of people is one of the least broached in diversity discussions. Social class and its products (for instance, real estate and who can afford to live where, who has access to quality education) divide people within every local context. The gap is widening between those students with access to education, technology, and medical care, and students without those assets— and the effects are dramatic. In many countries, the border between urban centers and rural communities is marked with more significance than borders that define nationalities. It's no wonder, then, that urban centers attract more youth every day—many without parents—all seeking better lives through better pay and its benefits. And for some youth, much of this money is sent back to family members living in the rural regions.

Imagine that someone moved cross-culturally to start a youth ministry in your context. Which of these intersections would be the least obvious to them at first? Which one would be the most crucial for them to navigate well?

Global Youth Ministry Is Holistic

In our own cultures, youth ministry's role is usually message-centered, and that message dominates our thinking. But global youth ministry reveals that all of human life intersects with faith, requiring responses that feature more than well-crafted messages or guitar-led worship songs with attractive multimedia backgrounds. We encounter the needs of people along the road of everyday life, often beaten up like the Jewish traveler in Jesus' parable of the good Samaritan.[15] We stand at this intersection, and the direction of our response will be telling. Do we sidestep holistic issues on our way to the meeting or study? Do we turn and avoid the need, engrossed in our book or the latest SMS on our mobile? Global youth ministry must move from the programmatic and information-dispensing moorings and catch the wind toward a more holistic and incarnational presence in communities and the youth and families who live there.

This list of intersections is not exhaustive, but the aforementioned have significant traffic and have caused others to get held up in their progress. There will be others, of course, but the reason many of us enter global youth ministry is that we believe that God has not only gifted us or called us, but also given us pioneering spirits. It's our hope to encourage you not to shrink back from the challenges, but to embrace them as you move into a new culture, press into unknown situations, and exercise great faith, prayer, wisdom, grace, and patience.

ESSENTIAL QUESTIONS FOR GLOBAL YOUTH MINISTRY

We are struck by the humility of those who seem to fare well in cross-cultural ministry—not just in regard to their leadership abilities, but their true ministry to others in a new culture. Those who experience success exhibit a dependence on God, a love of the culture and people, and a never-ending ability to ask and attempt to answer key questions.

There are several important questions that require exploration as one hears the voices of the contributors to a book such as this one. In fact, as you read this book, it will be helpful to keep a running list of questions as you learn about global youth ministry. The following are several essential questions that have helped others frame their learning and will be helpful for your own observation, reading, and reflections.

What recurring themes do you observe?

When you study youth ministry around the world, you encounter realities that most any youth worker can identify with—from the exuberant enthusiasm of youth to the emergence of teenage independent thinking. In the chapters that follow, you'll read about youth ministries that all sound very familiar, but are found in countries such as Norway, Cambodia, and Kenya. Nurturing relationships, providing places to belong, and living in dynamic tension with society mirror emphases in mainstream North American youth ministry (and elsewhere). And there's value in starting with the common themes across global youth ministry.

What do you learn about adolescent identity that seems consistent in most places globally? How do you interpret the influence of history, culture, and society upon what happens among youth? What's the relationship between the church at large and youth ministry? Pay attention to the common threads that appear from one place to another.

What thematic differences do you observe?

For many readers, particularly those from places like the United States, differences are often minimized because being different reflexively means being "bad" or "wrong." But the most interesting points of insight for youth ministry both nearby and far away are found by digging through the contrasts from one place to the next. Why are Japanese youth so fearful of their parents dying? What does courtship look like for Indian or Liberian youth? How does technology impact youth in rural China compared to those living in Beijing?

A number of European contexts have been included in the book. What differences emerge when comparing one European context to the next? How do the European perspectives and sections differ from other sections of the book? How does the history of a particular nation impact the way youth ministry functions? Does missionary activity in particular countries and contexts shape variances in youth ministry there?

How do cultural values shape and change the way youth ministry should occur? Lean into these differences and learn from them. Don't settle for simplistic explanations to these significant questions. Some differences might even appear to be contradictions. Remember: Figuring out what to do with the differences that emerge isn't nearly as important as taking the time to discover where the differences lie and then continually dig beneath them.

What's the role of the West?

As you read the contributions from our chorus of youth ministry leaders, consider what role places such as Australia, the United States, Canada,[16] and the United Kingdom should have in the global youth ministry arena. Some of the authors describe meaningful contributions from missionaries, while others aren't so sure that the influence of the West has been positive.

It's a foregone conclusion that the majority of Christians don't live in the Western world anymore. Most Christians today are people of color who live in Latin America, sub-Saharan Africa, southern India, and southern China. In fact, on the global scale, 70 percent of Christians live *outside* North America and Western Europe. However, the power hasn't shifted from the Western world of youth ministry to these places. Most of the decision-making, large youth ministry conferences, money, published books, and youth ministry networks are still led by and oriented toward English-speaking people in Western contexts. While Western churches should be involved in international youth ministry, we're to think carefully (and humbly) about what our role should be. Therefore, we recommend that you allow the global voices in this book to shape the way you consider what your future role may resemble.

Who gets to speak for youth ministry in a particular place?

To what degree can we obtain reliable accounts of youth ministry in various parts of the world? That question applies to the contributions in this book, and it applies to any of the discussions, conferences, and presentations about global youth ministry—ours included. The authors selected for this book were carefully chosen. We endeavored to find individuals who are well-connected to youth ministry in their contexts and would write not only about their specific organizations or ministries, but also rely upon data and broader networks to provide broader views of youth ministry in particular regions.

At the same time, we all have our biases and choose to emphasize our own experiences and observations. Therefore, we recommend that you discover the flavor of the personalities and cultures in each chapter and look for what you can learn about the local contexts through the authors' contributions. The same applies whenever you meet a missionary or youth worker from a particular part of the world. Listen carefully to what they say and file it away to compare with future things you learn about the place.

Among those working in China, there's a saying, "Whatever is said about China is probably true." In other words, China is so huge that you can probably find an example of something said somewhere about someone. Are Christians still being persecuted? Yes, in some precincts they are. Are Christians free to worship openly? Yes, in many cities they can freely worship. Do house churches and registered churches get along? In some places the underground church and registered church work together, and in other places they don't.

It takes deeper research to understand if what you hear is a norm for most of China. For instance, did you know that the world's largest printer of Bibles is located in China? Since 1988, they've printed more than 55 million Bibles for use all over the world—including North America. And more than 43 million of those Bibles have been printed for the church in China.[17]

Most countries aren't as large as China. But when you learn something about a place, ask yourself: Is it generally true about the place as a whole or is it an isolated example? Is it just one side of a story—or not true at all? Whose voices don't you hear in a particular culture? Think about that as you encounter snapshots of youth ministry in various places around the world. Then draw upon prevailing research to help answer those questions.

What's the role of short-term missions in global youth ministry?

We've both researched and written broadly on short-term missions.[18] The ongoing momentum behind short-term missions requires careful attention to what's going on in global youth ministry. Youth workers and churches around the world aren't simply waiting for foreigners' next visits to impart them with new knowledge and skills. As reflected in the following chapters, there are abundant examples of grassroots efforts in youth ministry around the world, led by dynamic and gifted local church leaders, parents, adults, and youth.

The global reality prompts reflection on how to better support these ecclesiological responses from within various cultures—but the answer isn't to abandon all short-term missions. The objective of short-term missions needs to be discerned in light of what's going on among youth globally. We each share an overarching value that there is much to learn from those who lead youth ministry in other cultures. This attitude differs from a philosophy of short-term missions where those who go are the experts—and this value also demands that we cannot completely answer this question on our own, but need to invite others to answer it with us. How can Western youth and their leaders develop reciprocal relationships with other youth and leaders globally? When planning short-term trips, how do we ensure that we're meeting a need on both sides of the border? How do we make sure we aren't simply exploiting the locals and ministries of the places we visit for merely our own benefit? These are the kinds of questions you'll be able to respond to more fully when hearing the voices that speak in the pages that follow.

What are my own perspectives on adolescence, and why is that important?

Scholars generally agree that Western culture significantly influences the way we view and discuss the adolescent period of life. So if you view youth as a period between childhood and adulthood during which we explore our identities, push back from the authority of Mom and Dad, and constantly hang out with our peers who dramatically influence our moral choices and direction in life—that's a Western ideal. As such, corporations market youthfulness as the ideal and use images to define what it means to be young. Because adolescence developed in the Western—and predominantly North American—culture, we often see it through that lens. If adolescence had emerged in tribal or Eastern culture, we'd be living in a very different world. Not wrong. Just different.

Though we worked for worldwide representation, this book reflects the Western-based history of youth ministry thought; the majority of authors originate from a Eurocentric/Western perspective. The obvious response is that we need to seek out and listen to rising youth ministry voices from the Southern Hemisphere and other often-overlooked regions in the world that are still rising fast.

For the global youth worker, danger lurks behind our actions in another culture. If we don't recognize our own biases and cultural perspectives, we risk offense, ineffectiveness, and more damage than good. And we may never know it when we're trespassing. Just as not every approach and model for youth ministry works in every setting within America, it's only more pronounced in the rest of the world. You'll see that tension from some of the authors as they discuss youth ministry in light of North American models. That's an important tension. Cultural effectiveness is a significant issue for global youth workers.

How do my cultural assumptions shape my worldview?

Just as we need to consider our perspectives about adolescence, we also need to apply the same kind of thoughtfulness to our overall cultural perspective. As noted earlier, we see everything through our own cultural lens—including youth ministry. This makes it difficult sometimes to separate what's cultural from what's a transcendent, biblical truth for youth ministry in all places. Therefore, trust the Holy Spirit to guide you along, study the Scriptures, and join with a culturally diverse community of believers to discern what's right, what's wrong, and what's merely "different."

As you read the following pages, more questions are likely to surface. Keep track of them and use the chapters that follow to nudge you forward in your journey to understand the mosaic of youth ministry around the world.

DISCUSSION QUESTIONS

1. What international experiences have you had? Write down every country you've visited for longer than three days. Next to each, list your reasons or motivations for going there. What has prompted you in the past to cross cultures?
2. Put a check next to those countries in which you watched or participated in a youth ministry while you were there. Reflect on those experiences and describe three observations about international youth ministry that you've made as a result.
3. Where does your interest in youth ministry intersect with your relationship with Jesus Christ? Do you feel as though God has called you to minister to the world of youth in some way?
4. Write down a few expectations that you have for this book. What do you want to gain by reading these pages? Once you've finished writing those down, imagine that a veteran youth worker from Thailand or Brazil is looking over your list and commenting freely on your expectations. What do you think he or she would say you should expect from reading this book?
5. Exercise: On a piece of paper, write down each of the subhead questions in this chapter. Then begin to fashion some answers that you can give to each.

RESOURCES

Brown, B. Bradford, Reed W. Larson, and T. S. Saraswathi, eds. *The World's Youth: Adolescence in Eight Regions of the Globe.* Cambridge, UK: Cambridge University Press, 2002.

Helve, Helena, and John Bynner, eds. *Youth and Social Capital.* London: The Tufnell Press, 2007.

Mortimer, Jeylan T., and Reed W. Larson, eds. *The Changing Adolescent Experience: Societal Trends and the Transition to Adulthood.* Cambridge, UK: Cambridge University Press, 2002.

Nilan, Pam and Carles Feixa, eds. *Global Youth?: Hybrid Identities, Plural Worlds.* London: Routledge, 2006.

Osmer, Richard R., and Kenda Creasy Dean, eds. *Youth, Religion and Globalization.* Münster, Germany: LIT Verlag, 2007.

CHAPTER TWO

YOUTH MINISTRY CHANGES MORE THAN YOU KNOW

JONNY BAKER

A quiet murmur began in youth ministry in the United Kingdom in the early 1980s. That murmur spread, multiplied, and rippled through the wider church to such an extent that the global environment has dramatically changed. Once again youth ministry is the back door for renewing the church and reorienting her toward its mission—and youth ministry changes more than you know.

The murmur, which I suspect was and is a tale being told not just in the United Kingdom, went something like this . . .

The predominant discipline of youth ministry based on working with church young people was running into problems. This model, which had been successful for decades, operated on the basis of growing a nucleus of young people, training them in Christian discipleship, and getting them to attract their friends—and then the group grew.[1] The success of the growth depended on developing a thick fringe so the young people in the nucleus had plenty of friends to invite. The young people were then socialised into church as adult Christians, and the cycle would repeat to pass on the faith to future generations and continue growing the church.

Soon questions were being asked about this model. In large part, this was fueled by a pattern of decline in church attendance. For example, between 1960 and 1985, the Church of England dwindled to not much more than half its previous size.[2] One statistic that caught the attention of the UK media was that 300 young people *per week* were leaving churches.[3]

This literally happened at Spring Harvest, a Christian festival in the United Kingdom. One evening Youth for Christ staged a walkout of 300 young people from the main worship service as a dramatic illustration of the numbers leaving every week. It was a call to prayer and a reminder of the need to invest in youth ministry.

Soon fewer and fewer young people opted into the nucleus of the dominant youth ministry model. Where a typical church youth group might have once boasted 30 young people in its nucleus, it was more typical to be leading a group of six to eight, if indeed there was an older teenage group at all in the church.

The murmur also reflected a growing awareness of the significance of culture and indeed various youth culture(s). Put simply, people began to talk about the gap between youth culture and church culture.[4] The idea that a church has a culture is commonplace now, but it was quite a radical theory then. Culture is only visible when you cross a border into another culture. But when you're already inside a culture—and never look beyond it—that culture just seems normal to you. This gap occurs in every generation to some degree.

There were two ways in which the issue seemed to heighten: First, 'Inside-Out' youth ministry failed to reach young people who didn't fit the typical middle-class group nucleus profile. Pete Ward added that the strength of the model 'like attracts like' is also its weakness.[5] In other words, unless they are exceptional young people, the skill of crossing cultures to attract different kinds of young people is simply too much to expect or ask. Further, it's not a skill that Christian adults often practise themselves.

The second way was that wider cultural changes variously documented as *postmodern, liquid modern, hyper-real, emerging, post Christendom, networked* (or whatever language you prefer to use) had found their way into youth ministry. The water in which young people (and indeed many of the youth workers themselves) were swimming in had a very different feel and makeup compared to the culture of church and the adults in them. There were huge changes taking place in the wider Western world that made many churches seem wedded to a bygone modern era. Rob Warner starkly put it this way, 'Embodiments of the gospel that work well in one era can become obstacles to it in another' and further that if the church gets stuck or time-warped 'the church is often the greatest hindrance to the gospel.'[6] This cultural shift has been widely recognised, though commentators describe it in different ways.[7] (While it's easy to focus on the details and nuances of the changes, the movement's significance doesn't lie solely in any one detail, but rather in the magnitude of the overall cultural shift, which is huge.)

> "Embodiments of the gospel that work well in one era can become obstacles to it in another."
>
> —Rob Warner

I tend to believe there are four significant contours of the new environment: (1) changes in communication technologies,[8] (2) shifting notions of truth,[9] (3) identity through consumption,[10] and (4) the global and multicultural contexts we now live in.

Communication and information technologies have rewired us in more ways than we know. I'm a big fan of the work of Marshall McLuhan who—perhaps more than any other writer—has demonstrated the significance of the medium of communication, not just the content of it.[11] Young people experience a world of connectivity, participation, access to information without needing experts (in other words, Google), self-publishing, and flat structured social networks where community is the content.[12] This environment shapes their reflexes and instincts in powerful ways.

For example, how might that affect the way they think about God and the body of Christ? Because we're all embedded, truth is more slippery than it used to be. By *embedded* I mean that we see only from where we stand, with our agendas and power games at play (that postmodern writers have laid bare). The objectivity that was so loved and sought after in the modern world isn't something that's available to us in the same way, so our gut instinct in the postmodern world is to be suspicious of truth claims—especially if we've been sold a lie before. The modern idea of solving the world's problems through science and technology and progress now seems a sick joke—how did we ever fall for that one?

Identity has shifted from production to consumption with sub-cultures predicated on taste. So one group of lads hang who they are on the peg of skating and indie and metal music; a group of girls' identities hang on the peg of R&B music and its accompanying smart dress clothes. (And this is true not only for young people, by the way—it's a game we're all playing. You need only to look in the church parking lot to work that out.)

Our community is obviously global now. I live in London, perhaps a more multicultural context than many; but the challenge is how to live with a plurality of cultures, faiths, and worldviews. In one school young Muslims, Christians, and non-Christians share the same class-room, all trying to work out how to live in consumer culture.

But it was the last part of the Inside-Out youth ministry model—socialising young people into church—that created the biggest ten-sion and sticking point for youth ministers. Because of these huge cultural changes, the gap between the world of young people and church culture now seems wider than ever. More than 20 years on, many still find it's their biggest challenge.

QUESTIONS TO PONDER:

1. How do youth ministries in your culture attempt to socialize young people into church?
2. What are the biggest "gaps" in your culture between the church and the youth?
3. What are some effective models you've observed that have effectively bridged gaps between church and youth?

Missiology came to the forefront as a platform for reimagining this practical dilemma.[13] In particular, stories of missionaries who crossed borders and faced the challenge of how to share Christ in a foreign culture caught the imagination.

The problem of the culture gap was resolved by growing faith in the soil of new cultures rather than expecting people to come and join the sending culture.

One example of the new interest in missiology was how the book *Christianity Rediscovered* by Vincent Donovan surprisingly became an essential read in youth ministry circles.[14] (I teach a module on mission and youth cultures for the Centre for Youth Ministry in Oxford, and I've observed that it's still one of the books my students find most inspiring.)

Donovan tells the story of a Catholic priest who goes to work as a missionary sharing Christ with the Maasai, a nomadic tribe in Central Africa. On arrival he finds the prevailing mission model doesn't work. The church has a mission compound with health care and a school. Children from the Maasai come to get an education and learn the catechumenate. But as far as Donovan can tell, no one has ever remained a follower of Christ upon returning to their nomadic tribe. So he writes a letter to the bishop saying he plans to meet with the tribes on a weekly basis to share the gospel with them in their culture. It's a very moving account.

As he enters this new culture, his Western take on who God is gets undone. The priest encounters the God of the Maasai. He's forced to recognise that the American God is as tribal as the God of the Maasai, but they need to journey together in search of the High God. He manages to improvise sharing the gospel in ways that incorporate the questions and insights of the Maasai. After a season some of the tribes decide to be baptised as a whole (very different from Western individualistic culture), and he shares Mass with them, creatively using their tribal rituals and customs. As he says, "An evangelist, a missionary must respect the culture of a people, not destroy it. The incarnation of the gospel, the flesh and blood which must grow on the gospel is up to the people of a culture."[15]

In the introduction to the book, Donovan reflects on the challenge of working with Western teenagers from his cross-cultural experience. He concludes that the journey requires neither calling young people to where we are or going to where they are, but rather going together to a place that neither the youth minister nor the youth have been. It's a very evocative description of the adventure of mission in youth ministry.

Even in this short account, you can see that there are rich themes and parallels for youth ministry and a whole host of questions we should raise:

- Do we expect young people to come to us, or do we go where they are?
- How do you start something from nothing?
- What language should you use to share Christ?
- Where is God already present in their culture, and how might their grasp of spirituality show you something about God that you didn't see before?
- Will they choose to follow together or as individuals? What will you do if their choice runs counter to your experience?
- Will you be prepared to leave the incarnation in their culture to them—or is it up to them? What might that look like?
- What is your role alongside them?
- Will God show up?
- Which of your traditions will you pass on to them and what will you ignore as cultural?
- When should you leave?

Youth ministers discovered a gold mine of wisdom in the area of missiology through facing these challenges—and not in foreign cultures either, but through working with young people in their own cities and villages. This approach was referred to as *relational youth ministry, incarnational youth ministry,* and more recently, *missional youth ministry.* The incarnation seemed to become a unifying theological theme across youth ministry; and mission was very much at the heart of these movements, rather than a peripheral concern.[16]

Perhaps it will help to give a few examples of practice informed by this growing murmur. "Church on the Edge" is a project in Devon and Somerset, a predominantly rural area in the South West of England.[17] The thinking behind this project is that a typical church in a village has an aging congregation and consequently expecting young people to join is simply unrealistic. Therefore, in terms of mission, a new strategy is needed. With the blessing and permission of more traditional churches, Church on the Edge seeks to engage and share Christ with young people outside the orbit of church. The goal is not to get people to fill the pews in existing churches; rather, it's to develop a new expression of Christian community in specific cultures.

> The goal is not to get people to fill the pews in existing churches; rather, it's to develop a new expression of Christian community in specific cultures.

In Chard, another small town in the South West of England, Richard Passmore has been doing detached (in other words, relational) work among skateboarders with no Christian background. He uses a framework for Church on the Edge that develops through five stages. Each stage is framed as a progression in the depth of relationship with and commitment to the growing community:

- Stage 1 is a contacting community where initial relationships and contacts happen.
- Stage 2 happens when time is spent together in activities and relationships deepen until it becomes a growing community.
- Stage 3 is a connected community in which deeper bonds form.
- In Stage 4 a community explores spirituality and expressions of the Christian faith and invites young people into deeper encounters with God.
- Stage 5 is a practicing ecclesial community in which the group has (however loosely) defined an expression of church.

In the first 12 months, the group forms deep relationships and goes on a couple of residential pilgrimage weekends. Additionally, in discussions around God and spirituality, Richard has suggested that "Flow" might be their language for God.

This has really taken off, and Richard has creatively reworked a few Scriptures and parables using Flow. His inspiration comes from stories of cross-cultural mission where the starting point is to try to see what God is doing and join in. Part of this involves naming God in the culture and developing a set of mission instincts to respond to and improvise around what God is doing.

Many of the skaters have decided to "go with the Flow" and develop Church on the Edge together. Richard's vision is of a community with a missional DNA at its core that will enable others to live out mission as part of discipleship.

Oxygen is a youth project set up and supported by more than 30 churches in the borough of Kingston in South West London.[18] The initial vision for the project was to develop a congregation for Christian teenagers, but local churches soon realised this would simply stem the flow, gathering young people they already know. So the churches decided to change focus and do something about young people *outside* the churches to bring about community transformation.

To facilitate this vision, teams of churched young people are recruited and encouraged to cross cultural boundaries in order to reach and engage their peers walking different life paths. As these young missionaries carry out this role, they not only see others come to discover and follow Jesus, but also, like Donovan, they come to discover a bigger Jesus for themselves.

This coming together of churched and unchurched young people has brokered and catalysed work with all kinds of groups of young people in different cultures, ranging from work on local estates to after-school clubs with university-bound 18-year-olds. It's included mentoring, youth cafés, homework clubs, adventure weekends, and big events. With an eight-year proven track record of cross-cultural youth engagement, Oxygen is now confronting the next challenge— what comes next?

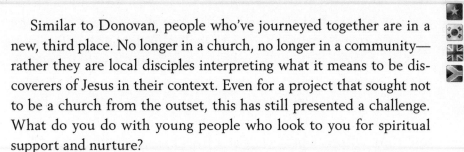

Similar to Donovan, people who've journeyed together are in a new, third place. No longer in a church, no longer in a community—rather they are local disciples interpreting what it means to be discoverers of Jesus in their context. Even for a project that sought not to be a church from the outset, this has still presented a challenge. What do you do with young people who look to you for spiritual support and nurture?

In addressing this dilemma, Oxygen has found surrounding churches to be willing participants in an exploration of something new. Since 2005, six people have been appointed 'external youth workers' who are paid by the local church but given the responsibility of going where Oxygen has engaged with young people and seeking to nurture discipleship into the community there.

This is a very different strategy than Church on the Edge uses, but through investment in an area-wide team, the problem of the culture gap between churches and young people is addressed in a different way. There is a dynamic network of young Christians spread out as an expression of church. Again, a different look to "church" than many of us experienced as youth, but this is what it looks like for them to be disciples in their culture.

The fluid nature of the loyalties and alliances across the churches doesn't seem to matter. Young people have managed to bolt together enough in the way of discipleship to grow as Christian disciples involved in evangelism themselves. This strategy of a citywide youth ministry project has been significant in many places in the United Kingdom, bringing creative and dynamic energy to the churches' work with young people.

Saint Laurence's Anglican Church in Reading was charged with a new mission focusing on work with teenagers in the city.[19] The mission statement on the Web site and on a plaque outside the church states, 'Living to see non-churched young people come to faith and creating new forms of church with them.' Even if you want to join the church, for example, you're discouraged to do so unless you share this passion. Chris Russell took on the role as vicar of the church with this agreement. An existing, dwindling congregation of five or six gradually moved elsewhere, and Chris grew a team passionate about youth ministry with young people outside the church.

Saint Laurence's has grown into a chaotic-but-wonderful church with a passionate heart for mission among young people with all sorts of youth ministry going on. In fact, the team has brokered work with young people relationally in schools, cinema clubs, pool halls, and through other projects—and lives have been changed. Chris reflected with me that as the church has grown, it's been important to keep its essential missional DNA with young people.

While these three models—Saint Laurence's, Oxygen, Church on the Edge—differ in structure, theology, and approach, they're all informed by this backdrop, this growing murmur of reaching out to young people with a missional approach. Yes, the contexts vary, but each is successfully reaching out to and sharing Christ with young people—and outside the existing groups of churched young people. And they are all reproducible models that the wider church would do well to consider investing in elsewhere.

In the last 10 years, we've seen this missional approach spread into the wider church—but not just as a youth issue. Many adults experience the same sort of gap between church and culture as young people do. So there has been a wave of experimentation in mission, church planting, and shapes and forms of church. And this has taken place predominantly in and around mainline denominations, not independent churches. Perhaps unsurprisingly, youth ministers who developed this approach with young people include many of the movement's leaders. It's been variously called *emerging church*, *missional communities*, and *fresh expressions*.[20]

We've seen a huge shift in the environment. The Church of England, for example, has recognised the need for a 'mixed economy' church that includes fresh expression churches to reach people who will never be at home in the culture of the traditional church.[21] The Church of England also has acknowledged the need for pioneer leaders with different kinds of giftings than typical church pastors and has begun to select and train them accordingly.[22]

While there is a wave of experimentation, newness, and a whole set of permissions, it's not devoid of challenges. For one, there still aren't many resources for this kind of pioneering work (though if there were, maybe it wouldn't be so pioneering!). And it's far from the case that the whole church has swung 'round on this. However, there are also increasing numbers of people focusing on church not as a refuge but as a community of mission disciples. About 25 to 30 years ago, if you'd suggested that murmurs in youth ministry might change things this much, I suspect no one would have believed you.

Youth ministry changes more than you know!

The implications for training in youth ministry are huge, too. In some ways, this parallels the challenges the church is facing in the United Kingdom around the training of ordained pioneer leaders. Colleges that have trained parish priests for centuries are now offering to train ordained pioneers. But rather than thinking in new and creative ways about training for the new context through the lens of cross-cultural mission, there has been a tendency to think that they had better be trained to be parish priests with a bit of pioneering added on top—a sort of 'priest plus.'

Lesslie Newbigin was one of the mission thinkers who began to help people in Western contexts look at what they do through a mission lens, rather than seeing mission as something that was focused overseas. He states:

> If the gospel is to be understood, if it is to be received as something which communicates the truth about the real human situation, if it is, as we say, to "make sense," it has to be communicated in the language of those to whom it is addressed and has to be clothed in symbols which are meaningful to them. And since the gospel does not come as a disembodied message, but as the message of a community which claims to live by it and which invites others to adhere to it, the community's life must be so ordered that it "makes sense" to those who are so invited. It must, as we say, "come alive." Those to whom it is addressed must be able to say," Yes, I see."[23]

I remember that when I first read this quote, I thought the problem was that church didn't make sense to young people and they didn't see. However, this more incarnational approach to growing faith in the soil of various youth cultures is extremely hopeful—even if it's a hard journey. In these ways perhaps young people, as Newbigin

suggests, will be afforded the opportunity to say that the gospel has come alive, makes sense—and yes, they do see.

DISCUSSION QUESTIONS

1. For missional youth workers, can the church be a hindrance? Some authors in this book say it's imperative for Christian youth workers to work with the church. What is your theological position about the role of the local organised church?
2. Jonny mentions four contours of the new environment. For each of the four, list ways that you've seen them to be true in your context.
3. In what ways do or don't the descriptions of British youth reflect what you experience among youth in your own context?
4. What are the educational responsibilities for youth ministry in your context? What should you teach (and not just preach)? Would that change if you were to lead a ministry in a new culture?
5. What's gained by viewing youth ministry through the lens of mission? How does that differ from socializing youth into church— the "Inside-Out" model?
6. In which of Baker's five stages for developing community is your youth group? List three to five reasons why you believe that's your current stage.

RESOURCES

Brierley, Peter. *Reaching and Keeping Teenagers*. Toronto: Monarch Books, 1993.

Brueggemann, Walter. *Texts Under Negotiation: The Bible and Postmodern Imagination*. Minneapolis: Augsburg Fortress, 1993.

Cray, Graham. *Postmodern Culture and Youth Discipleship: Commitment or Looking Cool?* Cambridge: Grove Books Ltd., 1998.

———. *Mission-Shaped Church: Church Planting and Fresh Expressions of Church in a Changing Context*. London: Church House Publishing, 2004.

Creasy Dean, Kenda, and Ron Foster. *The Godbearing Life: The Art of Soul Tending for Youth Ministry*. Nashville: Upper Room Books, 1998.

Davie, Grace. *Religion in Britain Since 1945: Believing Without Belonging*. Oxford, UK: Wiley-Blackwell, 1994.

Donovan, Vincent J. *Christianity Rediscovered*. London: SCM Press, 1982.

Harvey, David. *The Condition of Postmodernity*. Oxford, UK: Blackwell Publishers, 1990.

Jones, Tony. *Postmodern Youth Ministry*. Grand Rapids, MI: Zondervan/Youth Specialties, 2001.

Lyon, David. *Jesus in Disneyland: Religion in Postmodern Times*. Cambridge: UK: Polity Press, 2000.

McLuhan, Marshall. *The Medium is the Massage*. Berkeley, CA: Gingko Press, 2001.

Middleton, J. Richard, and Brian J. Walsh. *Truth Is Stranger Than It Used to Be*. London, UK: SPCK Publishing, 1995.

Newbigin, Lesslie. *The Gospel in a Pluralist Society*. London, UK: SPCK Publishing, 1989.

Passmore, Richard. *Meet Them Where They Are At*. Bletchley, UK: Scripture Union Publishing, 2003.

Riddell, Michael. *Threshold of the Future: Reforming the Church in the Post-Christian West*. London, UK: SPCK Publishing, 1998.

Shirky, Clay. *Here Comes Everybody: The Power of Organizing Without Organizations*. London, UK: Allen Lane, 2008.

Ward, Pete. *God at the Mall: Youth Ministry That Meets Kids Where They're At*. Peabody, MA: Hendrickson Publishers, 1999.

——— , ed. *The Church and Youth Ministry*. Oxford: Lynx, 1995.

——— , ed. *Relational Youthwork*. Oxford: Lynx, 1995.

——— . *Youth Culture and the Gospel*. Grand Rapids, MI: Zondervan, 1992.

Warner, Rob. *21st Century Church*. Eastbourne, UK: Kingsway Publications, 1999.

CHAPTER THREE

A WORLD OF IRISH YOUTH MINISTRY

ROZ STIRLING

I have a great inability to sleep during those long red-eye flights from the United States to my home in Ireland. So I watch movies or read a good book. However, as we approach the Irish coast, I am glued to the tiny window of the aircraft to get a look at the patchwork quilt of velvety green that tells me I will soon be home. It always captivates me even though I have gazed upon it many times before—field after field weaving together to create Ireland's famous '40 shades of green.'

But this interwoven and harmonious landscape hides the conflicted identities of the people who claim Ireland as home—a people bound together by their love for this small island, but who possess a set of opposed identities that are Protestant or Catholic, Nationalist or Unionist, Northern or Southern. And if colour accurately reflected these people's allegiances, we'd have not 40 shades of green, but rather a weaving together of either red, white, and blue; or green, white, and orange—the colours on the flags representing the two political jurisdictions in Ireland (in other words, the British Union flag and the Irish Tricolour).

Divisions in Ireland are all about religious, political, and cultural identity. Such divisions have conspired to divide an otherwise warm, hospitable people into two very distinct camps. Recognising that generalisations always create difficulty, there are nonetheless broad understandings of the means by which division has come to exist. For instance, if you were born into a Protestant family in the north-east, then the most likely political loyalty will be to some form of Unionism, which is best understood as a commitment to defend the six counties of northeastern Ireland as a British territory.

On the other hand, if born into a Catholic family—whether in the northern or the southern part of the country—then it's likely you'll commit to the politics of Nationalism, which for some means a vision for the reunification of the country as one state under the jurisdiction of the government of the Republic of Ireland, based in Dublin.

A small community of Protestant people in the Republic of Ireland—who often do not share the 'British' agenda of their fellow co-religionists in the North—bring a further hue to the colour of this complex Irish landscape.

Still, these sharp lines of division give no hint of the human stories that so often defy the expected norm. Catholic and Protestant women in Belfast working side by side on a factory floor—despite the intense animosity between their communities—became firm friends for life because of their commitment to Christian faith. Or the profound impact on a young Baptist girl as she listened to the prayers of an elderly Catholic neighbour whom the girl's mother had taken in to live in their home. Years later, at the height of the 'Troubles' in Northern Ireland, this same Baptist girl became a founding member of the 174 Trust reconciliation ministry in North Belfast.[1]

So to consider the world of youth ministry within Ireland, some knowledge of her people—as well as an adequate understanding of the evolution and challenges of ministry with Ireland's teens—is necessary. Furthermore, insight into the history of divided religious affiliation and contested political belonging will shed some light on the bewildering mix of religion, politics, and culture.

I asked local historian and author, Philip Orr, to describe the historical backdrop, and he provided this summary:—

> For many centuries the British Empire was in possession of Ireland, imposing its rules and values on the local people. This included religious values, as Britain was a Protestant nation and the native Irish

were Catholic. Those who were sent to Dublin to govern the people were Protestant . . . However, by the 20th Century the desire for independence from Britain had reached a peak within the Catholic population who predominated throughout most of Ireland.

After a bitter war for Irish independence in the 1920s, 26 southern counties were granted independence. The six northern counties, which had continued to be populated largely by Protestants, were allowed to remain as a part of the United Kingdom. Within this British part of Ireland was a substantial Catholic minority who felt cheated by the new arrangement.

By 1969, serious civil unrest had begun in Northern Ireland, leading in due course to the loss of over 3,000 lives. At the heart of the conflict was a campaign by the self-styled Irish Republican Army (IRA) to remove the British presence from Northern Ireland. After almost thirty years of violence, 1998 was a year of change, bringing new forms of local government, which involved power sharing between Protestant and Catholic in a Northern Irish parliament . . . A foundation for peace had been established. A peace that created for some Catholic and Protestant people an identity that was other than British or Irish; rather being "Northern Irish" became a real possibility.

Despite these positive changes, young Catholics and Protestants in Ireland often lead quite separate lives, worshipping apart, playing different sports and attending different schools, and [likely voting] for different political parties when they reach the age of 18.[2]

This is the historical context that the twenty-first–century Irish church must consider if it wants to keep her young. She must also embrace the challenge to reach the increasing number of teens who, unlike previous generations in Ireland, are growing up with little or no allegiance to the church. Statistics drawn from the records of the Presbyterian denomination illustrate this point. In 1970, church records document 69,604 young people in Sunday school and Bible class; by 2008, this number dropped to 26,291.[3] In a country where close to 30 percent of the population is under the age of 25,[4] it is essential that the older generations embrace their responsibility to pass on the faith to those coming after them, thereby fulfilling the biblical mandate.[5]

Let me set out my stall: After many years in youth ministry within the Irish context, it is my passionate belief that those called to work with young people will enter the heart of this crucial ministry only after addressing some key issues. Many aren't unique to Irish culture; but, when examined contextually, these four practices create a window to discern our contribution to the global discussion.

GET INTO THEIR WORLD AND UNDER THEIR SKIN

We must have an understanding of the cultural 'air' that young people breathe—and so create opportunities to demonstrate the unique capacity of the gospel to inhabit as well as transcend culture and time. Andy Hickford, senior minister at Maybridge Community Church in Worthing, writes:

> Culture is experienced more readily than it can be described. It is the air we breathe, the water we swim in. It is everything about our background and environment that shapes the people that we are.[6]

Using Hickford's descriptor and working from the 'given' that culture per se must be broken down and analysed from the stance of the prevailing dominant culture—and then the subcultures within—a close look at the world of the twenty-first–century Irish young person sets the stage for any conversation about effective youth ministry.

The 1990s provide an interesting launching pad for any discussion on the 'air they breathe.' In the Republic of Ireland, scandal was about to hit the Catholic Church like a maelstrom as bishops resigned and Catholic priests were charged with sexual abuse. During this same period, the well-documented 'Celtic tiger' meant unprecedented economic growth in Ireland, and young people were no longer forced to emigrate for work. In Northern Ireland, the much longed for 'peace process' found a beginning, but not before one of the most contentious periods further divided this already broken society—Protestant Orange Men claimed their right to walk a traditional route on their annual Twelfth of July parades, a route that took them through or past Catholic residential communities.[7]

If this has been the social context for Ireland's teens, what 'culture' and 'subcultures' have emerged? There are too many to identify here, but three areas provide useful insight.

Religious Fatigue and Disillusionment

In May 1992, Bishop Eamon Casey, then Bishop of Galway, resigned—a significant event. In the late 1970s, Casey was one of four who travelled to Rome in an attempt to secure a Papal visit to Ireland. The visit was agreed upon, and Casey organised the youth programme segment of the visit, culminating in the attendance of the young people at the Papal Mass, which took place in Galway on September 30, 1979. This was the first event in which the Catholic Church became directly involved in a ministry for young people outside of spiritual formation within Catholic schools.[8] Catholic leaders viewed the large attendance of young people as a 'National Awakening' among the young.

Fast-forward to the morning of May 7, 1992: The *Irish Times* ran the story of Bishop Casey's resignation. Revelations about his affair with an American divorcée and the existence of their son were momentous. Casey was a highly respected and progressive bishop. For some, this was regarded as the moment when the Catholic Church began to lose considerable influence over society and politics in the Irish Republic. The 1990s seemed to usher in an era of revelations of sexual misconduct, including many cases of child sex abuse. Plus, these scandals hit the public consciousness at the same time as Ireland's meteoric rise in economic prosperity.

The 1990s weren't the last decade in which the Catholic Church would reel from such revelations. The Ryan Report and the Murphy Report of 2009 brought even greater charges, culminating with all Irish bishops meeting with the Pope in Rome as out came painful stories of abuse within Catholic institutions over a 50-year period. And indifference toward the church in Northern Ireland was also on the increase, despite religious allegiance remaining strong for both the Catholic and the Protestant faith.

We must remind ourselves of the historical context, too: A claim to be Protestant or Catholic in Northern Ireland doesn't signify regular church attendance (although during the hardest years of the 'Troubles,' large sections of the population did attend church). Rather, such self-identifying claims represent cultural identity, political persuasion, and probably religious conviction. In a recent conversation with a group of teenagers of both Catholic and Protestant backgrounds, they recognized that to identify oneself as a Protestant or Catholic in Northern Ireland said, in the first instance, something about identity.

For the youth minister or pastor, therefore, the challenge of directing young people to the gospel, to the life lived under the lordship of Christ, is a demanding one. Many who grew up in the late 1980s, the 1990s, and throughout the last decade have looked back over their shoulders to the 'adult Christian population' with extreme disappointment. Young people have wondered about the lack of societal change when so many have claimed to be followers of Jesus. Despite the considerable political developments, sectarianism is still alive and well. Furthermore, they struggle to understand the involvement of Christian clergy in movements or organisations that have appeared to foster sectarianism rather than work for reform. And they have revolted against the form of faith they've seen in their parents and grandparents, as it isn't perceived to be a 'fit' for them. They long for an 'experience of faith'—not the cerebral certainty of belief that seems divorced from experiences and relationships. Religious fatigue and disillusionment has been proving an important condition among our young that we must address.

> Young people have wondered about the lack of societal change when so many have claimed to be followers of Jesus. . . . They long for an 'experience of faith'—not the cerebral certainty of belief that seems divorced from experiences and relationships.

Christian Subcultures

As noted earlier, young people from Catholic and Protestant backgrounds are often educated separately, play different sports, worship apart, and often live apart. When the question of passing on faith to the young is addressed, the strong theological convictions within the two traditions have led to well-defined youth subcultures. There is therefore no generic youth ministry within Northern Ireland.

This is exemplified by an examination of youth ministry practice within the evangelical tradition, where faith development begins with an under-fives 'children's church,' followed by 'early years' Sunday school, 'teen' Bible class, Sunday evening youth programmes, and midweek youth organisations, providing a church-centered spiritual nurture from toddlerhood to age 16, perhaps even 18. The summer months of any given year provide camps, outreach teams, and possibly an overseas mission experience. This pattern of spiritual nurture has provided great stability within the reformed context, nurturing young people in a very good understanding of Scripture and creating leadership opportunities for many.

One challenge evident within this cultural context is that evangelical outreach actually reaches only a small percentage of the teenage population—and those to whom it does minister are largely from the 'middle class' socioeconomic section of society. As such, these young people have been less impacted by Ireland's political-religious conflicts, thus creating an easier, unchallenged faith that needs no modification or contextualisation.

In addition, the challenge to decipher what is biblical from what is a cultural 'add-on' has been an issue within the church since the time of St. Paul. Where those who minister within this particular culture have embraced the call toward 'exegesis of the Word, exegesis of the world, exegesis of the self,' they have made connections with young people who otherwise would have disappeared from the care of the church.[9]

We Were Never Their Age

During a recent conversation with a youth pastor, he had this to say about the challenges he's facing in his ministry:

> A major feature of the lives of our teens is the fast pace at which their lives are lived. Instant downloads, annual mobile upgrades, instant messaging, social networking, and so the list goes on. Youth leaders and parents are continually adjusting to the pace of twenty-first–century life, but young people have never known anything

slower. They are growing up believing they can have what they want, when they want it, and whenever they decide they need it.[10]

This pastor's reflection indicates that—despite our unique historical, cultural, and political context—Irish young people are in the grip of the global, technological culture to the same degree that American, Canadian, or British youth are. The youth pastor must also understand and interpret what is taking place within popular culture, discerning where Christ is to be found and how and when he transcends it. Perhaps this comment on the enigma that is U2, arguably the world's greatest rock band, highlights the point:

> For those willing to take the time to look, popular music is brimming with songs of spiritually energized quests; some worth avoiding, but many worth engaging. . . . To those who do not consider themselves believers, this book will go a long way in helping explain why U2's music seems to scratch an unidentifiable itch.[11]

PASS ON HIS LOVE, NOT RELIGION

We must *know* the life-giving faith of Jesus Christ with both head *and* heart so that the treasure we pass on is a love of him, not a religious practice or culture that merely forms identity and defines *belonging*. As political stability takes root in Irish society and the *peace babies* search out the 'new wine,'[12] it seems that youth ministry may need to embrace its own prophetic voice that it so often spoke to the established church. As young people leave mainline denominations in favour of new churches, we must learn what they're looking for:

> We must *know* the life-giving faith of Jesus Christ with both head *and* heart so that the treasure we pass on is a love of him, not a religious practice or culture that merely forms identity and defines *belonging*.

The young people of the new millennium represent the experiential, feeling, 'walk the talk' generation. The churchgoing culture of previous generations in Ireland makes no sense to them, especially when attending a particular church is a statement of religious or theological identity rather than living faith.

The strong denominational ties of families and young people in the later decades of the twentieth century are gone. Beyond providing a cultural identity, there is no denominational loyalty in the 'peace baby' generation. They will express their belief and faith in a way and place where the experience tells them it's real. The fact that the old and new wine should not be competing with each other is a truth that they have yet to comprehend. Nor indeed is it a truth that their parents, ministers, priests, and pastors have yet comprehended. Here then is an opportunity for youth ministry to be a vehicle of reconciliation for those who will have ears to hear.

It's also significant that the *Emergent Church* movement hasn't affected Ireland for the most part.[13] Mainline denominations, though losing their young, still have the opportunity through the strength of their youth ministries to redress this balance. The Emergent experience speaks to this, albeit that redemption in Ireland will most likely follow a different path.

Create Authentic Communities of Faith

We must create communities where love of God is translated into a practical outworking of the counter-cultural values of God's kingdom; where each generational group is secure in its acceptance and belonging within its community, but equally where they affirm one another's expression and outworking of those kingdom values.

The story of the 'Summer Madness' festival—a Christian festival that grew out of the Church of Ireland's (Episcopal) youth department in the late 1980s—speaks to this. It was a response to young people struggling to find belonging within their local parish churches. John Kee, executive director of the Summer Madness charity, said that in the first year of Summer Madness, young people largely from within the Church of Ireland attended the camp, totaling 270 campers. In 2008 it was estimated that more than 3,200 young people from all denominations and backgrounds attended the festival.

In 2004, Summer Madness became an independent charity. The growing number of young people from across the spectrum of church denominations, including the Catholic Church, was the impetus for this decision. Within Northern Irish society, this is a great success story and an example of how youth ministry has spoken into the brokenness. Through the 'Summer Madness Street Reach' social action programme in the summer of 2007, more than 2,000 young people from Catholic and Protestant churches formed teams to serve in 27 venues across Belfast. Together they did garden work for the elderly, painted out sectarian graffiti, and organised cross-community football tournaments for kids who otherwise may have thrown bricks at one another.

Summer Madness has successfully created a very particular faith community that has enormous appeal to the 'peace babies.' 'We have made many mistakes,' Kee confesses, 'but these have certainly been inadvertent as we have simply attempted to provide a place of spiritual engagement for a generation of young people who were becoming so disillusioned with the mainline church that they were walking away in droves.'

The Catholic Church in Ireland similarly can testify to the 1970s grass-roots Charismatic Renewal Movement rushing in a whole new way of doing and experiencing church and its seminal influence on youth ministry. This, in turn, impacted the whole church.[14]

Summer Madness and Catholic Charismatic Renewal each tell a story of community that has worked within the youth peer group culture. But where are the examples within local church communities or any of the mainline denominations? Indeed you can find many local church communities throughout Ireland that are addressing the urgent need to reinvent themselves for the sake of the young.

As for denominational alertness, the Presbyterian Church, through the establishment of a Youth Assembly, have placed young people right at the heart of decision making within the denomination. The meeting of the Irish Presbyterian General Assembly in June 2009 adopted 14 resolutions from the Youth Assembly, all of which were expressions of concern and aspirations of the 230 young people who participated in the youth gathering.[15]

Authentic community that provides space to *belong* ahead of any expectation to *believe* is the context within which faith will flourish among youth in Ireland. Doctrine and belief are unmistakable central tenets of the Christian faith, but this feeling, experiencing generation won't grasp the significance of 'obedience to Christ' if its members are simply told it's what they must do in order to be a disciple of Jesus.

Recognise the Role of History in Shaping Individual and Community Consciousness

We have already noted the considerable importance of accounting for ministry context, as well as celebrating a healthy national identity (in our case being Irish or British) while directing youth to the higher calling of a disciple of Jesus where every allegiance (whether religious, political, or cultural) is subservient to his Lordship. When this is practiced in any troubled context, disciples of Jesus Christ will experience freedom from the tyranny of slavish national or religious identity.

But if it's not practiced, selective memories of past hurts and injustices will continue to inform religious practice and being. Even the most sincere believer may be guilty of excluding someone 'in Jesus' name,' rather than embracing that person out of love for Christ as a vehicle through which dialogue and understanding may take place.[16] However, such an embrace may be the journey of a lifetime, all the while becoming an outworking of the gospel call to 'love our enemies.'[17]

It is here that the courage of the four mainline churches in Northern Ireland (Presbyterian, Methodist, Church of Ireland, and Catholic) must be recognised. In 1991, they partnered in the formation of a unique inter-church youth service organisation, 'Youth Link.' This body provides support and training for youth workers and community relations experience for young people as described in their vision statement:

> Youth Link's vision is of Churches working together to develop excellence in youth work and ministry, enabling young people and youth practitioners to be agents of transformation in a divided society.[18]

Achievement of this vision is a testimony to the commitment of the church community within Northern Ireland to invest in the future of young people.

Further evidence of contextualisation of youth ministry within our particular historical experience is found in the programmes delivered by many of the denominational youth departments. For example, the Presbyterians developed a reconciliation ministry, Preparing Youth to be Peace Makers, which takes hundreds of young people through a discipleship course centered on peacemaking as a biblical imperative. The reputation of this course has stretched well beyond the Presbyterian denomination, finding a place within the curriculum of high schools, faith-based youth groups, and community volunteer groups working with young people in every conceivable context. The 'New Day' programme within the Catholic Church calls ministry pastors and priests to be peacemakers as well.

Both of these initiatives were built on the experience of many secular youth work programmes regarding the need to approach the reconciliation imperative within either a Protestant or a Catholic community prior to any cross-community programme of engagement.

Contextualise the Message

Perhaps the most universally shared issue among Western cultures is a well-developed secularism—on the rise since the rejection of objective truth and a 'God framework' to oversee and guide civic life. Another way of describing this shift is a 'new evangelical atheism.'[19] Within the Irish Republic, a major shift in values among large sections of the population led to the inevitable separation of church and state during the later decades of the twentieth century.[20] But these movements in societal thinking actually provide their own unique opportunity within youth ministry.

Today's teens have been so robbed of confidence in objective truth, due to our secular media-driven culture, that the only reference points for reality are . . . the teenagers themselves. Yet often they are surviving in a world that is desperately lonely, highly dysfunctional, constantly subjecting them to information overload, or peddling a version of happiness based on wealth or celebrity. Hence teens are suspicious of a 'saviour' who gives unconditional love or a faith where a deep, committed, loyal relationship with him—rather than self-determination—is the route to meaning, purpose, well-being, and happiness in life. This picture is a clear fit for the Irish teenager of the twenty-first century. What an opportunity for the church!

Throughout the course of the last two decades, Ireland has witnessed major changes in the development, experience, and delivery of youth ministry. The Irish church cares profoundly for the young and is deeply committed to the task of passing on the faith to them. The range of youth strategies and programmes or initiatives that take centre stage within all the Christian churches in Ireland are adequate testimony to this. In 2005, an audit of faith-based youth work in Northern Ireland revealed that 68 percent of government-registered youth groups were based in Christian churches.[21] The road, however, is steep and littered with obstacles. A new chapter in the history of this troubled island is currently being scripted as governments, churches, and communities reinvent themselves in this new era of 'peace.' May God grant his people humility, wisdom, discernment, and grace to bring his kingdom in among the young.

DISCUSSION QUESTIONS

1. Create three columns on a sheet of paper. In the left column, list the four key practices Roz notes in this chapter, leaving some vertical space between each entry. Use the center column to write down the Irish cultural issues that Roz notes these practices address. Then, in the third column, list the ways these four key practices might address particular issues in your cultural context.

2. In what ways has youth ministry been a prophetic voice in your church? In your community? In your country?

3. Roz writes that authentic community provides space to belong ahead of any expectation to believe. In what ways is this true about your ministry? In what ways is this not true? Why is this important in global youth ministry in various contexts?

4. Roz demonstrates a keen awareness of how historical events give shape and context to Irish youth ministry practices. What are the historical and cultural influences that shape youth ministry in your context? If someone from another culture spent time watching your youth ministry in action, what cultural factors would stand out to that person?

5. Roz and Jonny discuss creating "authentic communities." More than just meeting at a coffee shop, what does an authentic community look like? What can we learn from these two chapters that may advance our standards for an authentic community?

CHAPTER FOUR

FROM APARTHEID TO SAAMHEID

CREATING A CULTURALLY DIVERSE YOUTH MINISTRY

MARK TITTLEY

INTRODUCTION

Imagine walking into a youth group meeting room expecting to encounter a homogeneous collection of teenagers who love the same music, dress the same, come from the same socioeconomic level, and have leaders from the same culture—but instead you encounter diversity that takes your breath away. The kids clearly aren't from the same culture, they reflect all levels of the socioeconomic system, and the leaders engaging with the teens are as diverse as the teens themselves.

So where are you?

Would you believe South Africa?

Once a pariah of the world—isolated and ostracized for some of the worst crimes against humanity and one of the worst systems of segregation in recent history—this rainbow nation is now a beacon of hope for the celebration of diversity.

Would you believe it possible that in Johannesburg today, you can encounter a church community that is truly diverse, that reflects a population once deeply divided along racial and cultural lines? Well it is possible, and it's happening on the edge of the city of Johannesburg in a historically upper-class white suburb.

Still, the transition from *apartheid* (an Afrikaans word meaning "separateness") to *saamheid* (an Afrikaans word meaning "togetherness") is not a common feature of church life in this country that's just two decades into democratic rule. Clearly, diversity doesn't happen by osmosis: You cannot learn to sing by placing an iPod under your pillow while you sleep; you cannot lose weight by watching the exercise channel on television; you cannot have a safari experience by visiting a zoo; and you cannot experience diversity in youth ministry without taking specific, practical action.

Then again, should we be pursuing culturally diverse ministry? Doesn't it contradict what the church growth experts say about homogeneous units being a secret to growth? Let's explore the biblical basis for cultural diversity in ministry.

THE VISION FOR CULTURALLY DIVERSE YOUTH MINISTRY

The book of Revelation presents a vision of a united community of believers from diverse nations who worship in unity before the throne of God:

> [9]After this I looked, and there before me was a great multitude that no one could count, from every nation, tribe, people and language, standing before the throne and before the Lamb. They were wearing white robes and were holding palm branches in their hands. [10]And they cried out in a loud voice: "Salvation belongs to our God, who sits on the throne, and to the Lamb." (Revelation 7:9-10)

Imagine if people described your church with these words: *A large crowd from every nation, tribe, people, and language*. It would be a gathering of culturally diverse people representing many nations and with many languages spoken during the service—from greetings to worship to preaching.

What do we do with a vision like this? Historically, we've relegated it to an existence that lies beyond the grave where one day we will all live together in perfect harmony. But what if that vision is meant to be reflected here and now?

If we take seriously Jesus' passion for God's will to be done on earth as it is in heaven (Matthew 6:10)—indeed, for heaven to come on earth—then we have to pursue cultural diversity as a vision for ministry here and now. In other words, our mission is to transform our world so it reflects *God's* world, his eternal kingdom.

Sure, this may challenge our view of eschatology, particularly the belief that this world is a mess and we should shout out: "Beam me up, Scotty!" But instead of embracing an escapist view of life, we must embrace God's agenda and be salt and light in this world (Matthew 5:13-15). We should shine like stars in the universe (Philippians 2:14-15) and, like many examples from recent history (for example, William Wilberforce, Martin Luther King, Jr., and Nelson Mandela), work tirelessly to transform this world for the sake of the gospel of Jesus Christ.

Paul describes a church in which all walls of division are broken down—in fact, he says the death of Jesus went far beyond "just" the salvation of our souls. Read these words again from the book of Ephesians that describe our unity in Christ and the new way of living that Christ died for:

> [14]For he himself is our peace, who has made the two groups one and has destroyed the barrier, the dividing wall of hostility, [15]by setting aside in his flesh the law with its commands and regulations. His purpose was to create in himself one new humanity out of the two, thus making peace, [16]and in one body to reconcile both of them to God through the cross, by which he put to death their hostility. [17]He came and preached peace to you who were far away and peace to those who were near. [18]For through him we both have access to the Father by one Spirit. [19]Consequently, you are no longer foreigners and strangers, but fellow citizens with God's people and also members of his household, [20]built on the foundation of the apostles and prophets, with Christ Jesus himself as the chief cornerstone. [21]In him the whole building is joined together and rises to become a holy temple in the Lord. [22]And in him you too are being built together to become a dwelling in which God lives by his Spirit. (Ephesians 2:14-22)

Scripture clearly provides us with a mandate to pursue culturally diverse ministries, but how do we achieve it?

THE KEYS TO CULTURALLY DIVERSE YOUTH MINISTRY

What does it take to develop a church or youth ministry character-ized by cultural diversity? Here are five factors that will put you on track to reflect the reality in heaven here on earth and fulfill Christ's mandate.

Foster a Culturally Diverse Personal Lifestyle

David Livermore, in his book *Cultural Intelligence*, challenges his readers to "become more multicultural people so that we might better express love cross-culturally."[1] His emphasis is on preparing ourselves to engage in cross-cultural ministry through investigation and transformation. This is the starting point of a culturally diverse youth ministry. If our own lives don't reflect the kind of ministry we're seeking to create, it simply won't become a reality.

My own journey has been one of significant lifestyle adjustment. I grew up in a divided country, separated by the color of skin from anyone who looked different from me and with an older generation who accepted this division as just the way things were meant to be. So I embarked on a journey that put me at odds with the status quo. I visited and stayed in areas where I wasn't allowed to be (and many considered unwise to visit), intentionally created friendships across cultural lines for mutual enrichment, adopted a child from a differ-ent culture, and even made practical decisions about what books, music, or movies to engage.

Write a Culturally Diverse Mission Statement

Start by revising your current mission statement so it reflects a pas-sion for cultural diversity. It might just involve adding a preamble, something like: "Our mission is to be a culturally diverse community of believers who . . ." Then refine your list of core values by adding *cultural diversity* to the list. It's become popular in recent years to write values statements for life, family, work—and more recently, churches have begun to identify their core values as well. If your church has core values such as *lordship, evangelism, discipleship, spiri-tual family, leadership,* and *multigenerationalism,* you might consider adding *cultural diversity* to the list. When these values are visual (in other words, reflected on church signage, in images used on the property or in meeting venues, and in all publications) as well as verbal (spoken about by leaders in all contexts), they will consciously and subconsciously begin to shape the way people think and act in regard to cultural diversity.

In addition, the mission and values statements should ensure that diversity characterizes the way you do church; it should ensure that all gatherings are evaluated through the lens of cultural diversity. It may be necessary to set up a series of workshops and consultations that will facilitate transparent dialogue and help open hearts and minds toward living in unity with people of different cultures.

Build a Culturally Diverse Leadership Team

Someone once said that when people walk into a church, they quickly look at the stage to check for their culture group. If it's not represented there, they still might enjoy the service, but it won't feel as though this is the church for them.

The church leadership must increasingly reflect the diversity in the country and the community around the church. But be prepared: Inviting different cultures into your leadership will change the whole way you approach ministry. If it doesn't, then you aren't listening to the voices of the diverse leadership you've included.

It's important to adopt a proactive and intentional strategy to move toward a culturally diverse leadership team. This should be applied to every level, from senior church leadership to ministry leaders to adult volunteers and even down to teen leaders. In South Africa, the goal is to move toward a leadership team that reflects the demographics of the country.

Design a Culturally Diverse Ministry Environment

May it be said of your church that a sermon is preached on multi-culturalism long before a word is spoken from the pulpit. In other words, that "sermon" is preached by the diversity of the parking lot attendants, the diversity of the door greeters, the diversity reflected in the greetings given in many languages at the start of the service, the diversity of the worship team members, the diversity of the preachers, teachers, full-time church staff, and the diversity of the congregation as well.

Every aspect of a service must be evaluated for its diversity before the event is presented. Here are some sample questions to ask:

- Do our videos reflect cultural diversity?
- Do the images we project reflect cultural diversity?
- Do the stories we tell reflect cultural diversity?
- Do the songs we sing reflect cultural diversity?
- Do the people who speak and play and sing and support and work behind the scenes reflect cultural diversity?
- Do our words reflect cultural diversity?

Maybe the bottom line for a service is to ask, "Was everyone uncomfortable on at least one occasion during the event?" If the answer is no, then perhaps you're not being intentional enough about diversity.

Pursue a Culturally Diverse Feeder System

We realized early on in our process of diversification that we'd have to adjust to the inflow of teens into our ministry. Specifically, we needed to avoid targeting the advantaged and private schools— otherwise we'd remain a homogenous, monocultural youth ministry. So we set out to target government schools in our surrounding area, including a local primary school that had gone through radical cultural diversification in a short period of time. We also decided to target preteens in middle school, as they better reflected the demographics of our country. This began to have an immediate impact on the cultural diversity of our ministry.

It might be helpful to draw a five-to-10-mile circle around your local church and take a closer look to identify schools or community gathering points that attract different cultural groups. Then you can intentionally create a presence in that school or neighborhood. Doing so will begin to adjust the diversity levels of the people in your church.

THE CHALLENGES OF A CULTURALLY DIVERSE YOUTH MINISTRY

The Language Barrier

Here are some challenges that may arise: (1) Teens struggle to understand presented material due to the speed and complexity of communication; (2) Material used for discipleship is confusing (because it's written monoculturally); and, (3) Cliques develop as people with common languages are more likely to stick together.

In South Africa the solution that was adopted to deal with the language issue involved recognizing 11 languages as official languages. This approach has strengths—all cultures are affirmed, and people have access to education and commerce in their own language. This approach also has weaknesses—people struggle to communicate meaningfully with each other in the absence of a common language. A diverse leadership team and teaching staff (with translators, when necessary) can help in this regard, but language remains a significant barrier to true integration.

The Segregation Legacy

People often say that things have changed in South Africa (in other words, apartheid has been replaced by a democratic society), and therefore there is no excuse for people who were previously disadvantaged. However, there are some significant, lasting effects of apartheid, including:

1. **Identity Distortion.** Youth who grew up in segregated societies either have a sense of inferiority or superiority depending on which group they belonged to in those days. In South Africa the apartheid system classified people based on the color of their skin—effectively creating a hierarchy (from bottom to top) of Black folk, Colored folk, Indian folk, English White folk, and Afrikaans White folk. Resources for education, housing, and health were allocated based on this hierarchical system, which led to significant advantages and disadvantages. Being part of an advantaged group meant you viewed yourself

as superior to others; those from a disadvantaged group were socialized to view themselves as inferior.

2. **The Culture of Entitlement.** Previously disadvantaged youth tend to believe that it's their turn to be privileged and the previously advantaged must therefore give them everything they need to advance in life. This perspective may result in a lack of effort to rise from their current reality. Youth who were previously advantaged also have a culture of entitlement—they believe they deserve everything they have and resist any discussion about redressing the inequalities of the past.

3. **The Distrust of Authority.** Youth who believe that missionaries, church leaders, community leaders, and school teachers conspire together to create a system that enslaves the masses will find it hard to trust authority figures. Youth leaders must work much harder to earn and keep the trust of the teens they are leading.

The reality is that the legacy of years of segregation runs deep, and it will take generations for it to be thoroughly eradicated.

The Cultural Balance

Heading toward diversity is a challenge in and of itself, but attaining and maintaining a balance between different cultures must be continually addressed. The danger of losing one culture at the expense of another is always a possibility. Then there's always the chance that teens will leave because they don't relate to particular music or worship styles. When we pursue cultural diversity, we may find that we allow the pendulum to swing too far to one side or the other—and this will lead to a lack of diversity in the end.

Now, in case you're thinking that pursuing cultural diversity is too difficult, here are some words of encouragement by George Yancey:

> I am under no illusion that these are easy steps to take. I personally know the challenge of trying to find a multiracial church and of trying to impart a multiracial vision to members of a monoracial church. But the great difficulty associated with meeting this goal will also bring about tremendous rewards as we in the body of Christ begin to win the victories that multiracial congregations will

bring. It will be rewarding because we will see achievements that are beyond the abilities of humans, achievements that can only be obtained through God. We will see an enrichment of our fellowship we never thought possible. We will have the fruits of racial reconciliation at which the non-Christian world will marvel.[2]

LESSONS FOR CULTURALLY DIVERSE YOUTH MINISTRIES

Diversity Is Possible

Cultural diversity is not an elusive dream—it can happen. We cannot throw our hands in the air and say, "This is how things have always been—there is nothing we can do about it!" That's just not true—the many stories of transformation in modern society bear witness to the possibility of change, so it is possible.

Diversity Is Crafted

Cultural diversity does not just . . . happen. Youth ministry leaders pursue it through intentional actions, ongoing reflection, and course corrections. It is hard work—but if we want to create on earth the vision presented in Revelation 7, then it's worth all the effort that we put into making it a reality.

Diversity Is Vulnerable

Cultural diversity is always in danger of being lost once it's achieved. It remains an ongoing challenge to ensure that hard-earned gains aren't lost over time. Leaders will need periodic checkups to gain honest feedback. Just as Paul challenged church members in Ephesus to "make every effort to keep the unity of the Spirit through the bond of peace" (Ephesians 4:3), so we will have to expend effort to preserve diversity, which is a vulnerable commodity.

In my context, we know we're on a journey and in no way feel we've arrived. There are still many challenges; and often when we believe we've arrived, we discover attitudes from different sides that show how much work remains. As leaders, we're often a few steps ahead of the people in the congregation. So we should consider slow-ing down to ensure that others have forums for conversations that we're having as leaders.

FINAL CHALLENGE

May God give us wisdom and courage as we pursue his dream for a united community of believers from diverse nations who worship in oneness and peace before the throne—not just in heaven one day, but here on earth:

> [9]After this I looked, and there before me was a great multitude that no one could count, from every nation, tribe, people and language, standing before the throne and before the Lamb. They were wearing white robes and were holding palm branches in their hands. [10]And they cried out in a loud voice: "Salvation belongs to our God, who sits on the throne, and to the Lamb." (Revelation 7:9-10)

DISCUSSION QUESTIONS

1. What is the ethnic makeup of your community?
2. Have you been a part of a youth ministry that intentionally worked for cultural diversity? Why did they intentionally work for that goal?
3. Review the steps Mark provides for how to develop a youth ministry that welcomes diversity. What obvious "quick fixes" might you might need in your youth ministry? Craft a potential timeline for how you would implement these steps into your life and ministry.
4. How much do you know about cultural diversity and ways to promote it? EXERCISE: If your knowledge is lacking, do some research and develop a list of resources (books, DVDs, and Web sites) that can educate you on issues related to race, ethnicity, and diversity.
5. One of the issues related to diversity is power—who is in charge and allowed to set the vision/direction. In what ways might you benefit from collaborating with others to help grow your ministry's influence in your community and region?

RESOURCES

DeYoung, Curtiss Paul, Michael O. Emerson, George Yancey, and Karen Chai Kim. *United by Faith: The Multiracial Congregation as an Answer to the Problem of Race*. New York: Oxford University Press, 2004.

General Assembly Mission Council of the Presbyterian Church (U.S.A.). https://www.pcusa.org/multicultural/suggestedreadings.pdf (accessed December 1, 2009).

Johnson, Bill. *When Heaven Invades Earth: A Practical Guide to a Life of Miracles*. Fallon, MO: Treasure House Publishers, 2003.

Livermore, David A. *Cultural Intelligence: Improving Your CQ to Engage Our Multicultural World*, Grand Rapids, MI: Baker Academic, 2009.

Tittley, Mark. The Youth Ministry Resourcer at http://www.ymre-sourcer.com.

Yancey, George. *One Body, One Spirit: Principles of Successful Multi-racial Churches*. Downers Grove, IL: Intervarsity Press, 2003.

SPIRITUAL OBEDIENCE AS THE MARK OF MATURATION IN EAST AFRICA

EDWARD BURI

Given the growing fusion of world cultures, confusion is arising in regard to assessing maturity and when to celebrate the landmark movement of a young person from childhood. Communities in East Africa traditionally feature very elaborate, dramatic initiation practices involving wounding the immature body. However, the significance and effectiveness of traditional African initiations has been fading due to the competing understanding of "adulthood" between local and foreign cultures (especially in cities like Nairobi). Sadly, the decline of a rite-of-passage practice weakens the unique understanding of adulthood that the rites coded and articulated to the youth.

> Sadly, the decline of a rite-of-passage practice weakens the unique understanding of adulthood that the rites coded and articulated to the youth.

The uniqueness of youth is their *youthfulness*. While youthfulness implies energy and attractiveness, in light of the East African initiation process, it carries the taste of childishness that the community says cannot persist past some culturally defined point.

So when youth come of age, the community arranges for the shedding of childish skin and the accompanying childish treatment. Pre-initiation, youthfulness is associated with timidity, instability, and lack of wisdom—the uninitiated is not regarded with any seriousness. But immediately after initiation, youthfulness shifts to an embodiment of the community's boldness in the face of danger and the community's fertility (since the initiate can now marry and procreate). In this cultural perspective, any initiated youth caught doing "childish or uninitiated things" is shamed, labeled immature, and may be subjected to disciplinary treatment.

In most of East Africa, "youth" is a cultural understanding. Bodily changes are knit into the aspect of adult responsibility, and adolescence as a stage of life doesn't exist—one is either a child or an adult. For example, the Bantu communities of central, western, and coastal Kenya practice circumcision as a rite of passage to symbolize the transition. The young Bantu initiate in the Agikuyu community moves from childhood to adulthood as instantly as the swiftness of the circumciser's knife. The initiate enters the circumcision moment a child—and leaves it an adult. The community then holds wisdom sessions consisting of four weeks of counseling where life skills are passed along not to the *adolescents*, but to the fresh *adults*. Though the initiates are aged between 12 and 14, there is no provision for teenage mannerisms and habits. The initiation inaugurates adulthood immediately, and the initiate is given a new status in the community's wisdom hierarchy—an honor embodied through the responsibilities tasked as an adult.

The intersection of African rites of passage with Western culture creates confusion for the contemporary African dynamic. Teenageism is acknowledged while at the same time the initiation rite of passage is expected to yield its full adult effect. This leads to identity conflict—are they teenagers or adults? As a result, both the parents and youth use identity conveniently: Parents may demand better behavior from young people and ask, "Where is your maturity?" The same parents may turn down requests from their teenage children, saying, "I will allow that when you mature." On the other hand, young people may ask to spend a night out with friends by declaring, "I'm no longer a child." The same young people may challenge a parent's directive to "Quit going to night parties" by arguing, "Why won't you allow me to be young?" Such is the dilemma of an alloying culture—and adolescents must resolve the dilemma themselves. However, for the sake of cementing the identity of maturity, this dilemma cannot be avoided—it must be explained and appropriate conclusions drawn.

The church, however, possesses a reconciling stance that even reaches cultures with no elaborate initiation rituals. The church's articulation of maturity rooted in the biblical spirit even embraces girls (many of whom do not go through any formal initiation). This stance defines maturity as *a function of one's obedience to the Holy Spirit*. The mature young person knows God's will and is bold enough to step out and carry it out.

Samuel is an appropriate example of this in Scripture. As a young boy, Samuel heard the voice of God but was initially unable to discern it. But Eli—a much-older man who was also more mature in the faith and more experienced in discerning the voice of God—supported Samuel, saying, "If he calls you, say, 'Speak, LORD, for your servant is listening'" (1 Samuel 3:7-11). The message that followed from God wasn't child's play, but God knew Samuel could handle it. This definition of maturity aligns with an African understanding of *maturity as responsibility* and resembles an initiation moment.

The kind of maturity that God grants acknowledges the physiological and cultural status of young people and transcends those identities to provide them with new identities by enlisting them in God's mission. When Jesus Christ—the ultimate mature person—transforms a young life, the encounter produces one who's in the world but not of it, in the culture but beyond it, tasked by culture but with a higher task, labeled by society but bearing a greater label as well—a young person with an *un-young* identity. East Africa is just beginning to encounter Jesus' transforming power through our youth, a grace that transcends cultural markers of tradition, yet brings dignity to the rich cultures and people of East Africa.

DISCUSSION QUESTIONS

1. As Western (and more recently Eastern) nations seek their economic and political advancement through a presence in Africa, they are largely unaware of the confusing effect their cultural footprint has on the identity formation of African youth. The result of this disruption is a breed of non-Western westerners who thrive upon consciously and unconsciously negating their Africanness. As Africans take responsibility for this cultural corrosion, should not foreign nations take responsibility, too? What forms should the responsibility take?

2. The church as a symbol of hope for society expressly means that she must undertake her share of identity formation with young people in the community. What are some dead and dying cultural practices that the church can revise and champion that would be helpful in the Christly formation of young people?

3. Identity formation draws from several wells. This means the church cannot set out to be the sole identity shaper in society. What other institutions should the church deliberately strategize to co-work with in order to ensure the wholesome maturation of young people, making them responsible and productive citizens? What forms could this "co-working" take?

RESOURCES

Mbiti, John. *African Religions and Philosophy*. Nairobi: Heinemann, 1969.

Mugambi, J. N. K., and Anne Nasimiyu-Wasike, eds. *Moral and Ethical Issues in African Christianity: A Challenge for African Christianity*. Nairobi: Acton, 2003.

Mutie E. K., and Ndambuki P. *Guidance and Counseling for Schools and Colleges*. Nairobi: Oxford, 1999.

Thiong'o, Ngugi wa. *The River Between*. Johannesburg: Heinemann, 1965.

CHAPTER FIVE

AFRICAN REALITIES FOR YOUTH MINISTRY

BETH BALEKE

Most youth ministry in Africa focuses on adolescents in one of these categories: Families, churches, institutions, refugees affected by war or economic upheaval, street kids, or delinquents/youth offenders.

A recent continent-wide research project identified five significant issues that impact our young people in Africa today: Family breakdown, HIV/AIDS, globalization, poverty, and corruption.[1] In this chapter, I will focus on these five issues and offer hope for youth ministry amid these African realities.

FAMILY BREAKDOWN

Mukasa lost his father to AIDS when he was just a year old. His mother (from a different tribe than his father) abandoned Mukasa at his grandmother's door. Mukasa's grandmother then enrolled him in an organization that sponsors his education.

Mukasa, now a teenager, is also an orphan. Eager to study, he still isn't doing well in class. He is concerned about his future and desires to get a University education.

His report card shows he has to work on relationships as well as improve his grades. Mukasa frequently clashes with his guardian, and he struggles to submit to school authority. On his way home from school, he spends his little money and time in movie shacks that show violent films. If you asked, "Mukasa, what would you like your community to look like in the future?" he would quickly say:

1. Corruption-free with good leadership and justice
2. Security of life and property
3. No complaining about other tribes, races, and religions
4. Clean environment with sanitary water and good roads

Mukasa's story illustrates the impossible corner that many African youth find themselves in. Circumstances outside their control have dramatically altered their lives and eliminated many supporting institutions. And in Africa, if the family structure is absent, it is particularly difficult for youth to make it.

But Mukasa hopes. African youth hope.

Africa traditionally possessed communities of large extended-family networks that provided care, support, and safe environments. But this structure has been challenged by social change permeating Africa. Exacerbated by HIV/AIDS, economic turmoil, and migration, family networks have weakened, increasing pressure on other adults to adequately provide for vulnerable youth. The number of sub-Saharan youth orphaned before age 18 is expected to top 50 million this year.[2] In response, across the continent there has been a proliferation of orphanages and institutions now considered by many as the primary alternative-care systems in their communities.

> Africa traditionally possessed communities of large extended-family networks that provided care, support, and safe environments. But this structure has been challenged by social change permeating Africa.

Yet, mounting evidence demonstrates that institutionalized young people are often deprived of adequate opportunities for cognitive, emotional, physical, and social development that would otherwise help them grow to their full potential.[3] This should be of major concern to Christian workers envisioning ministry to youth in Africa. If we want to help transform individual lives, families, and regions of Africa, then it's urgent that we address the issue of institutionalized youth and their needs. My observation is that as we seek to reach out, we must pay attention to the larger family structure as the primary institution for influence upon an individual.

Jairus Mutebe, a prominent youth leader in Uganda, noted that youth and parents "held a vital link to young people's current and future well-being, development and [ability to find] meaningful placements and value in their lives."[4] Since millions of young people in Africa have lost their parents, however, youth workers must face the challenge to guide them to become responsible, godly parents themselves—a truly daunting challenge without any role models to follow. This starts now with guiding them into developing relationships and characteristics that will build their future families, hence the reality of Children and Youth Transforming Families and Nations of Africa.

HIV/AIDS

The tragedies young people face aren't merely personal—millions of young people like Mukasa strain the economic and social resources of families—and eventually communities. It's estimated that 12 million young people across sub-Saharan Africa have been orphaned by AIDS.[5] HIV/AIDS has affected entire communities and, consequently, many orphaned young people became burdens to other communities, further straining already weakened resources. Inadequate medical care and lack of protection from disease can result in increased social disorder, with profound implications for future political stability.

But several churches and FBOs (faith-based organizations such as World Vision, TASO, and others) are carrying out community-led care and support: Counseling, provision of food and nonfood items, provision of income-generating activities, and more are all in place to reach the young people between the ages of 5 and 18.

Many young people, especially females, face a disproportionate level of risk for exploitation, abuse, and HIV infection. The risk is highest among preadolescent and adolescent girls who've become the heads of their households. Often when the remaining parent dies of AIDS, the community's first response is to cater to the needs of the children and youth left behind, which translates into food, shelter, and maybe education. (Forget the grief and bitterness many orphaned youth may experience over their dead parents, their culture, and maybe even themselves.)

Only 16 years old, Veronica Nampala found out that her mother— her only family—was HIV-positive. Soon she was taking care of her ailing mum, and the experience is something she'll never forget. "I loved my mother, but it got to a point where I dreaded going to the hospital. There were times when she passed stool on the hospital floor and literally played with it, and each time I had to mop it up. I almost broke down. I went through a lot. I am scared of HIV/AIDS. I do not want my kids walking a similar path."

Years later, Nampala still nurses the wounds of this scourge.[6]

EDUCATION

A pressing need for the majority of African youth is effective education. However, as with Mukasa, school is the place where most of their needs rise to the surface.

The main approach to African education, in the majority of its formal institutions, has been knowledge-based—young people are fed information. The problem with this method is that many youth move away from school and end up loitering aimlessly without any practical skills. What's needed is an education that has positive values at heart but that also grooms responsible citizens for a world in need, in order to create a better world for all. What's needed are caring, respectful environments in which youth feel safe and are able to learn and grow.

Traditionally in Africa, older people imparted life skills to young people who worked alongside them during the day and spent additional time with them in the evenings around fireplaces using songs and stories. Today, this type of environment that nurtured such skills and positive qualities has been gradually disintegrating.

When I was growing up, my father used to sit us down in the evening and tell us stories and proverbs. I don't see that happening these days in the homes I visit. The gospel and basic core values used to be transmitted through the culture and its traditions, but now parents spend longer periods outside the home working. The challenge for youth workers today is to vigilantly explore how godly values should be best passed on in order to help youth bear fruit that will last (John 15:16).

POVERTY

Mukasa says he wishes to see a community that provides security of life and property along with a clean environment with sanitary water and good roads—but that is a rarity. In other words, poverty is experienced by most of Africa, and its effects may include feelings of hopelessness, worthlessness, lack of dignity, drug abuse (glue sniffing, marijuana, and so on), prostitution, theft, and violence. In addition, poor people are voiceless—they often have no way of protesting apart from using violence, which is usually dealt with harshly and without any positive results.

Since Jesus responded to people's physical and material needs, as well as spiritual needs, Christian workers should take care of the whole person as well. Today's youth workers should ask if their ministries are holistic—and if they are, to what degree? We should develop strategies that afford youth the opportunities to explore and develop their full potential, as well as offer them protection from violence. As a result, they will better be able to engage in their communities with respect, confidence, and purpose.

Such transformational youth ministry will exude godly, positive values at heart and groom responsible Christians who create a better world for all (Luke 2:51-52).

CORRUPTION

In Africa, youth often observe "bad" adults who are rewarded with wealth and fame. Tides of apathy and resentment wash away the idealism and hopes of youth with waves of corruption, greed, excesses, and injustice. The newspaper headlines across the continent report gross corruption by public officials—the same people who should be the keepers of justice. But there's a silent corruption killing parts of Africa, too. And as the world's economic machine comes to Africa in search of oil and other resources, the temptation for riches won't fade anytime soon.[7]

THE MINISTRY OF LIFE SKILLS

Despite the bleak picture I've just painted, there is one youth ministry strategy that many have successfully employed in African nations: Stepping into the young people's developmental voids and using the tool of life-skills education to make a substantial difference in local communities. With an overt Christian perspective, teaching life skills can help youth effectively resolve conflict without violence, think critically, develop self-awareness, and communicate effectively with adults. In fact, many youth and institutions that would normally resist the Christian faith are extremely receptive to it since witnessing the tangible results of this very practical ministry strategy. In the end youth develop self-esteem, sociability, tolerance, and self-control; become competent to take action; learn how to generate change; and develop agencies for their future decisions.

THE MINISTRY OF HOLISTIC PRACTICES

How do we communicate the gospel in the language of today's African youth? The challenge of helping children and youth take faith steps toward Christ and acquire moral values is no longer as simple as it used to be (when a good role model and a family tradition of honorable storytelling were sufficient). As Jacques Delors noted in her report to UNESCO, *Learning: A Treasure Within*, we mustn't just educate our children and youth "to know" and "to do," we must also educate them "to be" and "to live together."[8]

Therefore, youth ministries' working philosophies and practices should be holistic in nature, contributing to the development of the whole person. In our strategies, we must concern ourselves with our youths' intellectual, emotional, spiritual, and physical well-being (Luke 2:52). As we champion the advancements of God's kingdom, we should put efforts into and also network with those who provide guiding principles and tools for the development of the whole person to transform entire communities and sustain future Christian ministry.

In light of the fact that the majority of the African population consists of young people, we must take advantage of their energy, adventurous spirit, time, and passion. In order to generate youth who transform families, communities, and nations, we must help Christian young people live effectively in local communities with respect, confidence, and purpose. We should measure their impact not by how often they say, "I am saved—how about you?" but by the way they use their gifts and energy, as well as the witness of the fruits of the Spirit in the communities where they live. Understanding African youth dynamics and responding appropriately with evangelism and discipleship are the keys to transforming the families and nations of Africa.

DISCUSSION QUESTIONS

1. Given the widespread problems described in this chapter, what effect might they have on African youths' understanding of God as a father (parent) and provider?

2. How does the modern or current trend of living affect the behavior of young people, especially with regard to their faith? How does this affect the way they can be reached for effectiveness?

3. What are some possible strategies for working with youth in regions where there is much violence?

4. With some knowledge of issues affecting youth in Africa, how should we involve them in missions and discipleship?

5. Why do you suppose there is a seemingly ever-increasing tide of immorality and corruption on the continent of Africa? We need to continually offer meaningful ministry that has a lasting and significant impact on our young people.

CHAPTER SIX

MESSAGE FOR A MESS-AGE

MINISTRY TO YOUTH IN WEST AFRICA

DR. NUWOE-JAMES KIAMU

Since the 1960s, West Africa (and Liberia, in particular) has experienced vast political, social, economic, and spiritual changes. Some post-independent governments quickly collapsed as politics degenerated into militarism and dictatorship regimes. Scores of people died, and this significantly affected population parameters as wars and political upheavals literally decimated portions of countries' populations. As one generation rose up after another, its makeup became increasingly young as older persons died or left the country to travel to Western nations.

Let me use Liberia as a specific case to illustrate this generational phenomenon.

LIBERIA'S GENERATIONAL PHENOMENON

Although Liberia gained political independence in 1847 and for many decades made significant progress in self-governance, its political and social status quo may indeed be traced directly to the influence of persons born between the 1960s and 1990s. Those born in the 1960s, closely tutored by their predecessors born during earlier decades, formed the book-loving generation. For them, hard-earned formal education was the best route to better living. Education and success were equivalent because the former led naturally to the latter. This generation grew up expecting to earn certificates, diplomas, and degrees as success indicators. Such preparation would place them into positions of authority and trust in both public and private life. With decent incomes, they would settle down, get married, raise families, and pursue their lives' desires with much ease. Naturally, then, this group produced a significant school-going throng.

But as the '60s children became adolescents, older politicians organized them into social and political entities that would later drive our country to ruin. The people of this generation became strong candidates for social and political exploitation in the 1980s. And during those days, they acquired something they probably didn't consciously believe they would use—violence. At first there were vigorous university campus debates and political rallies, but soon brute force came into play. So as they became young adults, they naturally also became the passionate revolutionaries who desired and demanded political and economic changes—whatever the cost.

Although they did not participate directly in toppling the 133 years' political machinery through a bloody *coup d'état* on April 12, 1980, they witnessed first-hand much of its brutality. Their dissatisfaction and growing agitation played out in Liberia's civil war. As the war raged throughout the 1990s, the 1960s generation already had 30 years behind them, and they represented a prime civil-war fighting force.

They also recruited and trained teenagers to do what they themselves had acquired and were still perfecting—violence. They made those born mostly in the 1980s the infamous 'small soldiers' or child soldiers.

Now Liberia must deal with those born and trained in the violent structures of the 1990s—and these individuals are even more restless. They are in our high schools, colleges, universities, polytechnics, Bible schools, seminaries, and other institutions. Many of them peddle wares on the street or are serving time in prison. They experienced a mutilated childhood, forced into adulthood while still adolescents. They have no history of playing as children. They are survivors who fought for life. They did not grow naturally through adolescence—they leaped over it and became adults almost over-night. Yet, this group (and the generations of the 1960s through the 1990s) must rebuild their nation. That's both their honor and responsibility. This is the group we must disciple.

There are very distinct social and spiritual developments among young people in Liberia today. Socially, they are the illustrious danc-ing generation. Walk or drive anywhere in Monrovia or to any urban or rural community, and you will see two-year-olds jumping to their feet to dance to African music.

Place a music or video disc in one hand and a book in the other, and a large number of this group will naturally abandon the book. Many have no formal education, but they've perfected some skills, making them up as they go. They are creative, active, street smart, and forceful. Life for them must move on—fast and now. They are boisterous, fearless, unashamed, arrogant, and unapologetic. They are rebellious, defiant, and passion-driven. Youth don't seem to understand a culture in which authority (not power) and respect (not intimidation) prevail because their culture is power and action packed. They chase power and action wherever they can find them—sex, money, popularity, drugs, drinks, violence, spirituality, or sports and entertainment (for instance, European soccer or Nigerian mov-ies). School is considered to be a waste of time and resources. Quick, easy, and more desirable is fast fortune.

This group is most rife for manipulation, too, whether through roadside musicians or street-corner preachers, as both can attract a crowd and play on the missing parts in the listeners' lives.

> Youth don't seem to understand a culture in which authority (not power) and respect (not intimida-tion) prevail because their culture is power and action packed. They chase power and action wherever they can find them.

In spite of all these deficits, these young people seem to realize there's a certain spiritual vacuum in their lives, and most try to fill it with activities—although most prefer to stay away from church. But they're also Liberia's brave new adventurers who seem to be seeking fresh frontiers they can conquer. And with these challenging youth is the Liberian church's greatest opportunity to win, disciple, and transform the nation for Christ.

MESSAGE FOR A MESS-AGE

Mess is not a positive word to describe this group of Liberians. But many would quickly admit that adolescents in Liberia are confused and need direction and guidance into a safe haven. This state of confusion and the attendant moral decadence so widespread in Liberian society represents what I loosely describe as a mess. And the generations and periods so characterized by the mess become the mess-age.

Some might take issue with me for characterizing things in this way, but my aim is not to put down the group. Rather, it's to describe the group as accurately as possible while seeking to understand where and why they are what they are and explore positive options for leading them into safe haven. That's the message this generation needs—a message of hope and restoration; a message of God's transformative power in individuals, groups, and communities; a message of purposeful living in godliness; a message of critical reassessments and repositioning for productive living.

These messages should characterize whatever discipleship paradigms we seek for adolescents in Liberia, West Africa, and Africa as a whole because what's true in Liberia in these respects is incredibly true for the subregion and the continent overall, with variations only in intensity, styles, and depth as the entire continent is becoming increasingly young with every passing year. These people need a message to help them live and confront twenty-first–century problems with approaches best suited for them.

A GENERATION IN A MESS (JUDGES 2:10-15)

When Joshua took over the military command from Moses, the generation that followed did not know God.

> And all that generation also were gathered to their fathers. And there arose another generation after them who did not know the LORD or the work that he had done for Israel (Judges 2:10, ESV).

In other words, the generation had no personal experience of God—the kind that connects a person or people directly to the Almighty. Although on the outside they were God's people, on the inside they didn't even know who he is. How did this happen?

A steady, tragic progression of godlessness characterized this post-Joshua generation. They were completely dislodged from their center of gravity, their critical identity—Yahweh. As a result, this generation was steeply evil and idolatrous and so attracted God's wrath upon them (Judges 2:11-15). If we were to consider certain characteristics of this generation for a moment, it might become clearer as to why it was a mess and how God's relationship with Israel was the solution.

Characteristics of a Mess-Age

Ignorant about God. The generation described in Judges 2:10 was incredibly ignorant about the very Person about whom it should have been the most knowledgeable. The writer doesn't tell us why that generation was so ignorant about God, but he suggests that although Joshua and his generation lived to honor God, many in that generation didn't take very seriously their obligations to raise godly children A generation in a mess doesn't have God as a part of its consciousness.

Abandoning God. A mess-age abandons God willingly and willfully (2:12). In this generation's eyes, God consciousness has little or no significance to real life. God is irrelevant and meaningless, and pursuing and knowing God are futile and irrational ventures.

Notice also that this generation of Israelites refused to put their historical situation in proper, concrete perspective. Had they made the Exodus a pivotal historical referent, they would not have abandoned the Lord, the God of their fathers, so easily. But because they forgot God's awesome wonders on behalf of their ancestors, they spiraled downward.

Provoking God. "And they provoked the LORD to anger" (v. 12). Of course, why tolerate what one has abandoned? If God doesn't make sense, leave God. And if you leave God, do everything you can to upset what people or the holy texts say about him.

Substituting God. As a direct consequence of abandoning and provoking God, this generation identified and substituted "alternatives" for God. "They went after other gods, from among the gods of the peoples who were around them, and bowed down to them" (v. 12). "They abandoned the LORD and served the Baals and the Ashtaroth" (v. 13).

Doing evil against God. Doing evil in God's sight is the natural consequence of putting him out of a person's or nation's life. When people sin, that's a direct affront to God and constitutes evil against him. However, this generation did not get away with their actions.

Kindling God's anger. A generation of people who treat God as if he's not there must stand ready to meet him. "So the anger of the LORD was kindled against Israel, and he gave them over to plunderers, who plundered them. And he sold them into the hand of their surrounding enemies, so that they could no longer withstand their enemies" (v. 14). When God is angry with a people, God allows them to suffer all sorts of humiliation. This kind of suffering is not for righteousness or justice, but for evildoing. It demonstrates God's displeasure against a people.

Terrible distress. God's anger works out his purposes, but it's most unpleasant to experience. Israel witnessed this. "Whenever they marched out, the hand of the LORD was against them for harm, as the LORD had warned, and as the LORD had sworn to them. And they were in terrible distress" (v. 15). God's anger brings such outcomes to a generation in a mess. That's really tough news.

GOOD NEWS IN THE MIDDLE OF BAD NEWS

Believe it or not, there's good news regarding how this mess-age motif relates to Africa's adolescent population: The answer is working toward making disciples of these adolescents while they're seeking to discover their true identities. But before we get to that point, let me demonstrate how, in many respects, adolescent generations in Africa are very similar to the post-Joshua Israeli generation that did not know God.

Discipling Africa

Africans a generation or two older than today's youth generation won't hesitate to affirm that most African youths are in trouble. That's not to say that this generation has nothing good in or about them. It is to say, however, that much of what previous generations venerated is fast becoming intolerable to younger Africans.

Unknown gods. Deeply religious, Africans have always worshiped deities. But fear of the unknown, more than trust in the known, often accompanied this worship. Even today's Africans are still deeply religious overall, but the objects of their devotion aren't necessarily the same as those of their ancestors. For example, where just a few generations ago young men would pour drink offerings to the gods during shrine rituals, many no longer do so today. They are largely ignorant of their ancestors' gods; so in their place, they've substituted other gods or interests—sports, education, pleasure, activities, and so on.

In Liberia, a particular case in point concerns deep ignorance about the God of the Bible, the Bible itself, and Christianity in particular. Even though Liberians boast of their country's Christian heritage, display Bibles in public places, and so on, scores of Liberian adolescents remain ignorant of the Bible and the very Jesus they profess to know. Even Bible teachers in some public and private Christian schools reveal an incredible dearth of biblical knowledge and faith when they teach. In addition, some church practices—such as selling anointing oils and an excessive preoccupation with demonic forces, witches and wizards, the miraculous and spectacular, and so on—illustrate a lack of true Christian faith and knowledge based on the Bible and Christian traditions.

Irreverent living. Especially in countries where civil wars have ravaged and decimated populations, the newer generations tend to lead irreverent lifestyles, both toward deities and elders. "These days, children don't respect anyone," or a variation of this statement, comes quickly to older Liberians' lips when describing what their generation considers irreverence in the younger generation. This is largely due to the fact that role models are hard to find. Discipleship and modeling reverent living would help here.

God substitution. The gods of Africa are still very present. While some adolescents have renounced any relationship with their ancestors' gods for faith in either the God of the Bible or Islam, many still believe they can substitute the true God whenever it suits them. Especially in existential crisis situations, it's so easy to revert to ancestral gods for protection, position, power, and provision. And if they don't substitute God with another deity, then they just ignore God, for the most part, and drive their lives in the manner they see fit.

Evil living. Hardly any African needs convincing regarding the presence of evil in the world. They are at home with the spirit world's operations and the evils among living people. Many live in fear all of their lives, doing everything in their power to steer clear of situations, people, and influences they consider evil or against their well-being. Having gone through nearly two decades of brutal civil war, Liberians know evil; and many adolescents have witnessed or even participated in evil living. Certainly some young people desire change; they just don't know how to bring it about. But robberies, gang rapes, immorality, drunkenness, deceit, dishonesty, murders, bribery and extortion, disrespect toward authority figures, and the like are all too commonplace in Liberia. And Liberians don't hesitate to call these acts "evil." Disciplined, trained, and educated adolescent generations would secure a better national future.

WHAT IS HAPPENING?

Africa is experiencing a deeply spiritual and moral crisis. Politicians, economists, and educational authorities prefer to put it all on the economy. However, the crises are profoundly spiritual in scope. This perspective doesn't deny the hard facts of physical reality that show up through the economy, politics, and other societal situations. But when Africa breaks up its fallow ground because it's finally time to seek the LORD and pray that God rains righteousness upon us (Hosea 10:12-13, ESV), then transformation of this mess-age through God's message of Good News will come to pass.

Africa is fast realizing its need for spiritual transformation that meets people's physical and material needs. In countries such as Liberia and Sierra Leone where decades of civil unrest have left adolescents grasping at whatever glimpses of hope they perceive, adolescents stand ready to receive an old message in new garb. In a dancing country such as Liberia (and this is true for most of Africa), this message will have to take on more celebrative forms that speak primarily to the heart and then the head. Bold new ways of doing ministry will have to necessarily challenge more traditional forms and norms. This will require even bolder spirits who will challenge the status quo.

YOUTHFEST—A Discipleship Model

I propose a discipleship model—YOUTHFEST. It's a forum to motivate young people to celebrate adolescence from a Christian perspective. The celebrations would resonate with praise, admiration, adoration, awe, honor, and glory to God on the one hand, and lift up adolescents who are created in the image of God on the other. It seeks to help create a new self-awareness for adolescents steeped in Christ-centeredness.

YOUTHFEST would discover what connects with Liberian adolescents and align these things with biblical Christian perspectives. The adolescents could then deal with compelling alternatives and be motivated to make godly choices at different stages. YOUTHFEST would seek to meet adolescents wherever they are—schools, marketplaces, playgrounds, entertainment centers—thereby working with them and establishing discipleship cells where best suited (in real time and life situations) and striving at each point to discover how God's message can transform the adolescents' mess-age. Reconsidering and celebrating youth from godly perspectives may be an important way to help adolescents discover who they are in Christ and seek godly transformation.

CONCLUSION

Adolescents in Africa and in Liberia, specifically, need God's trans-forming message to pull them through their lives that the term "mess-age" suggests. And such a mess-age needs a message centered on Christ and his power to transform. If the church in Africa can do this for our adolescents, it would solve more than two-thirds of the social, political, economic, and other problems of the continent. YOUTHFEST might be an option for transformative discipleship that will help adolescents face themselves and their problems in light of God's great news for their age.

DISCUSSION QUESTIONS

1. How has the national and political situation in Liberia shaped Liberian youth? How do national and political influences shape your youth?
2. Reread the goals of YOUTHFEST. As you reflect on the descrip-tions of the Liberian context, what might YOUTHFEST look like when put into practice? What specific challenges does the Libe-rian context present?
3. If you had the chance to have a Liberian young person speak to youth in your context, what would you like him or her to share? Why?
4. How do you reconcile the vast presence of Western missions movement in places such as Liberia and Rwanda versus the atroci-ties that occurred in these "Christian" nations?

THE NEW LATIN AMERICA

FROM RENEWAL TO REVOLUTION

LUCAS LEYS

I remember a sleepless night, reading Matthew 16:8 in the traditional Spanish version, where it says of the church, "The gates of hell will not prevail against her." While I read, I imagined Satan battering a flimsy white church, which tried to survive and maintain its dignity. This image drove me to urgent prayer, and while I was praying, a new vision came to me:

Jesus taking the Latin American church into his hands and using it to pound violently against the gates of hell in order to liberate millions of captives.

The church in Latin America was for too long preoccupied exclusively with survival, protecting itself from the decadent world around it. This fortress mentality still affects it—but that's starting to change. For many decades the pattern in Spanish-speaking countries was defending itself from a wicked world that surrounded it. Thus, the castle gates were closed, and the focus turned within its own walls. To take up the colors of anyone outside the castle was an act of rebellion or immaturity.

To be holy was to wear distinctive garb; very few thought of holiness as preparation for extending the Kingdom of God, for transforming society, or for taking an active role in the broader culture.

Hence, not too long ago it seemed as though few in Latin America thought about strategic planning, spiritual warfare, contemporary worship, or "taking cities"—a phrase that today permeates our popular church language, regardless of denomination. Instead, the goal was to protect oneself and maintain a "joyful little huddle."

The new millennium, however, presents us with a church interested in building the Kingdom on Latin-American soil. It's a profoundly moving circumstance because only with such a frame of mind can we live the Christian life with passion and enthusiasm as opposed to solely maintaining ourselves "pure and without blemish" (Ephesians 5:27), becoming proud and dull.

It is toward this Kingdom effort that youth ministry now strives in Latin America and works within—and outside of—longstanding traditions in the Latin American Church.

WHAT CAN BE ACCOMPLISHED

Especialidades Juveniles was born in Buenos Aires, Argentina, in 2001. A continent-wide outreach focused on the needs of youth workers, and its first international convention drew 1,200 registrants from 10 Latin American countries. Since then it has grown steadily, with offices in Argentina, Chile, Uruguay, Paraguay, Peru, Guatemala, Costa Rica, Puerto Rico, Mexico, and the United States. The dream of *Especialidades Juveniles* has been to raise up a generation of Christian leaders who know how to meet the needs of Hispanic young people; leaders who would strive beyond attractive youth programs toward deep compassion for lost youth, discipling young people all the way to maturity in Christ.

In my workshops throughout Latin America, I show what can be accomplished through building a transformational youth *ministry* from the traditional maintenance of a youth *group*.

YOUTH GROUP	YOUTH MINISTRY
WHAT WE HAVE DONE UNTIL NOW.	WHAT WE COULD DO.
• Focused solely on the "spiritual"	• Holistic ministry
• Driven by activities	• Driven by biblical goals
• Leaders are self-serving	• Leaders serve
• Elite focus	• Compassion focused
• Cyclical growth	• Consistent growth
• Random songs and games	• Worship and attractive activities that are purpose driven
• Maintaining traditions	• Assessing if and why it's working
• Occupied by a local agenda	• Focused on Kingdom work

The chart highlights how maintenance ministry attempts to emphasize the spiritual but instead paradoxically neglects the whole person—i.e., the holistic approach modeled by Jesus. Latin America has a long history of unhealthy dualism, concentrating solely on the spiritual while neglecting the rest of what it means to be human. But thanks to Liberation Theology (which created a broader understanding of how to understand the gospel and pushed theological circles toward a more pragmatic view of the impact of their teachings) and other evangelical groups, this approach is finally changing.[1]

The second difference is with those who motivate solely by means of special events. A youth congress or camp meeting fires people up, and the group grows, but as time lapses without another big event, the group hits rock bottom. Why? Because the group was motivated by external rather than internal forces. To that end, we do need dynamic, stimulating activities, but more than that we need a genuine connection with our Lord who motivates us in our secret, interior places to reach and realize his purpose for our lives. When we plan activities and are convinced they equip us to excel spiritually—and that it doesn't matter if the biblical objective fails to permeate our work—then everything ends when the programmed activity stops.

As I've observed youth ministry throughout Latin America, I've noticed that those who focus on youth group maintenance seem to concentrate their efforts on popular students versus the needy. In this way, these leaders are just like the world—without a strategic plan that resembles the ministry of Christ and looking for quick solutions that rely on popularity versus Christ's transforming power. A maintenance ministry bases everything on what they like and what is easy, whereas the builders of the future of youth ministry focus on areas needed for consistent growth.

Another difference I see with those in maintenance ministry is that they tend to occupy themselves with self-defense and exposing the world's sins rather than preparing to extend the Kingdom of God in the world. Many times we forget the marvelous life which is God's alternative. We instead think of salvation as a passport to the future and we sing:

How beautiful when we get to heaven
and we are singing for eternity.

I listened to such lyrics during my adolescence and was discouraged. Is the only alternative to worldly pleasures to dream instead of singing on the other side? Thank God that we can start singing here and now! Making a difference in this world is the most fulfilling thing we can experience in this life, though doing so also means incorporating worship, and God wants to equip us for that as well. The youth leaders who facilitate the task of extending the Kingdom of God here and now to adolescents are the best loved, most respected, and most admired for what they hold dear.

Another characteristic of the leaders who just want to maintain what has been achieved to date is the way they lock onto traditions; but those who build constantly evaluate whether or not what they are doing is really reaching the goal they are pursuing. These youth workers ask themselves questions such as:

- "For years we have been electing a youth leader annually. Does this really help us or not?"

- "Sunday night meetings are geared toward evangelism, but rarely do we actually see conversion. Is there something better that we ought to be doing?"
- "It is incredible how many Latin American churches require their young people to dress up. What does that communicate to young people about priorities in the church?"
- "Those who preach in church are always men. Would we be more effective if we gave a place in the pulpit for women?"

There are occasions in which I use analogies to define what we should not be in youth ministry. The following are a few examples, along with my explanations of each:

A freezer. We should not think of our task as merely "keeping" the youth cold and stationary so they don't "spoil." Rather our task is to equip them to be salt and light of the world.

A circus. We are not here to provide safe entertainment for teenagers. Recreation can be an excellent tool, but updating methods doesn't mean we should make sure kids are comfortable and look toward their leaders as "popular." Instead the church needs to equip effective leaders who work for the transformation of this generation into the image of Christ.

A convent. We ought not to build such an alternative reality that our kids don't know how to dialogue mercifully with their non-Christian peers and lack the skill and knowledge necessary to offer understandable, reasonable answers concerning their faith. Local churches should be service stations where leaders refuel their young people with the virtues of the gospel so that they can dialogue with their culture and map out the path to God.

A school. We are not here simply to fill youth with biblical facts and knowledge. Our task is not so much informational as it is formational.

BRINGING METHODS UP TO DATE

Postmodernism undermined many methods that were effective during modernism. Some years ago, Malco Patterson said, "It's time to leave the methods of the fifties in the museum and to mobilize our young people to serve in the nineties."[2] Now more than a decade into the new millennium we should still ask ourselves, "Why are we doing what we are doing? Does it work?" If we agree that social trends change and vary, and that the adolescent problems of our times and places are unique, we will have to agree in affirming that our methods should be revised in order to make genuine contact with the reality of our context.

In some contexts, it is very easy to admit that activity planning should anticipate the use of applications appropriate to our era, though in Latin America it has cost us many a battle to achieve this. Pluralism, globalization, postmodernity, the new millennium, revolution, and variety are all concepts and realities that claim a major effort on our part when we design our methods. For this reason, our leaders who work with this emerging culture must be saturated with this type of mindset.

The following is a list of questions that Hispanic American youth leaders are asking so that the stagnant clouds don't fog their vision and strategies:

1. To what extent is my manner of working the result of my socioeconomic context and my religious tradition?
2. To what point am I willing to read, learn, and change in order to have an increasingly effective ministry?
3. What can I do to better understand my teenagers?
4. How can I better adjust my ministry to biblical objectives?
5. Is there a group or age level that is being overlooked or that needs distinct leadership?
6. What characteristics of an effective leader are weaknesses in my life, and how can I keep growing in those areas?
7. What paths are my youth following—and what paths are other students I would like to reach following?

If we as youth ministers keep on answering these questions with humility while putting into practice the necessary changes that boldly flow from the answers, it will be easier to keep advancing.

> Some years ago I listened to John Stott, "Every Christian needs two conversions: one from the world to Christ and another one back to the world *with* Christ."
>
> - John Stott

THE BEAUTY OF A RELEVANT CHRISTIANITY

Months ago I was talking with some youth leaders from Guatemala. When I told them my aim was to reflect on how one could start a postmodern youth ministry, their jaws dropped and looked at me as if in a stupor. In so doing, they reminded me of an incident from my childhood.

When I was little, my mother read me many stories. One night she read one with the word *terrícola* (which means "earthling"), and that really caught my attention, so I immediately learned the word. The next day I was playing with one of my little friends when I remembered the word and told him, "You are an earthling!" My friend looked at me, and told me I was stupid. I laughed since I realized he didn't understand the meaning of the word; and I repeated to him, "You are an earthling! You can ask your mom!" He looked at me even more upset and said a bad word that is very common in my country. At that I also became upset and went to his mother to have her tell him that he really was an earthling. I said, "Isn't it true that Fernando is an earthling?" Without knowing what was going on, his mother laughed and said, "Yes, of course!" My little friend began to cry.

The leaders were doing the same thing. We either like or don't like the words *postmodern* or *emergent*. But these are the times we live in, and there is an emerging Latin American leadership different from any the continent has seen to this point. For one, it's hierarchical and more oriented toward teamwork; in addition, it's more secure because it's coming out of success and not poverty. By God's design we live in this stage of human history, and it is to these generations that our youth ministries focus. The cultural codes of this postmodern generation are what we should use in dialogue with them. The well-known philosopher Voltaire used to say, "If you wish to communicate with me, you have to use my language."[3]

The story of the cradle and the cross is the most passionate tale in human history. It is the story of God becoming man to make himself relevant to humanity who needs him. Just by looking at Jesus' parables, we realize that he used a kind of code to reveal the truth. The Apostle Paul even used the altar to a god of pagans to attract the attention of a community to Christ (Acts 17:22-24). Your mission and mine is to raise up a generation of Jesus followers who leave behind the mentality of "a joyful people escaping from a filthy, nasty world" and understand that all they are and do should be sacrificed to bring the light of the Kingdom of God to earth.

JOINT PROJECTS

The whole world keeps moving toward a pluralistic society, and the call to globalization or "the global village" tends to diminish ideological defenses and draw together the various parts. The church should not lag behind in engaging this new reality. The ecclesiastical edge began among evangelicals with the appearance of various outreach movements, itinerant pastors, mass evangelism, non-denominational parachurches, and means of communication that didn't exist 20 years ago.

One of the imperatives for the future success in Latin America is for youth ministries to engage in joint projects, integrating and sharing human, economic, leadership, and strategic resources. For example, if a church has 10 young people, and 10 blocks away another church has 10 young people, those two groups should work together. Obviously a church need not surrender its identity, but to reach youth in each neighborhood more effectively with the transforming message of Christ, it is necessary for youth groups to work together. We're going to hear more and more about networks of youth ministries advancing across the continent, of youth leaders who dedicate themselves once and for all to approach fellow youth leaders in their cities or zones to plan joint activities and make better use of resources. It's amazing to see the enthusiasm from these youth ministers who think outside the box and begin to weave together energies to advance on a community (such as the campaigns *No More Violence*—held in the football stadiums of Argentina—as well as *One World* and "Youth Networks" in different countries of Latin America).

FROM RENEWAL TO REVOLUTION

While on other continents teenagers may be wholly apathetic and uninterested in the church, in Latin America many young people feel frustrated with their church leaders because they don't allow them enough opportunities to serve Christ. Nevertheless, since Pentecost there has never been a movement of adoration and worship comparable to what we are experiencing today. Thousands of people throughout the Latin American continent are praying for revival. Entire congregations are fasting that we will see a harvest beyond anything we have ever seen, and this is sensational. However, all this fervor must translate into a revolution of values, ethics, and social justice that mobilizes our youth to serve Jesus by serving the needy outside of our evangelical temples (Matthew 25). Inasmuch as this is feasible, youth ministers have a crucial role as protagonists; and for this reason it is a strategic moment to equip, link with, and inspire the youth leaders from the other America. Latin American youth leaders find themselves at the opportune time for passing from the liturgical revolution that we now see to a spiritual revolution that could change the history of Latin America forever.

—*chapter translated by Timothy Paul Erdel, Ph.D.*

DISCUSSION QUESTIONS

1. Write down a summary of the main points made regarding what youth ministry leaders need to do in Latin America.
2. How have you seen a "maintenance ministry" philosophy in action in youth ministry?

3. After reading this chapter, what analogies would you create for what youth ministry *should* be in Latin America?

4. In what particular ways has postmodernism affected Latin American culture?

5. Lucas briefly mentions the positive role liberation theology played in Latin America, even in evangelical circles. EXERCISE: Do a small research project on the contextual theology in Latin America. Use articles from the *Journal of Latin American Theology* and prominent books on the topic.

ANDRES

FROM "STREET URCHIN" TO STREET EVANGELIST IN BRAZIL

DR. CALENTHIA DOWDY

When I first met him, Andres was sitting on a crumbling, dusty curb in the City of God shantytown of Rio de Janeiro's west zone. A young man in his mid-twenties and of a brown hue (or what Brazilians might call "mulatto"), he was smartly outfitted in dress slacks, shirt, and shiny shoes. Gospel music blasted from the large speaker of his portable audio system as he sat there, unsmiling and serious—perhaps in deep meditative thought—holding that huge black Bible in his hands.

Andres called himself a street evangelist, saying he spent his life travelling around the streets of Brazil, sharing the gospel of Jesus Christ with the young people who lived on those harsh streets. His manner of dress and the way he comported himself clearly signified he was not a street thug or gang member. He was part of another team—God's team.

A life-changing event led Andres to do what he does today: He is one of the survivors of the well-known Candelaría street massacre of 1993. After midnight on July 23, Andres (then an adolescent) and approximately 60 other kids were sleeping on cardboard mats on the ground outside the large baroque façade of Our Lady of Candelaría Catholic Church in downtown Rio. They slept in front of the church every night after the priests served them food and taught them Bible lessons. Many people called Andres and his peers "street urchins"; they were considered useless and throwaways.

On this particular night, two unmarked cars passed by the sleeping horde of youth, and six men emerged from the cars to question the kids. An argument ensued, which ended with the men drawing their guns and shooting several of the boys in the head. Five were killed in front of the church, while the others scattered into the streets. Three more youth were killed a mile away from the church, indicating that the men ran after the children to continue their shooting spree.

Eight boys were killed that evening. It turned out that the bandits were rogue and retired Rio police officers. The worst part is that this wasn't a rare event in Rio. Millions of children live on the streets of Brazil, and many perish in executions each day. Residents of the city often support the work of vigilantes and rogue police officers in ridding the city of the nuisance of street youth. Some even view these slayings as a type of population control.

Andres survived that night and further violence, and he grew up to become a committed Christian and evangelist to other street kids. Anthropologists have studied the street youth population, gang membership, and religious conversion in Brazil, and some of the more compelling theories of survival come from John Burdick (1998) who writes that religion allows these young people to create new social identities. Donna M. Goldstein (2003) adds, "Religious belonging has become not only an indicator of faith but also a protective symbol of neutrality and nonparticipation in the escalating violence occurring among police, bandits, and police-bandits" (224).

The "belonging" element of faith communities is significant, but particularly in violent and impoverished communities where one can be assumed other. Generally, young men join gangs, and the women join the Pentecostal church—both alternative communities that offer safety, care, equality, and a sense of personal power within their otherwise unsafe, careless, unequal, and powerless realities.

Andres chose the church, and everything about him says something contrary to what his social condition tries to heap upon him.

He is valuable, he is not a throwaway youth, and he knows it. Jesus affirms his sense of dignity, and Andres hopes to offer street kids that same alternative, life-giving reality that he found.

DISCUSSION QUESTIONS

1. How should one determine the value of "street children" from a biblical perspective?
2. What would the biblical perspective you identified look like when lived and practiced daily on the streets of Rio de Janerio?
3. What changes would you need to make in your life and practice in order to embrace this perspective?
4. What should be the role of believers in terms of identifying, engaging, and changing socially challenging areas in our communities?

RESOURCES

Burdick, John. *Blessed Anastácia: Women, Race and Popular Christianity in Brazil.* New York: Routledge, 1998.

Burdick, John. *Looking for God in Brazil: The Progressive Catholic Church in Urban Brazil's Religious Arena.* Berkeley: University of California Press, 1993.

Goldstein, Donna M. *Laughter Out of Place: Race, Class, Violence, and Sexuality in a Rio Shantytown.* Berkeley: University of California Press, 2003.

LATIN AMERICAN YOUTH MINISTRY

JUNIOR ZAPATA

The term "Latin America" officially represents 20 countries and nine regions (or *dependencies*) in the continent of "America"—former colonies of empires whose languages were Spanish, Portuguese, or French. All of these languages derived from Latin, hence the name. However, most people use the term "Latin America" to describe those countries in America that speak Spanish.

Though Spanish is the shared language, that's where the "sharing" ends. Latin America is surprisingly huge and well populated, possessing a wide range of people groups and cultures. Each Latin American country is a cultural world in itself. A night world map reveals millions of bright lights of dense metropolitan cities, each light representing a soul, mind, and heart. Hugging those luminous cities like a black coat, the darkness of rain forests, mountains, and deserts are a testament to the vastness of the land where even more people live.

Most Latin American countries hold many cultures that melt in and out, constantly creating a potpourri of change woven together by a thin-but-strong thread of common values and shared pains. I believe this is where youth ministry in Latin America resonates the most—in those common values and shared pains of a diverse-but-analogous youth culture. The political scene throughout Latin America brings trends in economics and education that affect young people in all of our countries. Media and technology inject an abundant dose of homogenized pop culture into mainstream youth culture. Economy, politics, education, and technoculture influence attitudes and values across the land.

In general, Latin American society is very conservative due to its 500 years of Catholic heritage. However, we are rapidly becoming a post-Catholic culture, and young people under the age of 25 are the ones living this cultural shift. The Catholic Church's influence on government and society has diminished, making its opinions regarding contemporary issues less significant. Young people don't relate to their parents' traditional religion anymore, and they don't trust "the institution" of the church.

LATIN YOUTH MINISTRY

Youth pastors have a transcultural mission: They have to cross cultural borders to reach young people. In Latin America young people are disenfranchised from those aged 30-plus years and older—or maybe it's the other way around! This is because the world in which Latin American young people live is vastly different from the world of their parents, teachers, and pastors. And this reality strains relationships and shapes the way youth ministry is carried out. Youth leaders have to balance the parents' and pastors' expectations with the needs of today's young people.

As of 2010, in Latin America more than 150 million Internet users under the age of 30 spend an average of 12 hours a week online. They have an average of 53 friends online, of which 40 percent are from other countries.[4] Consequently, Latin American young people share most of the same music, celebrities, pop art, brands, and paradigms with their peers from around the world. From 2000 to 2009, the growth of Internet usage in Latin America more than doubled the growth rate of the rest of the world.[5] This connectivity has brought a profound change in the way young people learn and assimilate new information. Young people now learn in their

own way by seeking what they see to be valuable content, not from "experts" giving advice or telling them what to do.

The Latin American Church has yet to understand the effects of this new lifestyle.

The old learning paradigm was that an expert teacher "taught." It was a monologue. Today's paradigm is that users find content and talk to others about their questions. If they need to, they go to experts. *It's a conversation.* The traditional Latin American church is trying to grapple with this as more and more Latin American young people are searching for relevant ways of learning about spiritual matters.

But the impasse between church and culture often seems too deeply entrenched. For example, many churches in Latin America insist that their youth groups reserve "preaching" time when they meet because the Bible says "the Word has to be preached." However, youth pastors are discovering, through trial and error, that young people don't want to learn that way anymore.

I believe church and culture are spiraling down in a fight for supremacy. Culture, going more secular each day, advances issues and laws that make the church tremble. Society, influenced by mostly non-Judeo-Christian values, is promoting changes in all lifestyles. The traditional Latin American church wants to keep the boundary stone where it has been; culture and new expressions of Christian churches (and youth ministries) want to move it somewhere else.

At the center of this clash stands the youth pastor as the mass of the demographic leans toward the continent with the highest percentage of youth.[6] As we approach that day, some in the church in Latin America are already talking. Youth pastors and youth leaders are having conversations about the best ways to approach Latin American youth culture. "Youth ministry" is getting popular, and some church leaders have begun describing it as a "new movement."

Yet the picture has other scenes. There are young people in Latin America living in the most extreme poverty. There are young people whose lives have been dominated by violence and bloodthirsty gangs. Still, the Latin American church is dealing with these issues head on, and youth pastors all over the continent are finding ways to meet these challenges.

It's obvious that young people are a true concern to the Latin American church today, and while pastors have a genuine burden for young people, they're finding it a challenge to deal with "change." The emerging church is grappling with the issue. Youth pastors are developing a boldness of their own as they go about reaching Latin American young people while at the same time satisfying the traditional church's quest for remaining the same in a changing culture.

DISCUSSION QUESTIONS

1. How did Junior's depictions compare with your assumptions about Latin America?
2. Junior discusses the diversity within Latin America. Select a region of the world and perform a "people-group analysis" to discover the diversity among various groups living in that area. For those of us who look on the outside, the differences aren't noticeable. But to the residents, they are readily familiar and serve as strong social barriers.
3. What are the primary differences between *monolog* and *conversation*? How might conversation be used as a method for helping young people grasp biblical truth?
4. How could youth workers engage in conversation with teens in extreme poverty or violent gangs?

LEME

THE CHURCH AT THE BOTTOM OF THE HILL

DR. CALENTHIA DOWDY

Leme is the neighborhood of Rio de Janeiro that sits right next to Copacabana. It's quiet and has fewer people than Copa. Leme's beaches are pristine. If you're in the right apartment or hotel room, you get a full-scale view of the beach, ocean, and sky every time you look out your front window. Tourists soak up the sun, enjoy the food and drink of beachfront restaurants, shop, people-watch, jog, skate, and walk along *Avenida Atlantica* (Atlantic Avenue). It's a slice of heaven.

But one of the downsides to this slice of heaven happens to be the street kids who run barefoot along the beaches and in the streets, begging, stealing, working, and playing—all part of their daily hustle. I was in a taxi one night when the driver almost hit a tiny boy zipping between the fast-moving cars and trying to get across the six-lane avenue. The kid was quick, but we barely missed him.

I met Jorge on another evening as I was walking on the beachfront avenue and looking at the wares of street vendors. He had brown skin, looked to be about eight years old, and had bare feet and a sweet face. Jorge was meandering among the vendors and then slipped up beside me and started talking. I couldn't understand his fast-paced Portuguese, so I just looked at him. He spoke again, assuming perhaps I didn't hear him. When I finally spoke, he looked stunned. I was obviously a foreigner, not Brazilian. So Jorge asked me for money to buy some food. I asked where he lived and where his parents were. He said he had no parents and lived on the street.

"Well, Jorge," I said, "there's a church I know that might be able to help you, and it's right around the corner."

Friar Antonio is on staff at the Catholic church around the corner from the beach. Called *Paróquia Nossa Senhora do Rosário* (Our Lady of the Rosary Parish), it's the only Catholic church in the Leme neighborhood. The large traditional church building sits at the bottom of the hill between two shantytown communities, *Chapéu Mangueira* and *Babilônia*. Children in those communities adore Friar Antonio—a short, wiry, white Brazilian man about 50 years old.

As with all the Catholic churches in Brazil, there is no paid youth pastor. They rely on volunteers to work with children and teens. But functionally, Friar Antonio is the undeclared youth pastor for this parish. He walks up the steep, half-mile hill into the impoverished communities to meet and play with the children who live there. He invites them to come to church where he started a youth choir and teaches singing and Bible lessons. One Sunday each month is "youth Sunday" when the church tries to fill the huge sanctuary with young people. Children and teens read Scripture, sing songs, take offerings, and are recognized by the friar for something they've accomplished. Friar Antonio usually gives the mass on youth Sunday. After church, the youth are invited to the courtyard area of the church, where they're fed a meal and can choose from donated clothing and shoes.

The friars own several dogs and seven large turtles who wander around the courtyard. The children play with the turtles, eat, and select whatever clothing they may want. Friar Antonio also keeps a log of teenage girls who've become pregnant. He meets with them, encourages them, and makes sure they receive proper prenatal care so they can have healthy babies.

The work is difficult in the midst of crime and an enormous street youth population, but Friar Antonio hopes to offer presence, nurture, and stability that might make a difference in the lives of some of the youth in his parish. This is why I was sure my little street-friend Jorge could benefit long term from this church's ministry.

Jorge and I lost touch after that night. I don't know if he ever went around the corner to the Leme church the next morning. Maybe Jorge lived on top of the hill in one of the shantytowns and frequently passed by the church. In any case I would meet many more "Jorges" on the streets of Rio, and their stories were often similar: Hungry, no parents, no shoes, no money. I soon learned there were subcultures of street kids who generally behaved, dressed, held their bodies, socialized, spoke, and related to outsiders in specific ways—all of which specifically identified them as street kids (Oliveira, 2000). Many of them learned the con game of begging simply because they had to. Some of their stories were true, while others were slightly fabricated.

Street kids in Brazil can be categorized in at least two ways: Those who actually live on the streets alone, and those who work the streets in order to help whatever families they live with—either on the street or in a tiny *favela* shack. I never found out into which category Jorge fit.

The children I met in the shantytown communities on top of the hill were mostly connected with their families and had shelter at night. They all knew the church and knew Friar Antonio. Many seemed content to know that if nothing else, the friendly church at the bottom of the hill was always there to meet their physical and spiritual needs if their own hustling and begging resulted in nothing fruitful.

DISCUSSION QUESTIONS

1. *Identity:* Discuss the issue of identity in each of the ethnographic snapshots in this case study. How did these young people see or understand themselves, and why is identity important even in faith development?

2. *Community:* Discuss the issue of community in each of the ethnographic snapshots in this case study. Is community important? How might youth ministry play a part in creating particular communities?

3. *Holistic Gospel:* Discuss the lives of the young people in each ethnographic snapshot. How might youth ministry respond to the obvious physical and spiritual needs of these young people?

RESOURCES

Burdick, John. *Blessed Anastácia: Women, Race and Popular Christianity in Brazil*. New York: Routledge, 1998.

Burdick, John. *Looking for God in Brazil: The Progressive Catholic Church in Urban Brazil's Religious Arena*. Berkeley: University of California Press, 1993.

Goldstein, Donna M. *Laughter Out of Place: Race, Class, Violence, and Sexuality in a Rio Shantytown*. Berkeley: University of California Press, 2003.

Oliveira, Walter de. *Working with Children on the Streets of Brazil: Politics and Practice*. New York: The Haworth Press, Inc., 2000.

CHAPTER EIGHT

WE LIVE IN A PERIOD WHERE YOUNG PEOPLE ACTIVELY SEEK SPIRITUAL TRUTH— YEAH, RIGHT . . .

DR. SØREN OESTERGAARD

A story from Northern Europe on how research can change both the concept and the content of youth ministry.

You needn't be a youth ministry veteran to be aware of the discussion among youth workers in Scandinavia, a debate that asks, "What's the direction for future youth ministry in a context facing ongoing, rapid, radical change?" In many youth groups and churches, a figurative Under Construction sign hangs on the youth room door with a warning to "wear a safety helmet" because the future of youth ministry can be more than a little unstable and building bricks may fly through the air.

As youth workers, we're lucky to be experiencing this paradigm shift. The old maps—drawn when people believed in absolute truths, "human potential," and that all problems could be solved with the aid of technological developments—no longer seem useful as the territories undergo these changes.

You see, the majority of young people have grown up in a world in which:

- more than 1 billion human beings live below the "poverty line";
- climate change isn't just something we talk about, but something we experience in our everyday lives;
- we have to deal with AIDS, new versions of the flu, and the fact that millions of people still die from relatively harmless illnesses such as the measles, malaria, and diarrhea; and
- terrorism and regional wars confront us nearly every day by way of the media.

In addition, young people follow more of a socialized "midi-narrative." They believe in themselves and their close relationships, they're advocates of a pragmatic approach to life, and they don't feel a great need for a system or a "metanarrative" that provides "easy" answers to complicated questions. History has taught them that there are no easy answers. Therefore, if we want to communicate "the Story," then the big challenge globally, nationally, and locally is to dare to draw new maps that can help us navigate these new territories.

> Young people follow more of a socialized "midi-narrative." They believe in themselves and their close relationships, they're advocates of a pragmatic approach to life, and they don't feel a great need for a system or a "metanarrative" that provides "easy" answers to complicated questions.

In this chapter—based primarily on experiences in a Danish context—I'll attempt to demonstrate this paradigm shift in a Scandinavian context and with special focus on how an emphasis on research has been a major agent of change when applied to both the *concept* and *content* of youth ministry.

More specifically, this chapter will focus on answering these questions:

- What's on young people's agendas?
- What's on young Christians' agendas?
- What attracts young people with no Christian background to church?

Finally, I will note some of the overall challenges that youth workers will have to deal with in the years to come.

BACK IN THE '90S . . .

UK researcher Peter Brierley's 1993 book, *Reaching and Keeping Teenagers*, painted a disappointing picture of the church's ability to capture the attention of (and gain commitments from) UK teenagers. His book inspired a group of national youth workers to perform similar research in Denmark—a study detailing young people's everyday lives, struggles, and values, thereby producing a new approach to youth ministry.

This new approach shifted youth ministry from *assumptions* about what was going on in young people's lives to what was *truly happening*. In other words, we aimed to meet young people where they really were, not just where we hoped or thought they might be.

At that time most youth ministry in Denmark—and throughout Scandinavia—was either (1) activity-based (especially the church-based scout movement, church clubs, and the choir movement); (2) following the traditional "Bible, prayer, and refreshment" model—an attempt to copy the latest from the United States or United Kingdom (in particular the seeker-sensitive concept from Willow Creek and the Purpose Driven model from Saddleback); or (3) establishing youth churches.

Moreover, the number of youth workers was very limited (only a handful were in the free churches[1] and national youth organisations), and most lacked specific training in working with young people. Youth ministry was not a part of the curriculum in either theological colleges or universities where the majority of pastors and church workers were educated. In addition, only a few people wrote books about youth ministry, and the academic discussion on issues related to youth ministry was virtually nonexistent.

The Problem Is Not God . . .

The Danish version of Brierley's study was called *Teenagers and Their Beliefs* (Kier-Hansen 1995). Based on questionnaires answered by 1,300 teenagers between 13 and 16 years of age, their responses gave our churches something to consider:

- While 39 percent said they believe in God, only 20 percent stated they believe in God, Jesus as the Son of God, and the resurrection (very orthodox elements in Christian belief).
- When given 25 topics of interest and asked to list them in order of importance in their lives, topics such as the Bible, creation, and God got low priority. On the other hand, topics such as love, relationships, and hope made their top-three—topics that form key characteristics in God's kingdom.
- They evaluated the preaching in their churches with an F- but gave an A+ to the community they'd experienced in church during the year when most Danish youth attend confirmation class in the State Church.
- Only four percent of those who'd been "churchgoers" during their confirmation class stated that they stopped attending church because they'd lost their faith. The majority of these respondents said the primary reasons they stopped attending was because the church had a hard time communicating the gospel story to them in a meaningful and relevant way.
- The highest-prioritized things were relationships and being acknowledged by others.

These findings were an eye-opener for Danish youth workers, especially when:

- One in five teens said they believed in the constitutional elements of the Christian faith, yet less than two percent were active in Christian youth ministry.

- They were interested in some key elements that characterize the kingdom of God.
- Only a small number of young people stopped going to church because they lost their faith; rather, they stopped going because the church became irrelevant to their everyday lives, and finding their identity and forming relationships are their main concerns.

The book sent a clear message to the church in general—and more specifically to those in youth ministry—that the problem was *not* God, faith, spirituality, and what's going on in the everyday lives of young people. **Rather, the problem was heavily connected to a church that (a) failed to build meaningful bridges between "the Story" and the individual stories of the young people, (b) wasn't at eye level with young people, and (c) favoured a "you come to us" model rather than a "we'll go to you" model in which they might take the gospel to the various youth cultures of Denmark.**
The book initiated a new and more qualified debate on the role of youth ministry in the local church and in the church in general, and it became a catalyst for the following significant developments:

- An academic approach to youth ministry developed, and people began to ask "what" and "why" questions instead of just the "how-to" questions.
- A new commitment to a consistent focus on—and respect for—research was created.
- A network for national youth leaders formed in 1995 and has initiated important developments within Denmark's youth ministry.
- Denmark got into a process of internationalizing (for instance, youth workers from Denmark connected with IASYM, study trips were organized, and so on); and a few years later, youth workers from Scandinavian countries and Germany came to Denmark on study trips.
- The need to train youth workers theologically was acknowledged.
- Youth ministry has become a more integrated part of the national church agenda.

Also, a small group of people decided to conduct a youth-focused reality check—and it's now an important part of the Danish youth ministry DNA. In the following sections, some of the fruits of this reality check will be introduced.

THE CHALLENGE OF COPING WITH PROLONGED ADOLESCENCE

Adolescence – A Term That Has Lost Its Meaning

Adolescence is beginning earlier and earlier in life—and now it never seems to end! Forget for a moment the issue of teenagers never "graduating" to adulthood. One factor that's rarely considered is the adults in their lives who are more or less de facto teenagers themselves. This is why the term "down aging" has become integrated into young people's lives—they experience the so-called adults around them doing "younger and younger things as they get older and older." This means they quite often "play on the same playground" as their parents and other adults, and then these same adults try to teach youth in school and minister to them in church—a big problem. When adults and youth have the same values when it comes to consumption, hobbies, and the ideal body type, a 14-year-old daughter and her 42-year-old mother will work toward a BMI of 21. And a 14-year-old son and his 42-year-old father (or mother!) will listen to the same music while playing *World of Warcraft* together online.

Our research in Denmark shows that traditional "childhood" is now limited to eight years—and then children become "betweenagers" where they:

- consume the same products as their older sisters and brothers—even their parents;
- don't play with each other, but they do "hang out" with their friends;
- spend a growing percentage of their time in the virtual world—which for 7 out of 10 young people is a totally "parent-free zone"; and

- watch TV programs produced for a much older audience—but they'll often arrive at their own interpretation of the program. (Grube and Oestergaard 2008)

Unexamined Lives

Another consequence of prolonged youth is that many teenagers grow up in families where the parents ask, "What did you do?" but seldom ask, "Why did you do that?" The reason the "why" questions are absent in many families is that the parents are still asking themselves the same informative questions! Consequently, a growing number of young people grow up in "descriptive families." **In other words, we inform each other—often via Facebook or in text messages—about what we do, but we seldom ask, "Why?"** Therefore, a growing number of teenagers are moving away from analytical approaches to life (in other words, asking questions and taking time to seek answers through reflection, dialogue, and study).

If we want our teens' experiences to be more than *just* experiences and something they learn from instead, then we need to create spaces for reflection. These will come into existence only when adults dare to ask young people some of the important "why" and "what" questions. Young people need parents who'll ask, "What did you *learn* in school today?" instead of "What did you *do* in school today?" Similarly, teens need youth workers who challenge them by asking not only what they've been reading in their Bibles or experiencing at a camp, but also about the implications and consequences of their reading and experiences as it applies to both their personal lives and the community.

Why do the majority of young people need adults to facilitate a more analytical approach to life? Because even when they're in their "private spaces" with friends, teens won't ask each other the more important questions. And they won't do this because of a very interesting shift in the structures of peer groups. A few decades ago, young people typically grew up in neighbourhoods in which they spent time with kids both older and younger than themselves. Consequently, the older and more experienced kids in the group—who could also deal with the various questions of younger kids—usually introduced the others to new areas of life.

Today—especially given the specialized nature of the Internet—young people quite often become friends with people their age who are dealing with the same issues. And nobody really believes they have the right to question or challenge their friends concerning the issues that they themselves are struggling with or facing. Based on a six-month research project focused on teenagers and their friends, one of our main conclusions was that it resembled "the blind who tried to lead the deaf"! For example, when someone in the group shared how they did something really far out, we expected another group member to say, "Why on earth did you do that?" But instead the reaction was usually, "Cool! Did you really do that?" **The goal of acceptance and the fear of exclusion means teens don't ask each other some of the more unpleasant questions** (Grube & Oestergaard 2007).

But adults need to ask important questions of teens. A research project of 1,100 Danish high school students indicated quite clearly that parents move into something resembling a "department for logistics," and that the majority of high school youth lack even one adult voice that helps them create spaces for reflection (Grube & Oestergaard 2010).

A growing number of young people are actually pointing out that one of the things they found quite attractive about church is the openness toward asking important questions—and without needing to have all the answers. (Munksgaard & Oestergaard 2008) In other words, the church became attractive when it offered spaces for reflection and dialogue, rather than pushing teens into a process.

Has the Term *Youth Ministry* Lost Its Meaning, Too?

The prolongation of youth means that we have to ask whether *youth ministry* is the appropriate term to describe what we're doing. Is it really that meaningful when people at 15 and 45 are looking and longing for the same things? It's interesting to walk into an Internet café, an e-game event, or even a skater event in Oslo, Helsinki, Stockholm, or Copenhagen and observe people ages 15 to 40 doing things together in all three arenas. They aren't united by age anymore—only by their interests and values.

A few years ago, "youth churches" were a big focus in Denmark. Their aim was to reach out to young people ages 16 and older, but the challenge was that these youth churches attracted both young people and so-called "adults" who "felt much more at home" in the youth church than in the "big" church. The youth church's culture, set-up, and questions were relevant for them as well.

One of the questions youth workers have to deal with, then, surrounds the implications for youth when segmentation isn't rooted in age but according to interests, values, social subculture, and whether you're single or in a relationship.

So maybe *youth work*, *youth ministry*, and *youth workers* are no longer the right terms to use.

NO NEED FOR SIMPLE ANSWERS TO COMPLICATED QUESTIONS

When we ask "average" young people about their expectations when they attend church, only a very small number seem to long for simple answers to complicated questions. The majority actually look for "interpretation potentials" in relation to all the insecurity they experience. In other words, they're looking for various opinions *on top of* the opinions they may take in within a given context.

The challenge for youth workers in a Scandinavian context is to dare to deal with young peoples' insecurities by incorporating the ideas and words that have been placed on what could be defined as the church's "semantic stock paradox." To put it in another way, the church has an advantage with interpretation potentials that others don't have because its foundation is not merely of this world. Therefore, it can offer language and room for paradox, wonder, and even subjects difficult to understand (Qvortrup 2003).

By offering simple answers, we more or less relegate young Christians to homelessness because simple answers are part of a world that no longer exists. The challenge for Scandinavian youth workers is to help young people develop strategies that help make them capable of handling the insecurities that seem to be an integrated part of living in a postmodern context. It's not an easy task because it means we have to ask questions about our own foundations, values, and insecurities as youth workers.

However, the good news in this process seems to be that young people in Scandinavia don't look for experts. They look for *vulnerable pilgrims* whom they can join.

> The challenge for Scandinavian youth workers is to help young people develop strategies that help make them capable of handling the insecurities that seem to be an integrated part of living in a postmodern context.

ARE THEY THAT DIFFERENT?

In order to set up relevant programs for young people inside the church, researchers have conducted a few projects focusing primarily on the values and beliefs of those active in churches—and it would appear these young people aren't that different from their non-churchgoing peers.

A national research project conducted in 2007 and surveying more than 300 teens (ages 13 to 16) from evangelical and mainline churches asked questions previously used in the national survey that the Centre for Youth Studies and Christian Education conducts every five years. The 2007 project showed that—other than church activity—the primary differences between young people who've grown up in the church and their "non-church" friends are that:

• They don't spend much money on clothes.
• They're more reluctant to consider plastic surgery.
• They do their homework (yet the primary reason for this may be due to their middle-class backgrounds rather than their Christianity).

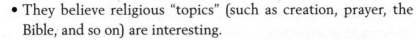

- They believe religious "topics" (such as creation, prayer, the Bible, and so on) are interesting.

In all other areas, the research found that churched and unchurched young people were pretty much alike, especially when it comes to areas such as relationships, the use of the Internet, views on the role of parents, and ethical questions. While it's true that churched teens believe in Christian principles, in practice they don't differ that much from their friends (Ehlers and Oestergaard 2007). When they were interviewed for the research, they were quite good at expressing some of the tensions they were facing. What they experienced in church seemed to be quite relevant for the arena of "faith" in their lives, but it didn't have any relevance for the others (in other words, arenas in which priorities involved relationships, being a part of a group, recognition, and identity). As one girl expressed it, "My youth pastor constantly challenged me to be a missionary at my junior high school; but as far as I know, I'm the only 'active' Christian in my school, and I really don't want to be lonely for the next three years" (Linda, age 16). So the fear of exclusion is significant. (Schroder & Oestergaard 2006)

This is true especially among young people who've grown up in "us and them" environments. For example—teens choosing an "assimilation approach" when attending school. Only when they're under pressure will they share that they are Christians because they're convinced that their church environment is so different and far off from their friends' everyday lives that revealing that part of themselves couldn't possibly benefit the process of introducing their school friends to "the Story." In other words, they just want to be normal kids! So they live somewhere between what they categorize as little "weird communities" (church) and the world outside.

This means some young people tend to be "situals"—in other words, whatever situation they find themselves in defines their values and navigation strategies. And that means it's actually possible for them to say yes to Jesus on Friday night and then say yes to sex on Saturday night and not feel any kind of conflict or regret. After all, it all seemed okay in the situation! Seen from the outside, it's not a very coherent approach to life, but when you talk to young people, it seems they experience some kind of coherence "because it was meaningful in the situation." (Grube & Oestergaard 2007)

Interestingly enough, it seems kids from more liberal "not that weird acting" churches (in other words, mainline) didn't experience the same problems as kids from other church traditions. In fact, the study painted quite a clear picture that young people from mainline churches tended to be more open about their faith and invite their friends to youth events and youth clubs more frequently. (Ehlers & Oestergaard 2007)

The Strategy of Silence

The same study also pointed to the fact that for a group of young people growing up in evangelical (or "free") churches, it seems "the faith of the tribe" is cracking a little. The majority respond by sticking to the strategy of silence because relationships are much more important than "truth"—and therefore, "Although I don't believe in talking serpents, I just pretend that I agree because I need to be accepted somewhere; and I use Christian vocabulary because it means something for my place in the 'hierarchy' . . . although I don't believe it's that meaningful. . . ." In other words, kids use the same strategy in church that they use in other arenas: They don't want to be excluded; therefore, they do what they believe will get them through. They *assimilate* instead of trying to *integrate*—in no small part because pulling off the latter is a big challenge. Indeed, for some it's too big, and they choose to give up altogether. (Grube & Oestergaard 2006)

For many European youth workers, the study was eye-opening because it exposed the fact that youth ministry equips teens for living in the world we *hope* they're living in—not for the world in which they're *actually* living. The issue becomes more complicated in the face of integration, as it clashes with the strategy that many middle-class churches have been using for decades—the strategy of "disintegration."

THE NEED FOR SOMEONE TO ACCOMPANY YOU ON THE JOURNEY

In order to become a bit more aware of what's really going on in the minds of young people who grew up in churches, we asked more than 600 young people between the ages of 18 and 24 about their experiences in church:

- 60 percent were still active in church (the percentage was a little higher for evangelical churches). Of this number, one in four had taken a break from activities in the church.
- More than half have never really experienced the church offering them any helpful tools to equip them for life in a postmodern context.
- Two out of three found worship to be irrelevant.

The study further showed that those still active in church could be separated into three categories:

- Those who've found "The Answer" (27 percent):
  - Nearly all of their important relationships are within the church.
  - Church is the only place where they meet people who share their worldview.
  - They honestly believe that church is relevant for people outside of church.
- Those who pick and choose (42 percent):
  - They have a typical social approach to faith and church—and they have close relationships both inside and outside of church.
  - They pick what they like when it comes to dogma, activities, and so on; and they mostly comprise their beliefs from "below," not from "above."
  - They believe in most of the foundational orthodox doctrines; but when it comes to "Christian morals and ethics," they're very selective in their praxis.
- Those who want to live close to Jesus and the culture (31 percent):

- It's important to stay authentic. They don't want to represent something with which they don't completely agree. Their "mantra" is to "stay true to myself"; they want to integrate and look for role models on how to do that.
- One in three is in an ongoing, internal debate regarding whether or not he should leave the church. The reason he hasn't left is often because he still has a dialogue partner inside the church with whom he dares share his questions (and who can cope with them). When there's nobody to talk with, the majority end up leaving the church.

The study shows that although we often tend to treat young people in church like a homogenous group, there is nothing remotely homogenous about them. The challenge for youth workers is to recognize where these young people are in their personal journeys and which approach they're using for learning and faith. Is it cognitive, social, or emotional? Then they should differentiate in personal interactions so young people experience that church (well, youth group, at least) is not a "sausage factory," but a place where people are valued and met where they are right now. (Willer & Oestergaard 2004)

WE'RE ON A MISSION . . . BUT WITH A SLIGHTLY DIFFERENT FOCUS THAN DURING THE "GOOD OL' DAYS"

Perhaps renewal of the church must come from the periphery. In 2006, a youth organization in Denmark did a qualitative study among 100 young people between the ages of 18 and 35 from "nonactive" Christian backgrounds who had since become "active believers." The study revealed quite an interesting profile of "new converts":

- Very few had actively been searching for "spiritual truth," and the percentage who started a search process during some kind of life crisis was very low. Most of them became Christians "by accident." In other words, they built relationships with Christians without knowing that their new friends were active Christians.

- Fewer than 10 percent had contact within a Christian community through "church activities," outreach events, and so on. The majority pointed to the fact that they'd become active Christians because they'd built relationships with Christians.
- 22 percent of "converts" see themselves as Christians who've just found a home.
- Most often they believed in the "foundational theology" of their churches, but very seldom did they believe in everything (and it really doesn't matter whether or not they do). Because their relationship to the church centers on human-to-human relationships, dogma is seldom a major focus or issue.
- 40 percent of the new converts consider leaving the church because they don't believe it's that relevant for the rest of their lives. Normally they'll stay in the church as long as the people who were the original bridges continue as a part of the community. If the bridge person leaves, however, these new converts often leave as well.

Many churches in Scandinavia stick to the thinking that activities attract and relationships make people stay. But research seems to show that relationships both attract *and* help people stay. Outreach activities seem to give meaning to those Christians who represent the disintegration-assimilation approach and need special occasions to share "the Story" because they have a hard time integrating it into their everyday lives. (Grube & Oestergaard 2006)

FROM KNOWLEDGE TO PRAXIS . . .

The focus on research in both Norway and Denmark has contributed some knowledge about some of the challenges youth ministry will face in the coming years in Scandinavia. We know a lot about adolescence, young people who've been raised in church, faith development, and related topics. Now we have to work on integrating our knowledge with praxis.

Among those involved with youth ministry, there is a desire to be inspired from the outside—and the inspiration primarily comes from leaders such as Kenda Creasy Dean, Pete Ward, Mark Yaconelli, and movements such as the Emergent Church and various models developed in the United Kingdom. At the same time, however, because of the failed attempts at copying *The Purpose-Driven Youth Ministry* approach, the "seeker sensitive" approach, the youth-church approach, and other models, it's evident that there's a strong focus on the idea that "we have to think for ourselves and develop a philosophy and praxis that takes our own unique context into consideration" (a process that will actually take some time).

There is a strong focus on putting "all the knowledge" into praxis in Norway because the government has decided to invest in youth ministry. Therefore, the experiences the youth workers are gaining in a Norwegian context will probably be the main influence in Scandinavian youth ministry in the years to come.

The Under Construction sign still stands outside most churches. And in a process like that, youth workers and youth organizations can choose either to *do nothing* (in other words, "do business as usual and hope for the best"), *ghettoize* (turn back to the old maps), or dare to *draw new maps*. And it seems as though this last option is the one most youth workers are going for—although it's "risky biznezz" because we don't know where we'll end up. Yet that seems to be the only unchangeable premise when doing youth ministry in a world of constant and rapid change.

DISCUSSION QUESTIONS

1. Søren used the term "prolongation of youth"—the idea that "youth" starts younger and younger and extends older and older. Do you experience the same development in your context? If you do, what are (a) the implications for youth ministry in general, and (b) the implications for your own personal ministry?

2. Is it also your experience that young Christians don't tend to be that different from average youth? Does the only major difference tend to be the fact that they "believe"?

3. In what ways might we be inadvertently promoting an "us versus them" environment by emphasizing youth group team building?

4. Søren writes that the majority of young people in church stick to the "strategy of silence" because relationships are much more

important than "truth." If the author is correct, this could have huge implications for the process of discipleship, assuming we should instead aim to meet teens where they are in their "faith journeys" and not where we hope they are. An important question is therefore whether or not we have an accurate picture of what young people in church really believe. Are there "faith arenas" where they stick more to the strategy of silence than the strategy of questioning?

RESOURCES

Birkedal, Erling. *"Noen ganger tror jeg på Gud, men . . .": En undersøkelse av gudtro og erfaring med religiøs praksis i tidlig ungdomsalder.* Forlaget Tapir, Trondheim, 2001.

Brierley, Peter. *Reaching and Keeping Teenagers in the Church.* London: MARC, 1993.

Brundstad, Paul Otto. *Ungdom og livstolkning: En studie av unge menneskers tro og fremtidsforv-entringer.* Tapir Forlag, Trondheim, 1998.

Giddens, Anthony. *Modernity and Self-Identity: Self and Society in the Late Modern Age.* Polity Press, Cambridge, 2001.

Grube, Kirsten, and Søren Oestergaard. *Mere end blot en søgen efter enkle svar: Et studie I danske unges søgen mod kirkelige fællesskaber,* Forlaget Unitas, Frederiksberg, 2006.

Grube, Kirsten. *Årgang 1992.* Forlaget Ungdomsanalyse.nu, Frederiksberg, 2007.

Grube, Kirsten. *Betweenagere: Et studie af 3-5.klassses hverdagsliv.* Forlaget Ungdomsanalyse.nu, Frederiksberg, 2009.

Grube, K., A. Eherls, and S. Oestergaard. *Are They really That Different: Et studie I hverdagsliv, værdier og livstolkning blandt unge, der er engagerede I kirkeligt borne og ungdomsarbejde,* CUR, 2007.

Gundelach, P., and E. Nørregaard Nielsen. *Hvornår er man ung?* Sociologi nr 3 2002.

Heggen, Kåre. *Ungdomsforskning og fremtidsorientering* i Ulstein, J: *Ungdomsi Rørsle ll,* Tapir Akademisk Forlag, Trondheim, 2004.

Holmqvist, Morten, ed. *Jeg tror jeg er lykkelig: Ung tro og hverdag.* Kloster Forlag, Trondheim, 2007.

Kier-Hansen, Finn, (red.) *Teenagere og Tro:* Forlaget SALT, Lemvig, 1995.

Lundgaard, B., and S. Oestergaard. *Teenagere & Tro ll: Et Studie i danske teenageres tro og vaerdir.* Forlaget Youth Resources, København, 2000.

Qvortrup, Lars. *Kirken i det hyperkomplekse samfund* i Ivernsen og Høisgaard: *Kirken og de diditale medier.* Forlaget Anis, Frederiksberg. 2003.

Schrøder, K., and S. Oestergaard. *Værdier i hverdagen: Og måske resten af livet.* Nyt Livs Forlag, Christiansfelt, 2006.

Skårhøj, Rie, and S. Oestergaard. *Generation Happy?: Et studie I dansske teenagers hverdagsliv, værdier og livstolkning.* Unitas Forlaget. Frederiksberg, 2005.

Willer, Thomas, and S. Oestergaard. *Generation Search: Et studie i danske unges livstrategier, værdier og livstolkning.* Forlaget Youth Ressources, København, 2001.

Willer, Thomas, and S. Oestergaard. *Jeg tror på det hele: Gud, Skæbnen og de syv bud.* Unitas Forlaget, Frederiksberg, 2004.

NORWAY: A CHURCH OF MANY MEMBERS BUT WITH EMPTY PEWS

ASTRID SANDSMARK

The Church of Norway lives in a strange juxtaposition: It is a facilitator for most Norwegians' rites of passage, and at the same time it is a vital community for believers. Around 81 percent of Norway's 4.8 million people are members of the national (Lutheran) Church of Norway, 77 percent have been christened there, and 67 percent of all the 14- and 15-year-olds in Norway are confirmed there. However, secularization and pluralism have weakened the traditional role of the church, and only three percent of Norwegians attend church services regularly.[1]

The state church system has been under attack for the last century. The basic question is whether a modern, democratic state should specifically connect to one particular religious community by constitutional directive. One implication of this system is that the government (*regjering*) appoints the bishops—a practice that's been in place for centuries but is now under debate.

During the last few centuries, the local parish, along with the priest, was responsible for the confirmation classes. The teaching methods were traditional, the youth learned about Luther's catechism, and this was usually the extent of church-based youth ministry—the active youth ministries were run by parachurch

organisations. But this is changing rapidly, and a dynamic growth of youth ministry is taking place in Norway as the church has realized the importance of youth ministry.

Believe it or not, the surge gained momentum thanks to the government.

In 2003, Parliament (*Storting*) gave the Church of Norway the responsibility to develop a systematic and continuous religious education for all the baptized children and youth. This dramatic decision gave local congregations and youth ministries a great challenge: What does faith-nurturing look like for today's youth? Since a large number of youth were coming to church for various confirmation activities (lectures, retreats, services, choir practices, and diaconal work for a whole year), this presents a great opportunity for the church—and its emerging youth ministries—to nurture a lasting faith.

NURTURING THE FAITH OF NORWEGIAN YOUTH

In two years, Anders will be 19—he wants to have a "gap year" so he can work in his youth group. But his family practices what Grace Davie describes as "vicarious religion."[2]

They belong without believing.

Anders grew up knowing little about Christianity and had quite a few prejudices toward the Christian faith. He chose to be confirmed as part of Norwegian tradition, however; and after a great camp experience, the adult youth leaders asked him to join the leadership development program and volunteer during the next year's camp.

"Everything changed," he said. "I became a Christian." He gained new friends at church and started playing the guitar in the worship band. "I meet God through the music," explains Anders. "The lyrics have started to mean something to me." He is now someone the confirmants seek out and ask, "Why are you a Christian?"

The average Norwegian young person, however, is not like Anders. When asked about their faith, teenagers' answers show the paradox of living in a country with a national church and a culture that's secular and individualistic. They tolerate other people's religious views but believe there are many different answers to life's big questions.

In some ways, the youth of Norway are content. Most of them live affluent lives. As one 13-year-old boy said, "I'm happy. We are doing all right. I go to school, I have friends and family and a roof over my head." Or another, "I think I'm happy. I'm very happy with my life. I live like all the others at school: TV, PC, go to school, go home, and go to bed. TV, PC, go to school, and so forth." The lack of spiritual need and questioning is a challenge the church hasn't fully comprehended. It brings up questions such as: *Do we need God in an affluent society? What is the "good news" to this generation?*

For most youth, their only experience of the Christian faith, church, and youth ministry is through confirmation. In the words of one 16-year-old girl, "I'm confirmed in church, but I don't believe in God. My dad is a Christian, so he is the one who wanted me confirmed in church. I'm baptised, but I don't believe."[3] This girl clearly states the challenge for the reformation of religious education in Norway: *How can we take advantage of the fact that most Norwegians have a connection to the church. yet work to make this membership mean something in their lives? How can confirmation be an actual meeting with God, with a community that loves Jesus and serves the Almighty God? How can confirmation be a way into church and not a passage out of it?*

DISCUSSION QUESTIONS

1. How can youth ministry "use" the traditions of confirmation and other liturgical practices and still stay true to the Christian faith?
2. In the United States, youth ministry grew when the government extended compulsory education in the 1930s and created age-segregated schooling. Decisions like that, and the one Astrid describes in Norway, have given dramatic shape to youth ministry practices. What do you think "youth" will look like in your culture in 50 years? In what ways will youth ministry be different then?

CHAPTER NINE

CONFESSIONS FROM A TRANSITIONAL COUNTRY—ONE CROATIAN YOUTH MINISTRY'S WORK IN PROGRESS

OR WHAT WE'VE BEEN THROUGH, WHAT WE'RE DOING, AND WHAT WE SHOULD BE DOING

IRENA DRAGAŠ

CONFESSION ONE: WE ARE IN TRANSITION

Panta rhei. Everything flows. A thought attributed to Heraclitus, it captures the reality that everything changes and nothing remains still.[1]

For those of us living in transitional countries, every system of belief and practice (political, economic, social, and moral) is being broken down and rapidly changed. A transitional country sees where it is while standing at a seam looking back at what was, and then plunges headfirst into what is to be. What was once taken for granted and considered a durable reality is now revealed to have almost been an illusion. So *panta rhei* is a particularly appropriate description.

I grew up trying to survive in a centrally planned economy, and now I try to keep my head above the raging waters of a free market. I was taught Marxism in school and Bible at home. Now the Bible is taught in schools, and Marxism is quietly praised only in one's home. For my country of Croatia, becoming an independent nation unfortunately meant war—and now we divide our transition history into three phases: Before the war, during the war, and after the war.

There is transition happening at every level of Croatian society. We are moving from socialism to capitalism while creating some sort of hybrid of the two. The politicians used to tell us that religion was the opiate of the masses. Now they flock to churches before elections and give speeches about how protecting our youth from drugs is their priority. Being a Christian used to mean you could never get a promotion at work. Now being a Christian (Roman Catholic, in this case) means you're a true Croatian.

David J. Bosch's *Transforming Mission* has become one of the standard reference books and textbooks on world mission. He writes:

> The events we have been experiencing at least since World War II and the consequent crisis in Christian mission are not to be understood as merely incidental and reversible. Rather, what has unfolded in theological and missionary circles during the last decades is the result of a fundamental paradigm shift, not only in mission or theology, but in the experience and thinking of the whole world.[2]

So I confess—Croatia is in transition.

CONFESSION TWO: WE NEED (YOUR) HELP

My parents attended a Billy Graham crusade in 1967 when he came to Yugoslavia—one of his few crusades in a communist country. A year later my parents were converted after hearing another American preacher. During communism, our ties to Western Christianity were a lifeline to the needy and growing church in Yugoslavia. Secluded from the world, we had to rely on our own resources and people—work was done by laypeople, not professional pastors and youth workers. Being part of the church meant you did not just receive.

When we became teenagers, we immediately became responsible for the youth group. No youth pastor, no volunteers, no interns, no youth program textbooks, no cool resources—just youth taking care of youth, leading Bible studies, organizing youth meetings, planning youth conferences and camps. An adult would occasionally help, but the youth were responsible for taking care of themselves.

> During communism, our ties to Western Christianity were a lifeline to the needy and growing church in Yugoslavia. Secluded from the world, we had to rely on our own resources and people—work was done by laypeople, not professional pastors and youth workers.

Then communism fell, and the war and religious freedom erupted. It was like standing at the bottom of a volcano just starting to spit out fire and lava. No matter how long you had feared or hoped that this might happen, once it did—you stood there petrified, not believing your eyes. The war created more needs and brought other forms of help. Humanitarian aid flooded Croatia. Church groups from other countries came to Croatia, brought material aid, and used this new window of opportunity to share the Good News. The foreigners had so much of what we needed, and they had different ways of doing things, which we immediately assumed were better. Yes, we needed help. We received help. And that help began to shape us.

CONFESSION THREE: WE DO NOT NEED (YOUR) HELP

It was during those war and post-war years that I participated in many youth events in which Croatians served as translators while the foreigners ran the show. They seemed happy running it, and we seemed happy to *just* translate—for a while. Because after the initial shock of hanging onto our bare lives while dodging grenades, hiding in basements, fleeing our homes, and becoming refugees, we faced another challenge—reclaiming and reinventing our identity. While hiding from snipers, we were intrigued by our newly established independence—no longer citizens of Yugoslavia but of the Republic of Croatia.

> After the initial shock of hanging onto our bare lives while dodging grenades, hiding in basements, fleeing our homes, and becoming refugees, we faced another challenge—reclaiming and reinventing our identity.

We realized we didn't need as much help as we first thought. We recognized the real needs versus the cultural need to please, and it took time to gather our courage to politely refuse what others graciously offered us because it wasn't what we desired or needed. We decided it might be time to take responsibility for our own needs and the work of rebuilding our country. Honestly, not everyone involved in a Christian ministry wanted to engage in this conversation. However, enough of us took the less traveled path to redefine our identity, and we encouraged each other to start a new "trend."

This is the time when I entered full-time ministry with a youth organization in Croatia. After receiving my Bible and literature degrees from an American Christian university, I was a national back in her own country. I knew the language and the culture, I had the education, I was willing and eager—I was ready to go.

CONFESSION FOUR: WE NEED TO BE AUTHENTIC

Perhaps my long intro is the first (and quite possibly the only) lesson a youth worker interested in international youth ministry should learn—spend time getting to know your new context. Get to know the country's history and how it shaped (and still shapes) its present.

We have to do the same thing here even though we're all nationals. As we grapple with the transitional history and our country's changing context, issues arise that we have to handle wisely. In those moments of cultural sensitivity, a pastoral response is necessary—it's the only response we know. And a crucial, nonnegotiable part of this response is authenticity.

DANIEL GENERATION

Though leadership development is important and essential, we didn't know where to start in terms of developing leaders in a post-war Croatian context. There were hardly any full-time pastors in churches, let alone youth pastors; so we couldn't hold a pastors' conference or a youth workers' convention. Still, we needed to educate, train, equip, and resource those who worked with young people—most of them volunteers and many still youths themselves.

We developed a five-day event called "Daniel Generation: Training for Young Leaders and Those Who Work With Youth," and we invited anyone involved with youth in a Christian youth ministry. This meant we attracted both teenagers (ages 17+) and 20-to-30-year-olds. Plus, a majority of those people attending would never call themselves "youth workers," just believers trying to "do something" to help youth.

We started out with mainline and evangelical Protestant churches, but soon realized that our work needed to spread into the ecumenical arena. One of the greatest needs in Croatia was to connect the Protestants and the Catholics. Daniel Generation (DG) became a place for networking and, most importantly, a time to meet the "other." Our joint organizing team of Protestants and Catholics was an example of the very principle we were trying to teach. But as I stated previously, we had to learn it first.

We had to learn how to work together and organize an event so we could have an authentic voice as we tried to teach others about the importance of meeting and working together. I still remember how our understanding and care for each other grew through the process as we determined the details of the program.

The annual event provided teaching, training, and exposure to new ideas and ministry models out of our own ministry experiences.

We highlighted new and field-tested Croatian youth ministry models, and participants left with free resources they could use in their churches, groups, and communities. DG became a reflection of our own journeys as we traveled toward an understanding of how youth work functions best in Croatia, toward an understanding of the tension between Protestants and Catholics, toward an understanding of the need to courageously risk with different traditions of the Christian faith, as well as our struggle to experience authentic worship and a desire to work with others and not build our own little ministry kingdoms within a small, divided country.

Our combined team membership grew. We challenged each other, built our team, dealt with differences, grappled with issues (such as postmodernism and men's and women's roles in the church), and then—together—presented the lessons we'd learned to the participants. Daniel Generation proved to be a pioneer event through which we began changing the idea of what church is or should be in Croatia.

Some principles made themselves obvious to us as we tried to figure out how to be Daniels in our generation and culture. For one, it seemed that Christians in Croatia responded better to ideas created in Croatia than those imported from other countries. Even though there is a certain fascination with foreign ideas and models, the DG participants kept saying it was refreshing and encouraging to see original Croatian ideas become the backbone of the event.

Second, having the organizing team model the principle of different organizations and denominations working together seemed to leave the most lasting impact on the participants. Third, we didn't just *tell* the young leaders at DG about models and resources they could use in their work, rather we let them *experience* them all. The whole event seemed more like a retreat because of the various activities. And they left there excited about what they'd experienced and wanted to share it with others. And they did. We still receive reports of people forming teams around Croatia to launch some of the models they got to experience at DG.

Finally, opportunities at DG to meet "others" resulted in long-term friendships and relationships that have positively changed the interaction between denominations in Croatia and specific communities.

APPROACHING THE THRONE

While in preparation for the Daniel Generation event, we started thinking about its "worship sessions"—that unavoidable component of every Christian gathering. So our team started asking questions about worship: *What is it? Is it supposed to move us to a response? How are we moved or challenged? How do we respond? What does it have to do with different personalities? What does it have to do with different faith traditions? What about our five senses? What about the rich traditions of the past? What about the common worship ground between Protestants and Catholics?*

> A key component of youth ministry in any context is worship, yet it can be one of the most culturally laden components of ministry. Many cross-cultural youth workers fail to recognize that every piece of music or artistic expression has a culture of origin. Despite the growth of a worldwide worship music culture and industry, there is no "one size fits all." As you read through Irena's account of how they worked through worship in Croatia, you may want to reflect on worship within your own culture. What is the story of how you've come to worship in the way that you do in your context?
>
> —Terry Linhart & David Livermore

We struggled, we asked questions, we felt confused, and we tried out new forms of "creative worship moments" that we called *Approaching the Throne.* We also created whole worship services in this new manner for various churches on Sunday evenings. We did this for a few years before we found that Christians all over the world were doing similar things and there was even a name for it—*alternative worship.* So we began to discover that there were actually more people like us in other countries. We were encouraged, and it was great to find more helpful resources. However, we were thrilled that *Approaching the Throne* came from within our context, rather than being somebody else's idea imported to us.

CHRISTIAN LABYRINTHS

We continued learning how to combine our youth organization's evangelical roots with our Catholic Croatian culture and our propensity toward postmodern eclectic expressions of faith. We often felt guilty for spending many hours talking within our team and discussing our questions about church, ministry, faith, personalities, tradition, and mission. Looking back, we now realize that without those honest times of sharing our questions, confusions, frustrations, discoveries, insights, and thoughts, we'd barely have had any ministry at all. Those times are what shaped us and our ministry and helped create ministry models that spoke in a truly recognizable Croatian voice—a voice that seemed to reflect all the sounds making up our history and our present. We hope this voice includes sounds of our respect for long-held Christian traditions, as well as our rebellious and reformation-prone restlessness; our awareness of how culture shapes the church and the church shapes the culture; and that many nations, ethnic groups, and faith traditions live in close proximity to each other—and the imperative for all those different groups to find a common language.

Perhaps history and geography have a major role in this. For how can one live in Croatia (and in Europe, for that matter)—right at the very meeting point of the borders between the Catholic Church, the Eastern Orthodox Church, Islamic nations, and the home of some of the first reformers—and not be aware that absolutes aren't as clear as some believe and not recognize the need to constantly redefine and transform the church? Not to mention the fact that communism nested in Croatia for decades, and personal faith was tried and tested here. You can't help but question the present state and desire to explore different expressions of faith in order to keep it alive and growing.

In the midst of this, we discovered the Labyrinth. Our like-minded friends in the United Kingdom added a modern slant to the ancient labyrinth and created an amazing interactive Christian spiritual exercise. It posed a challenge for Protestants, but it gave the braver ones an opportunity to explore new expressions of faith. Catholics thought it seemed close enough to their tradition, yet it posed a challenge with its fresh content, helping them connect tradition to the contemporary and everyday life. Atheists said this experience challenged their beliefs, while some long-time believers said they received answers to how to continue on the path with Christ. We also had new believers encouraged to persevere and stay courageous in exploring the expressions of faith that suited their personalities and family culture.

Through the labyrinth we seemed to have found a common point between Roman Catholics and Protestants that used to stand at opposite ends—now they both had a common place to meet.

And after a long personal struggle with this issue, we finally found a way to glue together the two parts that were tearing us apart internally—our Croatian Catholic heritage and our personal and family Protestant heritage.

One year we had a rather emotional Easter when we "embellished" the Stations of the Cross that a Franciscan monastery had placed on a hill near our city. We got permission from the monks to use the Stations of the Cross and add content, making each station interactive with texts, music, and hands-on exercises that used hammers, nails, photographs, candles, light, stones, and more. We stood at the bottom of the hill as people prayerfully encountered God through that experience. We could hear the sounds of nails being driven into wood echo through the night. Our team was moved to tears as we looked over the crowd and understood that the exhausting personal endeavor to connect the people of Croatia with a personal faith—what we'd been trying to translate into ministry practice (and what had brought us to the brink of absolute burnout)—was worth it after all.

We discovered that an eco-association had created stone labyrinths on one of the many beautiful Croatian islands. We fell in love with the island and wanted to help out with its preservation and use the labyrinths to do spiritual exercises based on long and wonderful Christian traditions. We could create a camp that was about more than entertainment. We could serve the people of the island and show in practical ways our appreciation and concern for God's creation. So we started a new kind of a camp. We felt more authentic as we did something to truly care for God's creation instead of just talking about it. And that opened up unexpected opportunities for us to share the Good News with others.

CONCLUSION

Saying goodbye to one ministry model opened the door for a new one, one that resonated with our souls, our culture, and God's blessing for our lives. It has been a long and difficult journey getting here, but it has been an exciting and fulfilling trip. If I had to summarize it in one principle, it would be this: **Know the context.** We believe this is the only way to do ministry. Well, actually, it's the only way to live. Learn about the place, the people, the history, the geography—ask questions about everything that puzzles you, confuses you, and strikes you as odd or wonderful.

There are reasons why people believe what they believe, do what they do, feel scared or hesitant about certain ideas or practices—and there are reasons why other practices and ideas make them feel comfortable. However, you won't learn any of this unless you're willing to risk and become aware of your own context as well—what you believe, why you believe it, why you learn a certain way, why certain paradigms scare you, and why you find certain ideas or traditions strange and different. So ask yourself questions and admit your fears, frustrations, and confusions. Revel in what brings you joy—a greater understanding of the love of God and God's teachings. All of this might lead you to pinpoint the important issues, and then, by working through them with a trusted team, you might discover the models of ministry that reflect both you and the synergy created by the intersection of the gospel and the relevant culture.

We're still learning how to stay committed to this principle—and who knows what awaits us as we continue our journey with God. Whatever happens, one thing's for certain: We can't wait to take the next step. These steps make us come to life and hopefully help others come to the source of Life.

DISCUSSION QUESTIONS

1. The chapter discusses a youth ministry model reflective of postwar Croatia. How has your culture impacted what your youth ministry looks like? Do you believe that the ways you think and talk about youth ministry are heavily influenced by your cultural upbringing?
2. To what degree have you conducted a cultural analysis of your own context?
3. In what ways can lessons learned in one cultural context be relevant to a different cultural context? Or is that even possible?
4. Since getting to know the context and translating it into ministry should be an ongoing process, how can one ensure that the process or the ministry don't get frozen in time?
5. What are some concrete steps you can take to help a person in ministry stay committed to a personal journey and an honest translation of that journey into how he does ministry?

CHAPTER TEN

MINISTRY TO THE DEAF

YOUTH MINISTRY IN AUSTRALIA IN THE NEW MILLENNIUM

DR. PAUL MCQUILLAN

The task of ministering to young people in Australia in some ways looks the same as ministry to young people all over the world; in other ways it looks the same as ministry to young people in some parts of the world . . . and in still other ways it's totally unique to our own part of the world.

Since the time of St. Paul, adapting the Jesus message to local circumstances has always been a challenge.[1] This chapter, therefore, will explore the precious gift of a unique Australian spirituality and suggest some ways in which youth ministry might nurture it.

Christian ministry is following in the footsteps of Jesus who invited all to come to him and exhorted those who followed him to go out to the whole world and tell the Good News.[2] This is the universal call of Jesus to all of humanity. Thus, Christian ministry is "in Christ and because of Christ."[3] Ultimately, those who work in youth ministry do so not because young people are Christians, but because *they* are. Yet, in all circumstances there is probably at least an underlying hope that this work will continue—that it will inspire at least some of those with whom we work to follow in our footsteps. The membership and commitment of youth is essential to build the future of every Christian church.

In Australia, many Christian churches are in crisis. This is similar to the situation in most of the English-speaking world.[4] Many of the mainstream Christian churches in Australia are sick, perhaps terminally. On the other hand, young people's search for an authentic spirituality, our capacity to know (and live according to the knowledge) that there is more to life than meets the eye,[5] and an understanding that our existence is part of a larger whole all remain a reality in search of expression.[6]

There is hope for Christian ministry, but in a secular society such as Australia, churches face significant competition in fields they once regarded as their own. Marriages and funerals are provided by civil celebrants, and pastoral care is offered by counselors or psychologists. Stolz defines this as "functionally close" competition.[7] There are also indirect alternatives to what churches provide. For instance, rather than attend church on a Sunday morning, one can go to the beach to seek spiritual well-being. Perhaps this has always been the case, but it hasn't always been so socially acceptable.

Plus, the exact definition of *spirituality* remains elusive. In some cultures it's ingrained in people's daily lives.[8] In the western Greek tradition, however, the spiritual has been divorced from daily life—particularly since the enlightenment.[9] So in the minds of young people, *spirituality* is associated in some way with "religion."[10] Christianity and its churches have certainly been the traditional means of expressing our fundamental human spirituality—our collective need to find and express meaning and belonging. But they no longer speak to the young, and, at least in the West, they are struggling.[11]

> In the western Greek tradition, however, the spiritual has been divorced from daily life—particularly since the enlightenment. So in the minds of young people, *spirituality* is associated in some way with "religion."

This search for spiritual experience among Australian youth provides a unique spiritual landscape for ministry. Gary Bouma writes of Australian spirituality as being a "shy hope in the heart."[12] He is clear that it's very different from the spirituality found in other countries and cultures. The next generation of young Australians, or at the very least the one that follows it, may well relate to a very different expression of Christianity—if it relates to Christianity at all. What will this mean for a future church, given that young people are vital to its future?

(Note: This chapter is based on the content of the course in "Ministry and Spirituality for Young People."[13] The course is part of the training for those who aspire to work as chaplains in schools or with young people in various settings. The course material addresses the major issues outlined previously:

- Many Christian churches in Australia are in crisis.
- Spirituality is a natural human condition.
- There is a disconnect between the need to express this in some way and mainstream Christian churches.)

YOUNG PEOPLE IN AUSTRALIA

In an earlier work, I compared young people in Australia today to the children of deaf adults.[14] Children born to two deaf parents usually have a natural capacity for speech, but they are surrounded by silence. Their natural language becomes signing, not English.

In the same way, young people in Australia are usually born into families with little religious affiliation. They have almost no experience of "church," so its language and practices are foreign. Their parents' generation has seen a remarkable decline in religious practice and affiliation.[15] Hence, Australian children are rarely inducted into Christian practice or teaching at home.

David Hay believes there's a "learned embarrassment" in Western culture regarding speaking openly about anything that may have a religious connotation.[16] Hay outlines in detail how, since the enlightenment, this embarrassment regarding overt religious discussion has developed in Western society. If parents and role models are embarrassed to speak openly about their beliefs, then young people's capacity for spiritual experience—what David Hay and Rebecca Nye term "relational consciousness"—cannot grow, at least not in the home.[17]

As a result, an Australian child's first contact with religious practice, belief, and the whole language of expression for Christianity never comes—or it comes only if she attends a religiously based school. That said, it's fascinating that religiously based schools in Australia now cater to nearly 30 percent of the population.[18] Large numbers of parents who may prefer not to talk openly about their personal spirituality or religious beliefs send their children to schools with a religious philosophy—in fact, they make an extra financial commitment for this to happen.[19]

It begs the question: Why are Australian churches nearly empty?

Sociologist Peter Berger concedes that the natural tendency for all formal religions is to reject the secularism that has characterised Western society since the enlightenment.[20] This rejection tends to be expressed in one of three ways: The first two involve "circling the wagons" by shutting out the world and reverting to sectarianism or religious fundamentalism. In the extreme, religious leaders might look to impose religious practices on whole populations by political means, as has been done in Iran and other countries.

Fortunately, however, Berger sees a third way that churches can react to secularization—and this is perhaps their way to survive: Adapt themselves to their culture. This response is, I believe, the only salvation for the mainstream church among young people in Australia today.

AUSTRALIAN SPIRITUALITY

Gary Bouma describes a uniquely Australian spirituality, largely formed by the history of development in Australia. Unlike the United States, Australia was never a haven for those wishing to freely express their religious beliefs; in fact, it was at first a church imposed on the early convict settlers (the Church of England) and later opposed by the same settlers—many of them Irish Catholics—as their own Irish clergy migrated to serve their spiritual needs. Hence, religion in early

Australian times was a sectarian battleground. It's no wonder that as waves of immigrants came from Europe, Asia, and South America over the last 40 to 50 years, they simply did not understand the battle and preferred to look for peace.

Bouma believes that "religion and spirituality have seeped out of the monopolistic control of formal organisations like churches."[21] On the other hand, for the majority of Australians, their personal spirituality remains "a shy hope in the heart." Australians are different. They do not readily express their beliefs and do not expect others to do so, either.

To trumpet spiritual experience in the way of an American televangelist would be for Bouma "an obscene dealing with what is so precious."[22] So the task of youth ministry in Australia is to assist in the expression of this precious gift while recognising the shyness and fragility of the gift for those who bear it.

> **Australians are different. They do not readily express their beliefs and do not expect others to do so, either. . . . So the task of youth ministry in Australia is to assist in the expression of this precious gift while recognising the shyness and fragility of the gift for those who bear it.**

Rituals and expressions of hope among Australians are largely secular. The resurgence of Anzac Day—and the remarkable attendance by the young at the Anzac ceremonies at Gallipoli—provide an example of a secular ritual that has gained extraordinary momentum in recent years. The recognition of Aboriginal culture is another example. There are few public ceremonies in Australia today that don't begin with a "welcome to country" that recognises the prior occupation of Aboriginal people in this land. The response of Australians in assisting those afflicted by natural disasters provides yet another example of what could be interpreted as spiritual searching expressed in a practical way.[23]

David Tacey, in his work with young people at Latrobe University, believes that although churches aren't connecting with young people, the pathways of spiritual seeking are crowded and wide.[24] However, he expresses the strong opinion that, ultimately, a person's spirituality cannot remain private.[25] While individuals can achieve their full potential only through relationships with others, it doesn't seem as though this can be achieved through gathering in churches unless the churches significantly adapt to a society that's largely moved on and left them behind.

Are Australian churches capable of this?

More importantly, are young people in Australia today capable of achieving their potential by joining with others and the society around them?

Although more than 50 percent of young people believe they have a sense of purpose and very positive relationships with friends and family, only 20 percent agree that there is "an inner being in each person that can be discovered"[26]—a theological concept with which most young people would have no familiarity.[27] Their attitudes regarding their wider society and the world at large are also less than positive. Only 20 percent agree that social justice is important and contribute to a better world through voluntary activities. Similar numbers are searching and asking big questions about life. Philip Hughes' research among 13-to-18-year-olds can be interpreted optimistically and pessimistically: They're either not engaging, or their nonengagement provides a flexible and fertile (but unploughed) field for youth ministry.[28]

Frost and Hirsch propose a "waterhole" approach to engaging youth—in other words, teens will quench their spiritual thirst as and how they choose to do so, rather than being fenced in by only one type of spirituality. Perhaps a more flexible approach would plant seeds to flourish in the future.

Other research detects a strong link between practical social ethics and the capacity to recognise and respond to those experiences in life that could be termed "religious."[29] Hay expresses a concern that our capacity to relate to the spiritual "relational consciousness" is being continually pushed underground in Western society.[30] Ministering to young people in Australia is, in many cases, akin to ministry to the "children of the deaf"—but perhaps it's even more like ministry to deaf children.[31]

Phil Rankin, working with young people in the United Kingdom, contends that they're inherently spiritual but have little space or opportunity to stop and reflect.[32] This may be just as true of Australian young people. Even more significantly, as their hopes are dashed perhaps they further hide their "shy hope in the heart" as they observe the world around them. Significantly, the values expressed in Australian society can be contradictory to basic Christian—and even human—values of community and the common good. Australian research has shown that many values expressed by Australian adults, such as "being a good member of society," are ruled by an underlying, deeper value of selfishness and self-enhancement.[33] To be a "good member of society" can be understood as a person being employed at the highest salary possible and the accompanying benefits, including the fast car and the large house. Yet youth unemployment is high, and access to the housing market is becoming more difficult for "entry level" participants.[34] Significant numbers of young people can see that this vision of society is one they may never reach.

According to Sohail Inayatullah, young people desire a world that works for everyone.[35] They are idealists, and yet their idealism does not come with an easily defined target. Idealism is more difficult to maintain, in fact, when the "enemy" is difficult to define—and we no longer have a communist threat, and fundamentalist Islam is remote from our peaceful society.

However, many young people can discover that the "system" is indeed a lie since it does not properly express their deeper human needs for spirituality and connectivity. Inayatullah asks what response young people could voice when they perceive the enormity of this lie. He sees four possibilities:

- First, they could run with it and join the MBA set, becoming both highly educated and highly affluent.
- Second, they could search for certainty in an uncertain world. (This results in fundamentalism of whatever type, be it religious

or secular, and the formation of a set of beliefs that provides certainty, thereby shutting out discussion and exploration.)

- As a third option, he sees depression and ultimately suicide as a pathway for some—and the suicide rate among young people in Australia, although decreasing marginally, indicates this indeed is a pathway for some.

- Finally, there are those who react against this "lie," whether or not they are able to express and understand their reaction, through violence. There have been numerous examples in Australian society over recent years, where violence has erupted in communities and among the young from what can appear to be very small and trivial triggers.

I suggest there could be a fifth response if churches can facilitate the spiritual search and walk beside the young in that search. To return to Berger, can the churches reject "secularism" and the "system" in a way that is relevant and encourages the spirituality of youth?

RESPONDING TO THE CHALLENGE

It's unlikely that the first of Berger's possible responses to secularism—that of a religious revolution—will ever be a phenomenon Down Under. Australians have a robust democracy, and any suggestion of revolution—particularly religious revolution—could hardly be taken seriously. On the other hand, churches even regaining the significance and influence they once had would be something of a revolution in itself.[36] It's more likely that churches will continue to respond to secularism by the Australian equivalent of "circling the wagons" rather than opening the doors and reaching out.

This chapter will briefly look at these first two options before moving on to consider Berger's third way, a change in which churches respond by changing themselves.

A POSSIBLE FUTURE FOR CHRISTIANITY OF AUSTRALIA

It may arrive via religious revival.

It's well-known that the young often rebel against the beliefs and values of their parents. Therefore, could rejection of parental secularism bring a revival of religious fervour among the young? The parents of Generation Y have experienced a significant decline in church attendance and outward expression of belief over the last 20 to 30 years.[37] So if young people take a different stance from their parents, the teens might become interested in (and attracted to) mainstream church practices in spite of their parents' collective indifference. They could become attracted to experiences to which their parents have never introduced them. This scenario sees churches remaining faithful to current expressions of practice and belief while seeing a resurgence of interest among the young sometime in the future and with a consequent increase in numbers.

In terms of providing meaning and direction for young people, would this "possible future" meet their needs? Probably—if only it would work! Many in Inayatullah's MBA set would no doubt refine their values and become churchgoers. Those who seek existential certainty would be satisfied, and, potentially, this return to the values of old through a resurgence in church attendance would see a consequent decline in depression and provide direction and meaning in life for youth.[38]

Unfortunately, Michael Mason and his colleagues found that Generation Y is the generation most like their parents in terms of attitudes and values when compared to other modern Australian generations.[39] They get on extremely well with their parents, share their beliefs, and indeed remain at home in a comfortable setting for years longer than previous generations. In Mason's opinion, their benchmark of church practice, already quite low, could see further dramatic declines if they follow the trends of their parents—so much so that church attendance among Generation Y believers could be minuscule in the future. Thus, resurgence from among the younger generation via rejection of parental beliefs and practices will have to wait for Generation Y to produce their own families. It will be a long wait.

Philip Hughes, on the other hand, believes that parents are actually the key to practice and attendance of the young in churches—

hence, churches are better served by working with families rather than concentrating only on the young.[40] But again, parents are conspicuous in churches by their overwhelming absence. A youth-based resurgence seems a long way off.

A Probable Future

A more probable future for the church in Australia is that current trends continue—in other words, a continued decline in church attendance. Robert Dixon found that church attendance for Catholics in 2001 was around 765,000 each weekend.[41] His figures are the most recent publicly published figures of Catholic church attendees, and he identifies a decline of around 20,000 per year in attendees from 1996 to 2001. Similar scenarios could be painted for other churches, while recognising that there is fast growth, albeit from a low base, among evangelical Christians. The capacity for these emerging churches to maintain allegiance over a long period of time still must be tested. It is clear, however, that the future of mainstream churches and for the Catholic Church in Australia seems very negative indeed.

Would the Australian equivalent of "circling the wagons" provide meaning and direction for the young? By its very description, it will provide for the needs of only a minority, most likely those who seek certainty in some type of fundamentalism. Meanwhile, the vast majority will go—as in the case with the MBA set—happily on their way and, in the case of a very significant number of others, continue with their alienation from society and church.

So how can it be that the probable future of churches in Australia is essentially to close down?

The Catholic Church, for instance, comprises the largest percentage (more than 27 percent) of the Australian population.[42] Catholic schools have more than 690,000 enrollments nationally, and a high percentage of these identify themselves as Catholic.[43] Yet their own church may not endorse their classification, tending to equate "Catholic" with being present at mass regularly, preferably weekly. They would be regarded as "marginal" at best.

Inayatullah's causal layered analysis (CLA), which I have mentioned in other publications, provides useful insight into the alternatives to both the possible and probable futures.[44] That analysis—in this case, the goal of attracting younger people to churches—can be compared to an iceberg: Only a very small portion of the problem is above the water line and readily observable (in other words, the lack of numbers in churches). Both the probable and possible futures address the problem at this level. If "success" equates with numbers, then both futures either increase or at least stabilise attendance. But do they address the real issues?

Below that level—under the water line—are a number of significant social causes (only some of which have been outlined in this chapter) that must be addressed if the piece above the waterline, numbers in church, is to change. Berger suggests that religion provides a "sacred canopy" to give a meaningful explanation to our lives.[45] However, there are in Australia today many such "sacred canopies" due to increasing migration from a multitude of different cultures. As outlined earlier there is also increasing secular competition for the services that churches have traditionally provided, such as marriage and funeral rites.[46] Deep, deep down below the surface is the real issue. And if the church is to have a preferred future in Australia, it should be aware of this definitional difference and adjust to it.

A Preferred Future—The Third Way

Churches and youth ministers following Berger's third way will adapt to their society. If Bouma is correct in identifying a deep spiritual culture among Australians, then the fields are ripe for the harvest. To respond, the churches must address spiritual needs and hence build their church communities to be in harmony with their surrounding culture. Berger believes the secularisation of religious expression does not equate to secularisation of personal religious consciousness.[47] This rings true because our underlying capacity to be "religious" is hard-wired into the human psyche, according to Alister Hardy.[48] The research of many in both Australia and the United Kingdom appears to confirm this.[49]

How to adapt? First, change the definition of what it means to be a member of a church. Attendance is necessary for survival, but churches must realise there will be many in a secular society who remain on the periphery, sampling church offerings only occasionally. Churches must begin to serve the needs of this group. Second, employ a theological language relevant in a secular society. Finally, understand young people and become comfortable with their culture. Perhaps being satisfied that larger groups happily join an event such as World Youth Day and not seeking allegiances that these people aren't yet prepared to give could provide a first step.

A wonderful metaphor representing how churches must change comes from Michael Frost and Alan Hirsch.[50] They speak of the Australian outback in their image of a new church. In the old established farming areas, the herd is fenced and their capacity to roam and explore is restricted; but in the outback, there are no fences. The herd is found only when it comes to the water—to quench its thirst. Thus, the water is constantly on offer, but only some of the water holes and wells will see members of the herd gathered around them at any one particular time. The membership will also change regularly—but the water still fulfills a real need.

A more contentious issue is how a renewed Christianity can find a language of expression that will both attract this fluid membership and provide a meaningful way to express that "shy hope of the heart" that is its personal spirituality. Churches themselves struggle with this question. Adrian Smith sees at one extreme those who believe they have the fullness of truth already and have stopped searching.[51] At the other extreme are theologians such as retired bishop John Shelby Spong who believes the current "religious understanding is doomed to die, no matter how frantically or hysterically people seek to defend it. It will not survive." [52] In the middle are those who both affirm the truth of our beliefs as Christians, but also realise there are "complex issues . . . raised in trying to understand the sense in which [our faith is] true."[53] As Smith says, "We no longer express ourselves nor understand our world as our [parents] did . . . Yet we are expected to believe in and worship a God with concepts that have remained unchanged since the Middle Ages."[54]

What does all of this mean for youth ministry? Inayatullah says the future is created by three forces. First, there is the push of technology and demographics. The inextricable rise of technology is significant in Australian society, as is the significant increase in population through overseas migration and shifts from one part of the country to another.[55] Second, there are deep structures within any society that are almost impossible to change. Bouma, referred to earlier, outlines these with regard to what he calls the "Australian soul."[56] Finally, there is the image of the future and how young people perceive it.

For youth ministry this third point is the key: Those who work with young people need to understand how they envision the future and encourage them to express that vision. A danger, from the point of view of the mainstream churches, is that young people's vision and expression of it may bear little relationship to mainstream Christianity (since mainstream Christianity has not yet changed its own expression of what it is and how it relates to the great God of the cosmos).

DISCUSSION QUESTIONS

1. How have you seen secularization affect religious expression in your context?
2. What churches in your community are experiencing the most significant growth?
3. How do immigrant churches respond to the dominant culture in your context?
4. If you could design a youth ministry that reached the most youth in your community in the most effective way—yet remained faithful to the gospel and had the blessing of local churches—what would you do?

AUSTRALIA

SCHOOL CHAPLAINCY: TAKING YOUTH MINISTRY OUTSIDE THE CHURCH

BILL HODGSON

Although an exceptionally secular country, Australia recognizes the vital contribution of religious organisations to society through welfare, pastoral care, and positive values for the community.

In 2006, the federal government launched a somewhat controversial initiative to help provide religious chaplains for schools that requested them. This move recognised the valid contribution and role of religion and spirituality to life development and education, funding grants for new chaplains for any school that applied.[1] Although the chaplains weren't required to be Christian, in the vast majority of cases, Christians were appointed as chaplains—an expansion of opportunity for a positive role of Christian workers in schools.[2] The new federal government (which was originally in opposition) reaffirmed the chaplain measure in 2009 after receiving overwhelmingly positive reports from principals of government schools who were involved in the original initiative.[3]

It's a paradox that this secular nation, where on any given Sunday only nine percent of the population is in church, is less Christian than American . . . yet more accommodating of Christianity in schools than the United States is.[4]

As such, many youth workers view school as nothing more than a fishing pond or target *group* for outreach activities launched from the church—a place to "get from" rather than to "invest in." This *outsider* approach fails to understand the nature of the school community and the opportunities it provides. A missional perspective views school as a complex community or village. The chaplaincy program potentially provides the most missional opportunity for youth workers to make an impact with the gospel in this highly secular country, legitimately working from the inside out, rather than from the outside in.

The government's chaplaincy legislation defines a school as "a *community* . . . students, parents, teachers, friends, former students, counselors, social workers, and other people connected with the school." Sociologically, schools are akin to the contemporary marketplace or city square. More than any other place in Australia, school is where people in a geographic area come together and connect in some regular way. Most Australians (parents and children alike) have no other shared social institution that rivals school in terms of providing a sense of collective identity—"our kids' school."

About 38 percent of all secondary students (ages 12 to 18) are enrolled in nongovernment (mostly Christian religious) schools, a number that's growing.[5] Nonreligious parents are increasingly seeking a Christian-based education for their children in schools that receive partial government funding in spite of their religious foundations.[6] This allows church and parachurch representatives to be involved in public schools for "voluntary religious education."[7]

Surveys of young people ages 13 to 18 in the United States and Australia reveal significant differences:[8]

- Whereas 84 percent of American youth believe in God, only 49 percent of Australian youth do.
- Weekly church attendance in the United States is 40 percent, but in Australia it's only 15 percent.
- In the United States, 51 percent of young people say that "religious faith is extremely important or very important in shaping daily life," but only 23 percent of Australian young people felt the same way.[9]

Youth ministers in Australia have to understand and work within this secular context. The exciting opportunity to develop youth ministry outside the church and into the secular context of Australian schools requires deliberate rethinking of prevailing assumptions. Youth workers must operate from a missional rather than a traditional mindset, with the humility of those representing the values and beliefs of a marginal minority, rather than some arrogant presumption of a majority (as seen in the uglier expressions of the Religious Right in America). While they have the right to be present, they must earn the right to be heard though the practical contribution of the gospel. This requires a perspective of influence rather than control, and through engaging the culture with love, grace, and truth, rather than judging it. In short, they must operate like Jesus—not the Pharisees—among tax collectors and sinners.[10]

The main venue for missional youth ministry (like the chaplaincy program) will not be an event, a program, or even a community of believers gathered on Sunday or Friday, but a community engaged in mission, sprinkled like salt and bringing light to otherwise dark places. The school is not a resource to building a better youth ministry; rather youth ministry is a resource for building a better school community through the transforming presence of Jesus changing lives and values.

> The school is not a resource to building a better youth ministry; rather youth ministry is a resource for building a better school community through the transforming presence of Jesus changing lives and values.

Over years of youth ministry leadership in Australia, I've discovered four biblical themes that are essential for effective youth ministry:

1. Be Salt and Light: Visibility with Credibility (Matthew 5:13-16)

Visibility is assured, credibility is earned. For instance, everybody knows and has an opinion about the chaplain in the local school. The challenge is to build and maintain credibility with the main three communities—students, staff, and parents. Ministry must add non-religious value to the community. Coupled with credibility, visibility is powerful and increases openness to the gospel.

Jesus said, "People [don't] light a lamp and put it under a bowl. Instead they put it on its stand and it gives light to everyone" (v. 15). In Australian youth ministry, there is no better "light stand" than schools. Though not everyone may ingest the "salt," they will all see the "light."

Jesus commissioned us to be "salt and light" (Matthew 5:13-16). We're "salt" when we uphold and live by biblical truth; we're "light" when we do "good works" demonstrating God's grace and love.

Light is more visible and self-evident than salt is. Light attracts while salt is about inner transformation. We cultivate openness to what we believe through showing its practical value in everyday life and community. Many skeptics and opponents of the appointment of chaplains have soon become vocal supporters, in effect saying, "I don't agree with her religious beliefs, but she's bloody good for the kids and the school. I can't imagine how we got by without a chappy!"

2. 'Lead' Like a Servant: By Influence Rather Than Control (Matthew 20:25-28)

True leadership means exerting influence to bring about beneficial outcomes. The secular setting does not afford a chaplain control or power. Australian culture values humility, self-sacrifice, loyalty, and service. Those who live and lead out of service have credibility and influence. Most principals and staff are dedicated to the welfare of students and desperate for resources and encouragement. If chaplains seek to serve as specialists, they add more value to school leaders' agendas and vision than anyone else from the community. Power and control reside in school leadership positions (the principal, senior teachers, board), and they will seek to exercise it toward the best interests of students and the school community. Youth workers with truly redemptive visions for their schools—determined to work under leadership—become allies, assets, and in many cases confidants to leaders hoping for a better future for students as well.[11]

3. Think Like a Friend: Intentionally Relational Rather Than Educational (1 Thessalonians 2:7-8)

Australian research shows that formal teaching in a religious education class has little influence on students' beliefs or their coming to faith.[12] Philip Hughes, author of *Putting Life Together*—the report on the findings of the Australian Youth Spirituality Research—concluded that adults in formal, institutionally designated positions are not where students go for personal help and spiritual answers.[13] Even those students in Christian schools will try to work it out themselves or turn to those with whom they already have *personal* relationships. Hughes writes, "What counted more [than a person's position] was the relationship that existed . . . of warmth and trust . . . It is necessary, then, for those who want to be available to young people to be proactive in building relationships."[14]

So a formal role as a chaplain provides access to a school—but not to the hearts of students, even students in real need of help. This access is reserved for those peers and adults whom students on their own designate as "friends." Chaplains should avoid primarily relating as classroom teachers, instead maintaining a more informal relational approach. Through involvement with students in and beyond school hours, genuine friendship can be established as these spiritual mentors cease to remain merely "the chaplain" and instead become trusted significant others who are *personally* interested in me.

4. Equip Like a Coach: Mobilize Students in Peer Ministry (Ephesians 4:11-14)

Model, equip, coach, and nurture students to intentionally extend friendship and reveal Jesus' love to their peers. Schools value students who are developing confidence and skills in communication, peer leadership, and community service. This requires specific training and modeling in regard to appropriate faith sharing and practical care for "their world." And actually, equipping committed students "for works of service" (as per Ephesians 4:11-14) will enhance the contribution of the chaplain in the eyes of the principal and staff.

Build a student-led movement with a strong sense of mission to change their world and reach their generation. However, wisdom and responsibility must be exercised to ensure their adolescent zeal is channeled appropriately given the school's secular context in contrast to their church youth group.

CONCLUSION

The opportunity of chaplaincy in government schools in a country as secular as Australia, though seemingly a paradox, has largely won over the critics and continues to invite a bold, creative, and pragmatic missional response from those truly committed to reaching this generation with the gospel.

It seems the perceived Christian contribution to secular youth is, at the same time, both increasingly marginal and practically central. The challenges are many, and the potential outcomes are huge: Every student could know not just basic information about the gospel, but also the name of an actual person who truly follows Jesus and demonstrates God's genuine love for them.

Youth ministry must adjust its primary paradigm, moving its centre of gravity from a ministry among the "faithful found" at the margins of society to a mission amid the lost at the centre of *their* world.

It's not about the survival of "our" churches but the expansion of God's kingdom through influencing this generation. Thoughtful chaplaincy provides that opportunity.

DISCUSSION QUESTIONS

1. What enduring principles and insights can be gained from this sidebar about Australian outreach that have practical implications for change in your present approaches and assumptions in ministry?

2. How might your approach and practice regarding school outreach change if you were to adopt the role of insider/advocate/encourager (rather than an outsider/adversary/critic) of local school officials in their commitment to students?

3. Make a list of the top-15 commitments or concerns that you as a youth ministry professional have for students' development and the school community. Now make a list of what you believe the top-15 commitments or concerns that a dedicated school principal and teachers would likely have for the development of their students and the school community. Identify the overlap and discuss how focusing on shared commitments and concerns for students' well-being and the school community's health could better position the contribution of Christian youth ministry.

CHAPTER ELEVEN

THE TEMPORARILY PARENTLESS GENERATION

OFW KIDS IN THE PHILIPPINES[1]

ANNE DE JESUS-ARDINA

JAMES' STORY

I hated my dad. As the youngest of six kids, I grew up without the presence of a father. Poverty forced him to seek greener pastures in the United States when I was only 10 months old. His earnings as a driver in the Philippines were not enough to sustain our family—so much so that my aunt adopted my older brother, and my mother tried to abort me when I was in her womb.

Although my dad provided for all of our material needs, I didn't feel like he actually existed. He was more like the voice of a big brother in a reality show, advising us on everyday life, scolding us based on reports from his "spies," and constantly reminding us that he was sacrificing so much just to give us a beautiful life back here in the Philippines.

A "beautiful life" for him meant having a large house and more money. But I was sure, even at an early age, that even more than money or possessions I needed a dad. There were many important occasions in my life that he missed: My first birthday; my graduations from preschool, elementary school, and high school; my circumcision; and my baptism.[2] Having no dad at my side made me feel so insecure and jealous of my classmates because their fathers were always there for them.

My brothers were lucky enough to have learned how to drive, fix the car, and do carpentry because my dad taught them while he was still around. But what really caused my anger with my dad was when I would hear him and my mom fighting when he called her on the phone.

People considered us fortunate. We had cars, a big house, a commercial building and convention center, a resort, and a farm because of my dad's hard work. But little did they know how pressured we were because we wanted to please our dad and make him proud of us.

—James, 18 years as an Overseas Foreign Worker's (OFW) kid

The trend of Filipinos working overseas began with the labor migration to the "promised land" of Saudi Arabia in 1974.[3] As the overseas labor phenomenon grew, it created a new dimension of the "temporary solo-parent." (Ortigas, 1996, 11) In a country of 96 million people, 10 to 12 percent of Filipinos are OFWs, with 72.4 percent of them distributed in the Middle East and 16.9 percent in Asia. The top-10 destinations for OFWs are Saudi Arabia, United Arab Emirates, Qatar, Hong Kong, Singapore, Kuwait, Taiwan, Italy, Canada, and Bahrain. (POEA, 2008) OFWs can be gone from home for two years or even a few decades. In addition:

- 209 countries have OFWs. (Sto. Tomas, 2002)
- Nearly 1.4 million Filipino families have mothers working abroad, and about 1.2 million more have fathers working abroad.
- 15 percent of Filipino families have children growing up without either parent.[4]
- 1.5 million Filipino children are left behind by mothers, while 3.75 million are left behind by fathers. In other words, 5.25 mil-

lion Filipino children are left behind by their migrant mothers and fathers. (Coronel, 2007)
- Those previous stats don't account for Filipino kids who are orphaned or grow up in broken homes due to legal separation or annulment.[5]

In a country that's very much family-oriented, the fabric of this basic unit of society is quickly unraveling as Filipino families divide due to distance and economics. OFW kids are often left with one parent, uncles or aunts, or grandparents. They may even live on their own. The main (and often, only) cause of the OFW phenomenon is poverty and the economic crisis the country has been experiencing for decades. The Philippines is the ninth poorest country in Asia, and there simply isn't enough work to go around.[6] One in three Filipinos is poor, and there are 4.7 million poor families. (Virola, 2008) Belen Medina observes, "The most common reason for migration is economic in nature. This is seen in the great exodus of all types of workers to other countries. The Philippines . . . is a major supplier of nurses to the United States, entertainers to Japan, and domestics to Hong Kong and Singapore." (2001, 284)

THE POSITIVE EFFECTS
Religious
Evangelistic Filipinos in diaspora are influencing their supervisors, colleagues, and subordinates for God's kingdom, gaining access even in restricted countries.[7] Some of them may be considered our new "missionaries" or tentmakers whose work abroad is incidental to their task of bringing Christ to the nations that prohibit professional missionaries. Many others become living testimonies of what a Christian looks and acts like. Others utilize friendship evangelism to win to Christ those in their spheres of influence.

Many times, too, OFWs are introduced to Christ in their host countries and then bring back their new faith and the Good News to their families. Family members—or even entire families—who become believers are then ushered into Bible-believing churches.

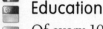

Education

Of every 100 Filipino kids who start grade one, 18 quit before completing grade two. By the end of grade four, another four leave school. Furthermore, 67 of the 100 finish sixth grade, and only 45 graduate from high school. Then 26 of those will go on to college, but only 12 to 13 of them will graduate. Of the dozen who graduate from college, however, only one comes from a poor family.[8]

To combat this, OFW parents earn the necessary funds to put their kids through school, even a private school, and go on to college. One former OFW kid (now a youth pastor) related, "My father said he would only come back home when we had all finished our college education."

Children's Independence

Some OFW kids learn to be independent at an early age, especially if they're left to fend for themselves without the care of an older relative or guardian. One former OFW kid told me that by age 13 he was handling all of the household and family responsibilities as the eldest son and second child. He helped take care of six siblings while both of his parents worked abroad. It's not uncommon for young daughters to assume the mother role if their mothers are OFWs. The same is true for young boys and fathers.

Economic

OFWs can grant their families basic needs—even luxuries. One former OFW child told me, "Even at the tender age of 10 back in the '80s, I concluded that if a family had a Betamax or VHS player, their father must be working in the Middle East." It seems one of the sure signs that a family has an OFW parent is the construction of a new house.

We cannot deny the larger economic benefits derived from global migration. The OFW remittances definitely have been instrumental to the Philippines' economic growth and its lower unemployment rate. The OFW phenomenon boosts the financial state of the Philippines through the $16.4 billion dollars it pumps into the economy each year.[9] Thus, OFWs are dubbed modern-day heroes in the Philippines.

But do these benefits outweigh the adverse impact, especially on the families and children?

THE NEGATIVE EFFECTS

There are allegations that migration and the OFW phenomenon have fostered a variety of ill effects, and its economic benefits are realized at a steep cost to families, children, and youth. Family breakdown, marital infidelity, marital dissolution[10], incestuous relations, and degradation of moral values have been noted as direct results of the prolonged absence of OFW parents. (Aquino, 2002; Coronel & Unterreiner, 2007; and Sto. Tomas, 2002)

Some even argue that the OFW phenomenon has eroded Filipino values such as *makabayan* (patriotism or love of country). Since most kids and young people aspire to work abroad, our best and brightest have been leaving our shores for years, causing a "brain drain" for our nation. The repercussions are felt even in churches where there can be a significant leadership vacuum.

Because some OFWs have been accused of taking "any" job abroad, they have been perceived as lacking *amor propio* (self-respect). It's common for teachers—even principals—to work as domestic helpers in other countries. Some doctors and dentists go back to school so they can apply as nurses abroad. Filipinos have long championed *pagtitipid* (frugality and conservation), a cultural value that is absent for many OFW youth who become materialistic, squandering their parents' hard-earned money.[11]

For the absentee OFW parent(s), there is a loss of closeness with their children, a loss of respect from their children, a danger of experiencing cruelty or injustices at the hands of their employers abroad, and suffering illnesses or injury away from home and their family's care.

When circumstances force OFW mothers to work abroad, cultural expectations compete with their need to provide for their families. Both options are seen as fulfilling their role in the home, yet they have to juggle which one is best. Although the father is the traditional breadwinner, the mother may either be more qualified to work abroad, or there are more opportunities available for women.

Filipino men are traditionally unaccustomed to being house-bound and taking on the role of "mother." Some may even feel it's tantamount to a castration. For the parent left behind, as with any single parent, caring for the kids alone is a challenge.

According to UNICEF, there are "negative emotional, physical, and psycho-social effects on [OFW] children."[12] OFW kids suffer from the painful lack of parental attention, affirmation, love, comfort, guidance, and protection. They are plagued with low self-esteem or loss of self-esteem. They often fear abandonment and feel empty, incomplete, vulnerable, helpless, and self-blame. If you talked with a group of OFW kids, you'd also discover high levels of instability, confusion, maladjustment, and denial.[13] These are also unfortunate by-products of the OFW phenomenon. One OFW kid commented, "The weirdest thing is that when they arrive back home, it's as if they never left. When they leave, it's as if they were never there."

Battling loneliness is a common experience, especially during important events. Hazel Russell recalled, "When I turned 18, a deb-utant, I didn't have a father-daughter dance. I almost cancelled the party because I thought everything was meaningless." Filipino youth ministry leader Randolph Velasquez boycotted his own graduation because both his parents were away as OFWs. Rigel Oro reflected on his days as a child of an OFW father and considers himself blessed since his father attended his high school graduation and spent two Christmases with them during the 25 years his dad worked overseas. A heartbreaking scenario is when OFW kids spend their Christmas holiday crying because their parents can't make it home.[14]

Social maladjustments in OFW kids may include problems related to discipline, increased juvenile delinquency,[15] becoming spoiled, and squandering their parents' money. Some OFW kids' academic performance suffers as well. (Medina, 2001) Bacon attests that "parental involvement in education has been victimized by a change in family structure" and mentions the high percentage of children in single-parent homes as one of these changes. (Ornstein and Hunkins, 1993, 46)

Is the money worth it? If you talk to many OFW kids, they'll say none of the benefits are worth their parents' absence.

YOUTH MINISTRY ISSUES

With about 60 percent of Asian populations below the age of 30, youth workers have their hands full. In the cities, universities and colleges teem with unsupervised young people coming from nearby towns and villages. Though they test their independence to its limits, they also search for meaningful relationships and the truth. Most Asian youth have become modernized and westernized, creating a cultural gap between them and their more traditional parents and elders.

In the Philippines there is still a dearth of youth ministers. Very few churches employ full-time youth ministers. Those who do work in churches often have other responsibilities besides youth ministry, and their designations may be associate pastor for music/youth, Christian education/youth, or evangelism/youth. I call this the "slash syndrome." It's always "youth minister-slash-something else."

With a minimal salary (if at all), some youth workers end up changing careers, especially if they have a family to support.[16] However, there are also passionate and sacrificial youth workers who have committed to youth ministry for the long haul. These "lifers" are found in churches, on campuses, and in communities all over the country.[17] Some have specialized ministries among the urban poor, street kids, gangs, and fraternities.

Youth ministers and adults who've either worked with or observed youth shared with me what they believe are the most pressing youth ministry issues in the Philippines.

Lack of Support from the Church

The issue in Thailand is representative of the Philippines. Thai church leader Wirot Khwanthong noted that "Thai churches generally overlook youth ministry. They don't have a program for the youth. Only a few churches have strong youth programs. Most missionary organizations do not have a clear program to reach young people."

One Filipino youth worker lamented, "It is so frustrating when the church does not support or at the least understand what the youth ministry is doing. I guess this stems from difference in ministry philosophies. Inevitably it hampers the ministry." Another shared a complaint frequently discussed among Filipino youth workers: "[There is] miscommunication and no support from the pastoral team."

Three overarching issues with churches affect youth ministry in the Philippines:

1. One veteran youth worker acknowledged, "Church leaders are not keen to discern the real needs of the youth. Most [of] what they see are only felt needs."

2. Few churches can support full-time youth workers. Another veteran youth worker said, "I often find myself all alone in the ministry work. Although the team of volunteers agrees on the plans and proposals I make, no one will step up to actively support and personally help me proceed with the plans and the implementation."

3. Lack of parental support or involvement. One youth pastor summarized the feelings of many others, "Most adults and parents are passive or take the ministry among the youth for granted."

Lack of Adults, Period

One of the realities particular to Filipinos and other Southeast Asian youth ministries is that *youth leader* is synonymous with a young person who's also a leader—not with an adult who works with youth (for example, adult youth pastors, youth ministers, or volunteers). In fact, it's extremely difficult to recruit adult volunteers in the Philippines. Thus, vocational youth workers regularly grapple with a lack of maturity, life experience, and dependability. Veteran youth worker and trainer Jean Galang observed, "With youth leaders in whom you've invested years of your life, you then face character issues, accountability issues, misplaced priorities, and intentional falling."

Lack of Resources

A lack of resources is arguably the most significant barrier to a fully developed youth ministry in the Philippines. And it's not just a lack of money (although that's usually the biggest and first obstacle), but rather a lack of time, people, and training. Asian leaders desperately need these resources, *but we need them to come from Asia*. Though some of the materials from the West are helpful, we need indigenous materials that are more relevant to our context. There have been efforts to produce such materials.[18] Excellent writers for youth abound, but some publishers are reluctant to invest in and produce materials for youth because they see it as a financial risk. Youth ministry isn't viewed as a viable market compared to women's ministry (since women possess more buying power).

Cultural Roadblocks

Filipinos tend to have an attitude of *ningas cogon*.[19] In other words, they tend to start with a bang—and then die out, unable to sustain the momentum. In general we also prefer to stay on the sidelines with a wait-and-see stance, playing it safe while the leaders do their thing. If we like what we see and it's working, then we jump on board. But if things aren't working well, we may turn around and mutter: "I knew it!" Then there's the *manana* habit of procrastinating.[20] We put things off until the last possible minute, and then crunch time forces out our creative juices. Each of the cultural attitudes limit the ability of Christian leaders to shepherd people around a new mission for the church. The underlying uncertainty that any plans will be successful with others creates a cycle of disappointment and frustration for Filipino youth workers.

ISSUES FACING ASIAN YOUTH

Asia hosts 61 percent of the world's youth population, with South Central Asia (not including China) accounting for more than 28 percent of the world's youth (ages 10 to 24).[21] For those of us working on this continent, we see the amazing successes of what God is doing through his church, and we also see the heartbreaking needs. In the Philippines—the only "Christian country" in Asia—many young people cling to an inherited faith but long for meaning in the rituals and traditions of the church.[22] Often there is syncretism as folk beliefs and superstition, misplaced fanaticism, other religions (such as Buddhism for Filipino-Chinese), as well as animism merge with the Christian faith. Many Christian Thai youth have been influenced by the Buddhist environment so much that they possess no distinctive Christian theology and actually resemble unbelievers. Northeast Indian youth have become more nationalistic and are directly affected by the movements around them, which can hamper a developed Christian faith. In the Philippines, the influence of the *barkada* (a Filipino colloquial term for "group of friends") is particularly important because of how much we value *pakikisama*—being harmonious with others and often yielding to the group's decision despite personal preferences.

Like their Western counterparts, Asian youth are mediavores and technoids—media and technology influences every area of their lives. Their perspective is Western,[23] their fashion is Japanese,[24] and their language is Korean.[25] Materialism spurred on by the media is rampant: Japanese youth choose style over comfort in a need to conform, "little emperors" of China are indulged with "an increasing amount of discretionary spending income,"[26] middle-class and upper-middle-class Indian youth are more prone to materialism compared to lower-middle and lower-class youths who deal more with an inferiority complex. (Pandya and Jayswal, 2007)

Filipino youth's addiction to Internet games has become a major concern of many parents and youth workers because some will go as far as skipping school in favor of playing the games at Internet cafes.[27] Plus, the shop owners don't feel obligated to report such truancy since there's no compulsory education for primary to secondary levels in the Philippines. In addition, 24-hour Internet cafes are popular, and although most youth will save on food and clothing expenses in order to be able to visit such venues,[28] some youth may resort to theft and even prostitution just to fund their vices.[29]

Identity development is a popular topic in youth ministry related conversations. Adults seem particularly concerned about the personal (internal) development of youth. Asian youth struggle with many of the same issues as youth living in other parts of the world. However, there are some cultural factors that are unique to Asian youth that youth workers need to be aware of.

First, they grapple with their image and a preoccupation with cosmetics and beauty. At the time of this writing, *Kikay* bags are an indispensable accessory of young Filipinas.[30] Even metrosexual young men have been known to have their *kikoy* bags as well.[31] They say beauty is in the eye of the beholder. While westerners strive to look bronzed and tanned, many Asians are obsessed with white skin as this connotes wealth, a high social status, and beauty.[32] As such, whitening soaps, lotions, pills, and injectables are used on a regular basis; and dermatologists are making much profit from the whitening industry.

Just like western youths, Asian youths strive to individuate from their parents; but their cultures don't provide an avenue for this natural development. Families (nuclear and extended) are tight-knit, sometimes to the point of enmeshed relationships. The youth are torn between their culture and family traditions and the twenty-first–century western world in which they are growing up. Asians who pride themselves on close family ties face the harsh reality of families splitting up. Damaged family ties have collectively registered on the Filipino psyche and touched off deep longings. (Sto Thomas, 2002, p. 173)

Poverty is an all-too-familiar face in Asian countries. It drives the youth in Cambodia to work hard by selling items to tourists; Indian youth from poorer castes find jobs with foreign companies if they're able to read, write, and speak English; generations of young Filipinos have left the country's shores to seek better opportunities abroad—and because many Filipino parents cannot afford to send their children to school, 11.6 million are OSYs (out of school youths).[33] Some young people (many of whom are street children) deal with their poverty and hunger by using illegal substances—for instance, *rugby boys* sniff the solvent "rugby" to get high. There were 3.4 million drug dependents in 2002, with more than half of these between the ages of 15 and 27. (CIBAC, 2007)

HOW YOUTH MINISTRY CAN MATTER IN ASIA

Asian youth are generally warm and outgoing. Filipino youths in particular have a high "social quotient" coming from the "Text Messaging Capital of the World,"[34] and they have among the largest number of Social Networking Site members in the world.[35] Because they long for meaningful relationships, it's quite easy to establish friendships with Asian youths that could influence them for Christ.

Filipino national hero Jose Rizal once said that the youth are "*bella esperanza de la Patria mia*" ("fair hope of my fatherland").[36] The youth of today are not only the hope of our nations . . . they will not just become the leaders of our churches, communities, and countries tomorrow, but they are our leaders even today. A cursory look at our Asian churches shows evidence of young people stepping up as praise-and-worship leaders and Sunday school or VBS teachers. They are actively involved in the ministries of music, dance, and drama. They are rising fast on the corporate ladder as well. And in local and national governments, we see younger and younger politicians and officials.

Stronger, smarter . . . eager and enthusiastic . . . more creative and innovative, Asian youth of today are in their prime. And this is the best time to help them come to Christ and grow in faith and grace so God can use them to their full potential. With their wanderlust and adventurous spirit, they make ideal agents to bring the gospel not only to their compatriots, but to other lands and people groups as well. As the Western part of the world turns post-Christian, those in the East are rising as the Son reaches out to them. And the missionary venture comes full circle as Asians bring Christ once more to the West.

When I preach to adults or challenge them about youth and youth ministry, I tell them to invest in the youth by discipling and mentoring them, as well as providing for their physical, emotional, social, and financial needs. We need to be role models and show them how to translate faith to life and what it means to be a Christian in the real world from Monday to Saturday—not just our Sunday best in church. We cannot take youth for granted or underestimate them because when we do, we put a limit on God's transforming power.

Despite all the challenges that we face as youth ministers in Asia, our hope and passion does not diminish because we know that through God's help, we are making a dent—however small it may be.

But lives are being changed. Families are touched. Society is transformed. And above all, God is glorified.

EPILOGUE: JAMES' STORY CONTINUED

It took a stroke to finally bring Dad back home, and I saw him for the first time in 18 years. Here he learned that a "beautiful life" is not just having all the wealth but having God and a complete family.

Dad's subsequent paralysis turned out to be a blessing in disguise because it humbled him and made him realize that God is the Owner of everything. And I was able to spend quality time with him as his caregiver. Ironically, I did things for him that he failed to do for me as I was growing up: Bathing him, brushing his teeth, waking up in the middle of the night to attend to his needs, giving him medicine, massaging him, leading him to pray, and many more. In a short span of time, we became best friends because we were together 24/7 and shared a lot of secrets.

My father eventually died. I am just thankful he didn't die while he was in the United States because I wouldn't have had the chance to know him and spend time with him. Besides, he wouldn't have had his family to take care of him. Thank God for allowing me to experience having a dad even if it was just for a short time. Because of that, I was finally able to understand him, forgive him, value him, and show my love to him. Now I can say that I am complete.

DISCUSSION QUESTIONS

1. Are there "parentless" kids in your youth group? What category of being "parentless" would they fit into? (For example, are their parents hardly ever around? Are the parents emotionally absent, psychologically absent, or temporarily absent? Did the parents abandon their kids?) Are there other categories you can think of?
2. How would you as a youth worker relate to or deal with youth who are "parentless"?

3. How could you help bridge the gap between parents and their adolescent kids in this context?
4. How could the church as a body of Christ respond to the needs of the "parentless" youths in your church? In your community?
5. How would you counsel a "James" from this chapter's prologue? (In other words, before his father came home, and as he came to some realizations later in his adult life.)

RESOURCES

Aquino, C. "Family and Values: Changes and Challenges in Shaping the Youth." In *The Changing Face of the Filipino: A Salesian Tribute to the Youth of the Philippines* (pp. 109-116). Makati City, Philippines: Salesian Society of Don Bosco, 2002.

Bacon, K. H. "Philosophical Foundations of Curriculum" in *Curriculum: Foundations, Principles, and Issues.* 2nd ed. Edited by A. C. Ornstein and F. P. Hunkins. Boston, MA: Allyn and Bacon, 1993.

Citizens Battle Against Corruption (CIBAC). "Profile of the Filipino Youth." CIBAC Briefing Papers, 2007. http://www.cibac.org/index2. php?option=com_content&do_pdf=1&id=12.

Coronel, F. K. and F. Unterreiner. *Increasing the Impact of Remittances on Children's Rights: Philippines Paper, 2007.* Retrieved on April 19, 2010 from http://www.unicef.org/policyanalysis/files/increasing_ the_impact_of_remittances_ on_childrens_rights_pdf.

De Jesus-Ardina, A. "What Is it Like to Be an OFW Parent or Kid?" *Light Touch Magazine, 13,* 3 (2009).

Good News Balikbayan. "Save Our "New Heroes": The Filipino OFWs and Their Families." http://goodnewsbalikbayan.com/advocacy/ save-our-"new-heroes"-the-filipino-ofws-and-their-families/.

Medina, B. T. G. *The Filipino Family.* Quezon City, Philippines: University of the Philippines Press, 2001.

Ortigas, C. D. *The Solo-Parent Experience: A Growing Social Phenomenon.* Quezon City, Philippines: Ateneo De Manila University, 1996.

OFW—Overseas Filipino News Worldwide. "DOLE:

Good Traits Make Pinoys Preferred Abroad. (Posted October 22, 2009.) http://pinoyoverseas.net/news/uncategorized/dole-good-traits-make-pinoys-preferred-abroad/.

Pandya, B. U. and M. M. Jayswal. "Materialism among Adolescent: Understanding Conceptual Framework and Imperatives for Marketers and Society for New Horizons." International Marketing Conference on Marketing & Society, IIMK. (2007) Retrieved on October 9, 2010 from http://dspace.iimk.ac.in/bitstream/2259/318/1/673-701.pdf.

Philippine Overseas Employees Agency (POEA). *Compendium of OF Statistics—2008*. http://www.poea.gov.ph/stats/2008_stats.pdf.

Sandoval, Gerardo, Mahar Mangahas, and Linda Luz Guerrero. "The Situation of Filipino Youth: A National Survey" (by Social Weather Stations). Paper presented at the 14th World Congress of Sociology, Working Group 3 / Sociology of Childhood at Montreal Canada on July 26–August 1, 1998. Retrieved on October 6, 2010, from http://www.sws.org.ph/youth.htm.

Sto. Tomas, P. "Overseas Employment and Its Social Impact on the Youth. In *The Changing Face of the Filipino: A Salesian Tribute to the Youth of the Philippines* (pp. 165–175). Makati City, Philippines: Salesian Society of Don Bosco, 2002.

Virola, Romulo A. "Poverty Worsens between 2003 and 2006." Press release of the National Statistical Coordination Board. (March 2008). Retrieved on October 4, 2010, from http://www.nscb.gov.ph/pressreleases/2008/PR-200803-SS2-02_pov.asp.

CHAPTER TWELVE

WHAT DOES YOUTH MINISTRY LOOK LIKE IN ASIA?

JUDY FOO

Asia as a continent is too complex in terms of culture, religion, language, and so on, to make any over-generalizations about all youth ministry here. It's not feasible for me, even after 16 years of leading youth ministry in Southeast Asia, to compose a list of do's and don'ts or a set of uniform principles and practices for successful youth ministry here. However, I want to suggest some "Asian" values and characteristics that I've discovered through my own journey as an Asian youth worker and connect them to biblical values. As Paul exhorted the church in Corinth, I trust that as we continue to work faithfully in this field of youth ministry, God will cause the growth of well-discipled youth. (1 Corinthians 3:5-9)

But before I share these characteristics of Asian youth, there are three "snapshots" that paint a portrait of my youth ministry experience.

SINGAPORE

Singaporean Christians are often "churched" in terms of ecclesiastical traditions and rites of passage, but they lack the "substance" of faith in their daily living. Christian parents are often more concerned with their children's academic and financial success than seeing them sold out for Christ. Most of the teens in my youth ministry here came from upper-middle-class homes. The church parking lot sparkled with church members' Mercedes and BMWs, and most of the youth and families took exotic vacations in Bali, South Africa, and Europe.

Our youth group was relatively large, nearly 100 members. Our ministry strategy revolved around weekly cell groups and a corporate youth worship time. It also included prayer meetings, occasional evangelistic events, and yearly youth camps. One time one of my youth asked me, "Is there more to the Christian life than what I'm experiencing now?" He felt "something" was missing with his practice of Christianity, and he longed for something different. Similar to what I hear from many of my North American friends, he felt as though being a second-generation Christian was a disadvantage. The Christian life just felt so mundane and disconnected from his academics and time with friends. He'd grown up in a godly Christian home and had faithfully attended church since he was a child. He went on to do well in school and in his career, but he stopped attending church regularly. It just didn't "do" anything for him.

CAMBODIA

In many countries like Cambodia, the challenge for Christian workers doesn't merely involve the conversion of souls but discipling converts while surrounded by systemic corruption and injustice that pervades every level of society. I spoke with a group of Christian Khmer youth in an orphanage, discussing the implications of Christ's lordship upon daily living. Some of the issues we discussed include: *What does lordship look like in an impoverished environment where the primary struggle for youth is simply survival? How do Christian Khmer youth live out the lordship of Christ when they have to pay their teachers to teach the other half of the syllabus because the teachers don't teach everything during class time? (The "extra" income is needed for their livelihood as they have a meager salary.) Should they tell a friend who has run afoul of the law to surrender to the police, even though they know more injustice will be committed against his friend in jail?* There are no simple answers to these questions.

JAPAN

A typical church service in rural Japan consists of about 10 people, most of whom are women and children. Most of these children drop out of church when they reach junior high. Even if there were regular youth meetings, youth can't participate due to weekend extracurricular activities that 'clash' with church activities. The dearth of a core group of young people in the Japanese Church makes it difficult to sustain effective youth ministry. And many rural churches are pastored by elderly pastors or missionaries who may not necessarily be strong in reaching the youth.

> Even if there were regular youth meetings in Japan, youth can't participate due to weekend extracurricular activities that 'clash' with church activities.

TRAITS AND CHARACTERISTICS OF THE ASIAN WORLD

Large youth population. More than 60 percent of the world's youth reside in Asia. Cambodia is one of the most "youthful" populations with 36 percent between the ages of 10 and 24; the median age is 22.[1]

Christianity is NOT the dominant religion. Asia is home to three of the world's major religions—Buddhism, Hinduism, and Islam. Christians are consistently the *minority*, with many countries having 10 percent or fewer. In Singapore, it's 15 percent; Japan, 2 percent; Cambodia, fewer than 1 percent.[2] Historically, the Asian population has viewed Christianity as a "Western" religion, and so a large segment resists the Christian message.

Multiethnic/lingual/political landscape. Asia is filled with many ethnic and religious groups that speak many different languages. Most have lived harmoniously alongside each other, although it is common to hear of ethnic strivings against other more dominant groups. Democracy as we know it in the West is not a given in the

Asian political milieu. Asia has one of the world's largest communist blocs (albeit "opened") in China, and there are a number of autocratic governments holding power over millions. Corruption and injustice commonly prevail in every level of society in many countries.

Traditional Asian Values

Effective ministry to Asian youth must understand traditional Asian values such as filial piety (the respect for authority/elders), a foundational value from the Confucian tradition in Chinese culture. Most Asian cultures also center on relationships between individuals and groups. The notion of *guanxi* ("relationships") often opens or closes doors to access opportunities for career, education, and even marriage in the Chinese society. The connection through relationship is a much higher value than the task at hand, a stark difference from a more Western focus on completing a job. Fortunately, because the global economy is coming to China, there are numerous resources available to aid in understanding Chinese culture.

WHAT IS PERCEIVED AS SUCCESSFUL YOUTH MINISTRY?

Many youth ministry models that have been brought to Asia seem to suggest that a "successful" youth ministry must have:

- Loud, emotionally stirring worship with a full-piece band and vocals
- Dramatic, theatrical preaching
- "Fun," wholesome activities to rival and replace "worldly" activities
- Structured Bible study groups or cell groups (for instance, the 4 Ws—worship, word, witness, walk)

Hillsong, well known for its worship songs (and sometimes for its church services), is drawing many Christian youth worldwide. And Asia is no exception. Even in less-developed countries like Cambodia, I've observed that the Hillsong style is gaining popularity. The energies released and passions stirred are great to guide youth toward deeper love for God and greater obedience to him in Christian living. But we need to question if it's culturally acceptable and technically feasible to go this route in worship. In some places—especially more conservative and rural settings—the Hillsong style of worship may alienate youth instead of draw them into a deeper worship of God. In essence, the authentic expression of youth ministry in Asia must take into consideration Asian identity and characteristics, while remaining biblically grounded.

WHAT SHOULD YOUTH MINISTRY IN ASIA LOOK LIKE?

Relationships must be central. Family relationships are more important than anything else in Asia. The closeness of one's relationship (how "thick" you are with the person—or your shared *guanxi*) determines the mutual trust level, that "blood is thicker than water."[3] Once you have gained trust, you will be treated like a family member. And that close relationship, like family, will open up the doors to various aspects of life, ranging from businesses to sharing of secrets.

Similarly, in a Christian discipling relationship, the closeness of the relationship—and the level of trust established—helps the discipler to gain access into the youth's heart and mind, which can lead to opportunities to speak to, encourage, teach, and even rebuke where necessary. This close relationship takes time to grow, but it's important to take the time, especially in Asia.

There must be *a personal encounter* with God in Jesus Christ and ownership of your faith. In many traditional Asian families, religious belief is passed down from one generation to the next through rituals. For the most part, there is little explanation regarding what's behind the beliefs—children are simply expected to accept and continue religious observances. As such, there is little conviction about or personal ownership of our faith.

Youth from Christian homes also face similar challenges to owning their faith. As they enter the stage in life where they need to make sense of what they were taught to believe, they also need freedom with support to come to their own convictions.

This is a frightening time for Asian parents because they're fearful of not only letting go, but also seeing their children stray, which would bring shame on the family. Knowing God personally is foundational to helping them navigate through some rough terrain in the adolescent years.

Thus, the challenge of youth ministry is to help youth—both Christians and non-Christians—encounter God, understand the message of the gospel, and personally acknowledge Jesus Christ as their God and Saviour.

Youth ministry should be open and ready to practice *power encounters.* This includes spiritual warfare in intercessions, healing, and deliverance. The Asian worldview recognizes the activities of spirits in our everyday lives. For example, spirit houses are common in our landscape, offerings to gods at the start of the workday are common in many businesses, and there is a month in the year dedicated to the appeasing of spirits and ghosts in the Chinese community.

Therefore, we must be mindful that many of our youth encounter such spiritual activities (and others) in their daily lives. Occult practices, *feng shui* (divination using geomancy), as well as fortunetelling and astrology, are prevalent—even among nominal Christians.

But I've observed youth ministry curricula rarely focus on the teaching and practice of power encounters. I feel it's important for our youth to be informed and understand the incompatibility of occult practices with the Christian faith—specifically Christians' authority to be delivered and set free from spiritual bondage. There may be doctrinal differences toward this issue in various denominations, but there is no running away from having to address the reality of the spirit world so prevalent across the Asian landscape.

A holistic youth ministry in Asia will do well to teach youth about the authority and power of a true disciple of Jesus Christ to confront and overcome the spiritual forces of darkness, just like the Gospels and rest of the New Testament proclaim.

Youth ministry in Asia should be a community where the biblical values of love and acceptance, forgiveness and reconciliation, and respect and honor for one another are championed, lived out, and passed down to the generations. In a place like Asia where the group's interests and general welfare are valued above the individual's, I believe the Christian community and what it stands for can become a viable alternative—one that youth can more confidently and expectantly "conform" to.

For example, in places such as Singapore and Japan where much of one's identity and worth is tied to academic excellence, this perspective has created undue pressure on youth. The failure to perform well in school often results in a sense of personal failure and rejection by society, and it likely affects one's prospects for future career development. Pressures to do well in school and to "save face" have been linked to the high incidence of teen suicides in these countries. Youth ministry could provide an accepting and embracing environment where youths can learn the true source of their identity and worth, and find strength and encouragement from others to work through their struggles together.

The power of community can also be seen in places like Cambodia where missionaries have started orphanages and Christian hostels. In the less-developed and less-urbanized parts of Asia, it is quite common to hear of orphans being adopted and brought up by relatives and neighbours. But adopted children and youth brought up in Christian homes are discipled in biblical truths and values—a big added benefit. The Christian foundation in their lives will help them navigate the challenges of the harsh world they'll eventually enter.

This is easier said than done, especially because of the Asian mindset that Christianity is a "Western" religion. There is much suspicion and misunderstanding to overcome. Besides, changing the mindset of a people is one of the hardest and most time-consuming tasks. It will take many generations of intentional discipling in these communities before we see transformation toward biblical values and standards in society.

CONCLUSION

I've shared four values and characteristics for doing youth ministry in Asia: (1) relationship is central; (2) opportunity for personal encounter with God; (3) opportunity for power encounters; and (4) community where biblical values are imparted and shared. These came from numerous interactions with youth in Singapore and other parts of Asia.

Although Asia is very diverse socially and culturally, I have tried to identify some common values that are understood by most in Asia. Regardless, youth ministry calls for the long-term investment of time, energy, and sensitivity to the Holy Spirit in whatever context you serve. As we remain faithful, we will see the transformation of generations of well-discipled youth who know and love Jesus and live for his glory wherever God has placed them.

DISCUSSION QUESTIONS

1. What does the growth of Christianity in Asia look like? How have Asian cultures worked to claim Christianity as "their own" versus a far-off "Western" value?
2. Do you believe close relationships can be developed between people of significant age differences? Why or why not? How might it be more difficult in some cultures than others?
3. How has the church in China been misunderstood? It would be a worthy exercise to research the various expressions of the Christian church in China from as many different perspectives as possible. What accounts for the various perspectives people give to the church in China?

JAPANESE YOUTH ARE THE CHURCH

YOSHITO NOGUCHI

Despite our material wealth, most Japanese have never heard the gospel and suffer from spiritual bankruptcy. Since 1998, there have been more than 30,000 suicides; and among youth between the ages of 10 and 19, suicides tend to grow.[4] Though the church is the only light to shine through the darkness and share God's transforming and glorifying power, many churches ignore our youth and have lost the passion to reach the next generation. According to an article in *JP News*—a Christian newspaper in Japan—about half of Japanese Christians feel that churches aren't trying to connect to outsiders, and most church youth groups eventually close down.[5] Those who do attempt to reach them often use Western-like programs and events, but they've seen little success. This is the reality of youth ministry in Japan.

Even though teenagers attended our Sunday services, they struggled to find a place in ministry and missions. When I saw this problem, I decided to spend time with several students in order to pray with and disciple them. It was during our prayer time that God spoke to us from Mark 16:15, "[Jesus] said to them, 'Go into all the world and preach the gospel to all creation.'"

Through this verse God gave us a vision to train and send out Christian students to plant a church led by youth to effectively reach other youth.

Three questions guided our thinking:

- What would happen if students had a chance to *be* the church instead of just attending their parents' churches?
- What if all the students used their spiritual gifts together for a mission?
- What if we sent our youth to do missions among their peers?

Just as Christ became flesh and lived among the people, we believed that high school students could plant a church and become the light in their own nation. By living out their faith, they could change Japan.

> Just as Christ became flesh and lived among the people, we believed that high school students could plant a church and become the light in their own nation. By living out their faith, they could change Japan.

Since we planted the youth church in 2004, we have seen students achieve many things that we didn't see when they were attending their parents' churches. Students have developed Christ-like love for one another, teaching and building each other up. During weekly worship services, young people freely worship God in their own styles and express their love for him with their hearts in a way that they can't in a mixed-age situation. And they are reaching their peers who live in the youth culture.

One of the underlying principles reminds us that the Holy Spirit promises spiritual gifts to all believers, without any prejudice to age. Since youth have gifts, they need to use them and not "bury" them. That's what we've seen—God transforming these students in a spiritually "stagnant" culture into leaders, teachers, givers, encouragers, hosts, prayer warriors, and evangelists. They aren't just being saved—they are *becoming the church* through the power of the gospel.

WHY DOES THE YOUTH CHURCH MODEL WORK IN JAPAN AT THIS TIME?

The first reason is that people value traditions very strongly in Japanese culture. Older leaders in all organizations are slow to give responsibility to younger leaders for fear that those traditions that the older leaders hold dear won't be upheld correctly. This makes it difficult for the established church to connect with youth who are living in a different culture. It also makes it difficult to raise next-generation leaders.

Second, youth are very busy with many things (schoolwork, sports activities, cram school,[6] and so on). So their peer groups—with whom they spend the majority of their time—become kind of their entire world. Youth in Japan tend to listen to their peers more than they listen to adults, so it makes more sense to utilize the youth to connect to their peers. Also, we cannot expect to pull them away from all of the activities they're already busy with so they can attend more "church programs." Instead, we teach youth to be missional in everyday life.

As we have been leading youth church in Japan, we have learned from our mistakes. **First, we learned that young people cannot be totally separated from the adult congregation.** Yes, they are a youth church, but they need the fellowship and encouragement of adult Christians, too. That older, more mature leaders must pray for and support us would be true in any context. But there's also the importance in our culture of demonstrating respect for our elders and wanting to support the value of our intergenerational emphasis.

A second important lesson is to **teach youth correct theology.** Japan is a polytheistic culture, and people have many different ideas about gods. If we teach them only how to maintain acceptable moral and spiritual behavior, then they won't learn who God is and what Jesus Christ has done for them. Such a scenario can easily lead them to different gods.

In Japanese culture it's easy for students to be motivated by a desire to be accepted, popular, and especially praised. **Youth ministry leaders must be very careful not to create a "performance trap"** where students express their talents for their own purposes and not for the transforming truth of the gospel. But young people are who they are through the power of the gospel, not the power of their performance. This is the right motive for mission—and what we need to continue to teach, or else we'll fail to reach the next generation of Japanese believers (and the rest of the nations) with the gospel message.

We have a student, Tatsuya,[7] who came to know Jesus when he was in the ninth grade. He'd been bullied at school and believed his life was meaningless. But when he found the church, he saw the love of Christ and realized what his life had been missing. After he was baptized, his parents strongly opposed his being a Christian. Tatsuya's father told him he needed to worship their ancestors and stay away from his Christian friends.

At first, Tatsuya hated his father for not accepting his Christian commitment. But as he grew and understood God's mission to the world, Tatsuya now wants his father to know Jesus also. He now lives with a mission.

One of Tatsuya's friends also became a Christian and said, "When I came to the youth church, I saw a difference in you guys. Thank you for accepting me more than a year ago—even though I did not have any interest in God. But through your love, I now see him and am able to believe the Savior who is described in the Bible." We as a church praise God for what he has done in and through these students.

We are learning and growing through being a church sent by God, and God has been patient with us and blessed us because of our faithfulness. My prayer is that one day people from all over the world will confess Christ as Lord because many youth are living the gospel. God's kingdom will come—and your heart matters to God.

KOREAN YOUTH MINISTRY

DR. YOUNG WOON LEE

Korea has a long cultural history, much like China, recorded for more than 5,000 years. Korea's monocultural background and shared language provide a deep sense of ethnic pride. After becoming a republic in the early 1900s, most of the world learned about Korea through the Korean War (1950–1952). Due to a more recent period of expansive economic growth, South Korea has become a key participant in the global economy, a huge step for this once-silent kingdom. The 1988 Olympics (Seoul) and the 2002 FIFA World Cup helped Korean society become more progressive and move away from its monoethnic roots.[8] As the numbers of multicultural families increase, Korean monoethnic cultural society is changing slowly. As Korean society changes, this will require Korean churches to consider how to reach out to the new and various multicultural and ethnic groups, as well as the theological and educational implications of ministering to them.

UNDERSTANDING KOREAN YOUTH CULTURE

"Pressure, Perfectionism, and Performance"[9] are key concepts to understand in Korean youth culture. These are values that youth have internalized from the standards placed on them by society and family structures. However, these are not entirely external factors—youth culture projects these standards of perfection as well. Korean youths have developed a slang vocabulary which is otherwise unacceptable to the historical use of the Korean language. The word *jjang* carries its own meaning of "perfect" or "best," especially when related to contemporary culture. So to say, "He is *jjang*," means "He represents perfection in that area."

As *"Jjang"* culture and perfectionism is spread among them, Korean youths focus on being the best—perfection only. They respect Olympic gold medalists and look unfavorably on silver or bronze medalists in sports or other competitions. Due to this trend, youth display the same fashion styles within their culture (for instance, clothing, shoes, hairstyles, brands of makeup, and so on). Even hip-hop dancing has taken on a competitive nature in Korea, where "b-boy" dance groups are celebrated for winning international competitions.

Based on its Confucian cultural background, Korean respect for education and the educated is matched only by its corresponding disdain for the uneducated—so much so that higher degree holders implicitly command more respect and rights.[10] Discrimination against the less educated offspring of poorer families is one of the central patterns of class conflict in Korea. The idea of "getting into university to avoid becoming a laborer" still dominates the society. Without a college degree, it seems one cannot maintain a meaningful life, and so Christian youth ministry must understand and be sensitive to this societal pressure.

> Based on its Confucian cultural background, Korean respect for education and the educated is matched only by its corresponding disdain for the uneducated—so much so that higher degree holders implicitly command more respect and rights.

Because of this cultural pressure for education, most youth attend a *hakwon*—a private after-school tutoring institute. *Hakwons* hire private teachers to work with students on different subjects, usually English or mathematics, in order to prepare for university entrance. More than just about studies, though, the *hakwon* is a gathering place to socialize. And youth usually spend more of their time at school and at *hakwons* than they do at home. The importance of this educational system shines a light on Korean cultural dependence on the perceived stability offered by formal education (through which jobs, financial security, and even family structures are supposed to follow).

First, the youth pastor must be sensitive to the time demands upon youth who are dedicated to securing their futures. The youth pastor who pulls too much time away from his students' studies will face unhappy parents (and elders in the church) who pride themselves on having educated children.

Second, understanding the cost of extended education has led churches to open after-school programs for children who can't easily afford the more expensive *hakwons*. These programs may be as simple as providing a place where students can study or being visible at volunteer programs where members of the church can tutor students and provide help for assignments—or as complicated as running a *hakwon*-style program within the church for reduced fees.

Third, churches must also provide alternative programs to minister to youth who are *not* college bound. These might happen through sports and similar fellowship programs that are open to all and will minimize the differences between those who are well-educated and those who are not. Other programs might include volunteer opportunities in which youth can take active roles in their communities despite the educational disparity.

YOUTH MINISTRY IN KOREA

In the 2000s, Korean young adult and high school groups developed short-term mission trips to international mission fields. Korean churches see short-term mission work as both training for the youth as future missionaries, as well an opportunity to build up their faith and spiritual growth. These mission trips are often conducted in nearby Asian countries, preferably English-speaking ones, due to the difficulty of raising funds and the lack of financial support from adult congregations. Rather than providing professional ministry support, the young people are often expected to provide the physical labor that the local churches in that area might not be able to handle on their own, thereby allowing the youth to see the practical needs of ministry in these foreign countries.

Most youth ministry groups have focused on perfect performance styles in the worship service. Due to the Korean cultural and communal pressure, youth ministry in Korea has focused on becoming more performance-oriented within Protestant churches. This includes café nights that highlight praise or poetry and place emphasis on performance styles, public prayer meetings for university entrance, and other shared group ministry events. Korean youth ministry developed performance-based outreach programs such as Street Evangelism using contemporary Christian music (CCM) and contemporary Christian dance (CCD) aimed at youth and young adults.

THE FUTURE CHALLENGE

Youth will be coming up against a system of prosperity, perfectionism, and performance orientation. **To encourage youth and society to become Christ-oriented and people-oriented, rather than program- or performance-oriented, is the primary challenge of Korean youth ministry. The challenge is not to be "less perfect" or to perform worse, but rather to pursue an attitude of purpose (where these ends are put in their proper place as forms of worship) and to respect the individual's relationship with Christ.**

As Korean society moves from its monoethnic roots to a multicultural society—and since Korean churches have historically been the centers for the poor, the weak, and any minority groups—youth ministry will need to focus on the development of individuals and community in order to become more loving and caring.

Increasing numbers of Korean elementary schools nationwide have had children with multicultural or interracial backgrounds since the early 2000s. When these children become adolescents, youth ministry will face significant multicultural issues. Youth ministry will need to change from a collective societal orientation to one that works with each student's unique circumstances. The Church will need to support and encourage youth to respect their education as an act of stewardship, rather than for their own sake or for their own prosperity.

CONCLUSION

Those who come to Korea from the West need to educate themselves regarding Asian culture and the inherent pressures of the family system. They need to understand that youth are drawn to fulfill their commitments to pressure, perfectionism, and performance. And there are two questions to keep in mind—ones that confront Korean youth and their families as they participate in youth ministry: (1) As teens develop their faith in Christ against other concerns, will they see the need for a deeper faith, or will they find a shallow expression of Christianity to be acceptable? (2) Will parents find it acceptable for their children to prioritize Christ over academics and financial stability?

Like all ministry, the challenge lies in the integration of the gospel into the changing world to come. Korea's developing multiculturalism indicates a change from a communal, family, and male-oriented society to one that celebrates the individual and smaller family, as in the West. The church must be a loving and caring community for everyone, not just for elite youth. If perfectionism or a "*Jjang*" culture focuses on more elite groups, then other youth won't come to church and the free grace offered by Christ for all will have been lost to churches with implicit standards of perfection that keep anyone who is less than perfect—that is, everybody—from knowing Christ.

DISCUSSION QUESTIONS

1. What similarities and differences did you observe between the Spotlight on Japan and this essay on Korean youth ministry?
2. What cultural aspects seem different from yours?
3. In what way might cultural traditions in your context play a positive role in youth ministry?
4. How does this Korean approach to short-term missions compare to the use of short-term mission trips in your context?
5. Review the titles of books and journal articles that focus on youth ministry. What are the main themes that concern Korean youth ministry leaders?

RESOURCES

Armstrong, C. K. *The Korea*. New York: Routledge, 2007.

Clark, Allen D. *A History of the Church in Korea*. Seoul: Christian Literature Society of Korea, 1971.

Kang, Wi Jo. *Christ and Caesar in Modern Korea*. New York: State University of New York Press, 1997.

Lee, K. *A New History of Korea*. Translated by Edward W. Wagner. Cambridge, MA: Harvard University Press, 1984.

Tokunaga, Paul. "Pressure, Perfectionism and Performance." Chap. 1 in *Following Jesus Without Dishonoring Your Parents: Asian American Discipleship* by Jeanette Yep, Peter Cha, Susan Cho Van Riesen, Greg Jao, and Paul Tokunaga. Downers Grove, IL: IVP Books, 1998.

Weinberg, Meyer. *Asian-American Education: Historical Background and Current Realities*. Mahwah, NJ: Lawrence Erlbaum Associates, Publisher, 1997.

CHAPTER THIRTEEN

BACK TO THE FUTURE

LOOKING AHEAD AND BEYOND

JACOB G. ISAAC

"If you know what the youth want, they'll want what you have"[1]

"The youngest nation in the world," declared former Prime Minister A. B. Vajpayee in 2008 as India's population touched an all-time high of 540 million under the age of 25. Of this growing population, more than 300 million are between the ages of 15 and 25.

What does this mean for the world's largest democracy, which was called, until recently, a "Third World" country? Does the word *development* spell signs of woes to come? Or do the 300 million youth in India have an understanding of the "abundant life" that the Word of God talks about? Is it enough to do youth ministry in India like it was done a decade or two ago? Is youth ministry only about evangelistic rallies that were so popular in the early '60s and '70s? Is it any longer about tracts being thrust into the hands of passersby? Is there something missing in our approaches, styles of presentation, communication methodology, and creative use of resources?

THE CHANGING INDIAN CONTEXT

India has huge cash reserves and is the most preferred investment destination of rich and developed nations. Many multinational businesses have set up BPOs (Business Process Outsourcing) as well as ITES (Information Technology Enabled Services) industries. India's middle-income group is believed to be larger than the population of the United States. Today, India is where gobi manchurian (a traditional Indian Chinese dish) and paneer masala pizza (Indian flavoured pizza) go hand in hand with the Coke and Pepsi generation, where hand-pulled rickshaws and bullock carts move with ease alongside the Toyota Camry and the Honda City.

India is a land of diversity. Attitudes, behaviours, and expectations of youth vary throughout the country. Each major city is influenced by the predominant ideology of the larger subculture of that city. For example, the city of Chennai in southern India possesses a predominantly traditional cultural and religious outlook owing to her historical importance. This is reflected in the habits, attitudes, and lifestyles of the youth from this city. As one Indian newsmagazine aptly stated, "Inner directed change is evolutionary, outer directed change is revolutionary." Wearing a pair of Nikes may transform him outwardly, but the thinking is still the same.

Big Changes over the Last 15 Years

Rapid economic growth has changed the lifestyle and expectations of youth. Nearly 32 percent of the workforce in India is young, thereby increasing the average earning (and spending) capacities of the more than 200 million Indian youth.

The *average age of sexual activity* has dropped rapidly, giving rise to personality and emotional issues related to sexual abuse, teenage pregnancy, and teenage rape. Addictions to substances, technology, and pornography are not showing any downward trends. Psychological disturbances such as depression and anxiety are still not addressed effectively in India.

Educational indices show a proliferation of avenues for education—for those who can afford it. About 87 percent of all youth are enrolled in primary school,[2] with 94 percent completing primary school (which is up 15 percent from 15 years ago).[3] However, for a section of urban youth consisting of migrant workers, education is still not a realistic pursuit. At the same time, urban youth aspire to lead better lives and are open to finding avenues that make life meaningful through education.

India's diversity is mirrored in its *pluralism among major religions*. Of the just over 1 billion people in India, 800 million are Hindus and 140 million are Muslims, and there has been significant violence among religious groups.[4] India has more people groups with no Christians, churches, or workers than any other part of the world. No surprise that the expanding youth population of India is one of the largest unreached people groups on earth.

> India has more people groups with no Christians, churches, or workers than any other part of the world. No surprise that the expanding youth population of India is one of the largest unreached people groups on earth.

It is in this context that I have raised some issues that affect youth in India today. The age-old racism and caste issues still plague our society, and the recent rise in moral policing of 'Westernisation' practices and values is meant to head off the global culture from influencing the 'Indian value' system. For instance, the celebration of Valentine's Day is considered a Western concept and strongly opposed by fundamentalist groups. In addition, Christians' minority status restricts their equal opportunities and the growth of Christianity in the country, as we see in the excessive government scrutiny of foreign funds to Christian groups. Finally, the Hindutva (fundamentalist Hindu groups that say everything non-Hindu does not belong in India) propaganda threaten to curb the freedom of expression and fundamental rights provided in the Constitution.[5]

YOUTH MINISTRY IN INDIA TODAY

Youth ministry in India is complex as we navigate religious pluralism, strong traditions, and a global urban culture that seeks to redefine our values. Most youth ministries follow ideas and methodologies that have been used over the years by Western missionaries. Though the West has been helpful in India for supporting many ministries and aiding their success, the effectiveness emerged from ideas and approaches generated from within India. Effective youth ministry has to be marked by personal attention and creative methodology focused on those from other faiths. But music programs, summer camps, and youth rallies have become platforms to preach at the masses while ignoring the personal. So a large percentage of our youth work is confined to churches, leaving many un-churched— especially those from non-Christian traditions—without the gospel.

John Amalraj of the Indian Mission Association criticizes youth ministry in India because of its primary focus on young people 18 and older. He hopes that a network can develop to serve 15-to-18-year-olds because churches and most mission agencies are missing the target. Billy Verghese of the Union of Evangelical Students of India adds, "The empowerment of the student must start at an early age." Young people can then be given strong Bible-based teaching that builds convictions to impact the church and society. Highlighting their model, he describes it as "ministry of the students, by the students, and for the students." Youth workers in this model serve as facilitators, coaches, and catalysts who empower student initiative.

Barring a few attempts, Indian youth ministry is still caught in a traditional outlook, unwilling to test new avenues of communicating the gospel. The **media** revolution of the '80s gave every Indian home access to satellite cable television. Living rooms came alive with music and movies due to the large Indian-based "Bollywood" industry. With literally millions hooked on TV, media can be another effective approach to youth ministry because of its appeal and good recall factor. Quality talk shows, stories with high moral values, interviews of celebrities and personalities with sound Christian values, case studies of transformed lives, and Christian music videos can be used effectively to capture a readily available audience. We need to offer youth workers and church youth groups opportunities to work alongside mission agencies that are using radio, television, the Internet, and CDs and DVDs to reach large groups in school and college campuses.

Another popular approach is the existence of up-and-coming **rock bands**. Youth love to come together and show off their talents through music, but the biggest problems have been the lack of venues for bands to perform (as non-Christian youths may not attend a concert on the church premises). Moreover, unwillingness to promote events outside church buildings and the unfortunate preoccupation on a "questionable" medium (even if the message is biblically sound) puts undue pressure on young aspirants. With very little or no financial (or other) support, youth don't see attempting this as a worthwhile ministry strategy.

An Assemblies of God church that lays a strong emphasis on **youth leadership training** has helped it grow. Pastor Jacob says that there are two tracks—a core discipleship program combined with regular outreach events full of creative programming that helps the church connect with non-Christians. One of the components of the discipleship program is one-on-one training and group evangelism. Though the core is a commitment to discipleship (which keeps the group stable), the focus is impacting the community through a variety of methods.

An approach that's been tried and is working well is the **"Awareness Program"**—educational sessions often conducted in schools and colleges that bring awareness to issues related to sexuality, drug abuse, effects of alcohol, and child sexual abuse. A youth worker could approach an institution and ask for an opportunity to make a presentation to the students.

In many cases, youth ministry is tied to old traditional methods and may not be relevant to the emerging youth culture of India today. Dr. Tony Sam George of Christ University in Bangalore said:

> Youth work in India follows traditional approaches which are usually based on contexts outside the Indian culture. This leads to a misfit between the message of the gospel and the realities that young people in India are facing. Their social, psychological, spiritual, and relational issues are often separated from the gospel, making it hard for them to understand the message of the gospel in their

lives. Youth work in India needs to be dynamic and related to the needs of youth. This can happen only when we decide to take steps to understand what works and what does not work. The power of the gospel is wasted due to the application of traditional methods that do not work anymore.

> Youth work in India follows traditional approaches which are usually based on contexts outside the Indian culture. This leads to a misfit between the message of the gospel and the realities that young people in India are facing.
>
> —Dr. Tony Sam George

I am burdened that youth ministry in India should evaluate strategies and develop those that work, making sure they're contextual to the needs of youth and attractive to them. This leads us to youth work **research and development**. By participating in the evaluation process, youth workers can empathize with the needs of the youth in their community and discard personal or traditional notions of what they believe will truly impact them with the gospel. Arriving at effective strategies, tools, and training will enable us to more effectively engage and empower today's younger youth leaders in India.

OBSTACLES TO YOUTH MINISTRY

In the face of all of these possibilities, there are some obstacles we need to be aware of:

- Church hierarchies often stifle or ignore the energy of youth.
- Leaders' high spiritual expectations put undue pressure on youth.
- Heretical groups challenge teens' regular youth group attendance.
- Church leaders' unwillingness to cooperate or network with

specialists outside the church leadership deprives youth of input from the wider body of Christ.

- Traditional worship patterns and irrelevant and outdated methodology discourages church attendance.
- There's a lack of trained personnel within church leadership.

In addition, family work pressures keep the adults preoccupied, causing a decline in their active participation in their children's lives. Another growing concern is the rise of 'Ghetto culture,' which perpetuates a holier-than-others attitude. This attitude of spiritual pride and contentment hinders organisational networking, cooperation, and growth. Also, a shift from a people-orientation to a programme- and events-orientation has caused a decline in qualitative discipleship. In addition, gender inequality is another grave concern. Traditional Indian values keep women confined to the home and prevent them from being actively involved in ministry—and they have also stifled youth groups from growing. And heavy bureaucracy keeps youth workers from giving adequate attention to other matters, thereby limiting their full potential.

> Students are fast emerging as trendsetters, be it in fashion, ideas, and even thought processes. Therefore, youth workers should have the cutting edge at their fingertips and be trailblazers in regard to innovation and creativity, training their minds and looking for opportunities to read and interpret cultural trends.

Furthermore, financial struggles—due to the policy of independence on the one hand, and the accusation that youth ministries live off others' money—have curbed more specialised youth ministries from emerging.

MY DREAMS FOR FUTURE YOUTH MINISTRY IN INDIA

I dream of youth workers who are Christlike and relational. Our very existence is due to relational practices—and no youth worker or youth ministry can be fruitful without them. So I wish that our training institutions will develop youth workers with exceptionally good relational skills. They also should be incarnational and form youth ministries that are just like the early church was. They should be compassionate, and their ministries should be grass-roots oriented.

I dream of youth ministries that are lively and vibrant, attractive and appealing to those outside the church, and sensitive to the needs of youth no matter what their age or background. They should also be transformatively powerful, as adolescence is when we make many important life decisions. Youth ministries should be creative and radical in style and approach so that we bring glory and honour to the God of all creation and creativity. We need to be professional in approach—well-managed organisations that help widen their scopes beyond church walls. We need to be unselfish but maintain a healthy competition that fosters overall growth.

I dream of youth ministries that are visible in mainstream society so the Christian ethos and principles can permeate the culture; our "Christ fragrance" should be smelled all around us as well.

I dream of youth ministries that incorporate multiplying principles to speed growth and develop transferable concepts to aid other aspiring youth workers to start new ventures that can reach the community.

Finally, I dream of youth ministries that empower younger leaders to flourish under our guidance and not become leader-driven or authoritative—something that has been a bane of our ministry through the ages.

WIDENING THE SCOPE OF YOUTH MINISTRIES

For youth ministry to be effective in India, it will have to follow some distinct paths amid the pluralism and pressures of our culture. First, it has to be Christian, which means it should be about biblical, sound teaching. Youth workers should be marked by their call and commitment and truly express Christlike compassion and care for youth. These points may seem obvious, but they aren't always present.

Second, the maturity and commitment of youth workers is crucial for a mentoring ministry focused on the discipleship of young believers. Youth workers should be exceptional in every way, exhibiting a high sensitivity to the needs of youth. They should be creative in their approach, and the programs they churn out should be dynamic and engaging to the youth.

I also see the need to train and develop capable leaders to serve in unreached areas of India. An emphasis on pioneering youth ministry efforts must be maintained, as there are many unconventional areas of youth ministry we haven't yet entered. These pioneers need to build networks and develop partnerships that can make youth ministry a less-stressful effort as we join hands to reach the unreached millions.

After the 'IT Boom' at the beginning of the new millennium, 'call centres' exploded upon the Indian landscape, helping many thousands of youth find jobs and earn the kinds of incomes that were so elusive until then. Thus began a consumer culture driven by Indian youth's newfound financial freedom. Unfortunately, the church spent a considerable amount of time criticising the trend and did very little to engage youth toward more spiritual pursuits.

I consider this an important turning point in the history of India (and in youth ministry) as we encounter a whole new generation of youth waiting to hear the gospel. These young people are professionals, entrepreneurs, and students migrating from other cities in search of more advanced academics and employment. We also see many training institutes providing fast-track training to cash in on new business opportunities; a large number of youth who don't have the money to attend university have settled for these study programs.

A MISSION THAT NEEDS OUR ATTENTION

I also dream of youth ministries that would adopt bivocational lifestyles or ministries to work and earn their way (literally) into the hearts of the young they want to reach. There have been a few attempts. The first was Kerygma, a coffee shop established in 1997 in Bangalore City, in southern India. Believing that youth would find it easier to walk into a coffeehouse than a church, Kerygma provided a space and ambience that connected with the youth's relaxed and social world—and it also connected youth to key ministry staff who worked at Kerygma. The ministry featured creative programs that used media, theatre, the creative arts, talk shows, interviews with important personalities, music concerts, and art exhibits to lead young people through an exciting journey in which they could discover God in a new way.

An emerging model is setting up call centres that provide income and opportunities to nurture hundreds of young professionals. Organized and supervised by Christians, the ministry would be holistic, helping young people earn an income, develop effective life and communication skills in a Christian environment, and provide opportunities to share the gospel with workers at the centre.

Finally, there's the "Business as Mission" (BAM) model for ministry and becoming a human resource (HR) manager.[6] An HR professional is involved in developing individuals' life skills, training them in behavioural and organisational development.

Training and Development of Youth Workers

Training for youth ministry has not been a priority in our country. This is because of the traditional understanding of mission and the notion that a basic degree in biblical theology would suffice. But it doesn't. Youth workers should receive specialised training in apologetics and homiletics as an added asset. In addition, basic training in psychology and behavioural sciences—especially for at-risk kids—would be of additional value. Accurately understanding and interpreting issues means that training in critical thinking is a must. Training young entrepreneurs to start business ventures would be an added benefit, as would business and organisational management training and sound communication and writing skills. The ability to raise funds can be of great help, as would be the ability to research and analyse youth ministry trends to stay ahead.

Develop a National Network of Youth Ministries in India[7]

I believe we must harness local networks of youth workers in order to reach youth in every state of India, especially its most unreached communities. A diverse cross-section of youth workers would be encouraged to share resources, develop and implement cooperative strategies, and enhance relationships. Much like the political world and its division along caste and communal lines, India would be divided among ministries toward a consensus of reaching India. Therefore, we must unite in recognition that reaching and discipling each student cannot be accomplished by any one organization—only when youth workers and ministries work together.

Specialised ministries (for example, college campuses, urban and rural missions, youth at risk, and research and technology institutes) and creative approaches such as coffee shops, camping ministries, and dance and drama are some affinity groups that must come together periodically to analyse and understand changing trends for more effectiveness.

And clearly we must identify and develop many more youth workers. We need to understand the necessity of youth workers' presence in the whole mission of the church, and prepare them to pass the baton smoothly and seamlessly to the next generation. India has the resources and people to reach neighbouring countries—and they're even more in need of organised youth ministries that make a difference in their social and political contexts.

CONCLUSION[8]

As wealth increases in developing nations, as we've seen happen in India, it's poverty of another nature that stares us in the face. Unlike our parents who belonged to a generation of limited resources, today's Indian youth are enjoying the fruit of their parents' labour. This is leading to laziness, lack of direction, consumerism, addiction, and even crime. Millions are at risk because of poverty, but millions are also at risk because of prosperity! Many young people today have everything to live *with*, but nothing to live *for*. Poverty—at its deepest level—is what happens to people with no meaningful relationships (or whose relationships fail to work for their well-being). A person's well-being is rooted in wholesome relationships.

Young adolescents can contribute much to a positive social change. What often prevents this from occurring is an absence of adults who believe in them. As a consequence, many young people do not believe in themselves. Nevertheless, most young people respond well to challenges and can participate in opportunities to better their surroundings and their societies. When wise adults give a significant challenge to young people (intentionally or "accidentally" through necessity or disaster or obligation), they usually readily adapt to such demands. The ministry challenge, therefore, is about encouraging and equipping youth to use their gifts and potential as agents in transforming the world. They represent an enormous untapped pool of influencers with sensitivity to the voice of God and willingness to embark on his mission. God can and does use young people—their prayers, their insights, their hands, and their feet—in changing the hearts of humankind.

DISCUSSION QUESTIONS

1. What are the unique elements to India that prompt Jacob to say that "youth ministry in India is very complex"?
2. What are the new ways of communicating the gospel that many in India are unwilling to test?
3. What are the economic needs of youth in your culture? In what ways do youth ministries in your context address those needs?
4. What are the various urban subcultures in your country?
5. To what extent are you familiar with what is happening in India? It would be a worthwhile project to do a cultural summary of India.

CHAPTER FOURTEEN

CHRISTIAN IDENTITY IN A GLOBAL AGE

SNAPSHOTS FROM NORTH AMERICAN YOUTH MINISTRY[1]

DR. KENDA CREASY DEAN

As teenagers in America "grow up global," ideologies can become more divisive than time or distance. As young people grow more accustomed to other cultures, cultural identities seem to homogenize, at least on the surface. However, this is more a product of American naiveté than an actual reflection of the state of the world. Deep cultural differences exist beneath the surface, although globalization shies away from pointing these out. Globalization tells American youth that borders are irrelevant, time is inconsequential, the world is a single place, identity is shapeless, and that all of this is good.

Globalization has vast implications for youth ministry because young people arguably constitute the population most affected by globalization. The economic practices of late capitalism target adolescents to socialize them into the values of consumerism, and globalization presents serious challenges to identity, the development of which is necessary for every youth.

In spite of dismal statistics that might suggest otherwise, countless ministries address young people who are "growing up global" with faithfulness, sensitivity, and integrity. This was one of the things examined in the Princeton Project on Globalization, Youth, and the Church. We were interested in exploring the way ministries intentionally address globalization's impact on youth. None of the ministries we surveyed set out to address globalization itself; they all set out to address *young people* representing the church in more or less formal venues. But regardless of educational approach, governing theology, or style of leadership, all of these ministries shared three core convictions:

1. Youth ministry—in our age and in every age—requires the church to develop a deep and critical appreciation of our culture.
2. The church is called to proclaim, decisively, identity in Jesus Christ as an alternative to the local and global culture's proposals for adolescent identity.
3. The church is most effective in addressing young people who are "growing up global" when it emphasizes relationships, mediated through face-to-face communities of significant peers and adults.

Three of the ministries studied are included here. They were chosen partly because they illustrate the range of effective ministries in a global age: an urban African American congregation in the Midwest; an urban Eastern parachurch ministry; and a suburban Western age-segregated ministry. On the one hand, we would have liked to have discovered new paradigms for ministry in a global age in these case studies, but we did not. What we found were unremarkable ministries that infused young people with remarkable faith that changed in remarkable ways the way these young people approach global culture. The most significant shared emphasis among ministries that prepare young people for faith in a global age appears to be human relationships, imagined in these ministries as "surrogate families," "neighbors," and "deep friendships." In the end, ministry is about people, not about globalization.

> The most significant shared emphasis among ministries that prepare young people for faith in a global age appears to be human relationships, imagined in these ministries as "surrogate families," "neighbors," and "deep friendships." In the end, ministry is about people, not about globalization.

However, the fact remains that introducing young people to Jesus Christ *does* prepare them for global culture. Christ calls the church to gather people around a common table to alleviate suffering, expand our concept of *neighbor*, and embrace the "other." Ministries that address the kinds of issues globalization brings to the surface—such as social fragmentation, dehumanization, and cultural pluralism—seem increasingly apt to use ancient forms of Christian discipleship to do so. Perhaps this suggests that globalization has always been with us. Or perhaps it suggests that the gospel has always had a globalizing impact. Whatever the case, globalization seems to beg the church's response.

The three ministries profiled differ in dozens of objective ways—demographics, size and range of programs, theological dispositions, style of leadership—but they share similar skeletons. To different degrees, they all function as "monastic communities" in the sense that their energy is derived from small communities of committed Christians who self-consciously enact an alternative way of being in the world to that which is proposed by global culture. They all rely on the central importance of face-to-face relationships that are intended to model a personal relationship with God in Jesus Christ. Each of these ministries emphasizes the radical nature of Christian commitment. Finally, all three ministries assume that authentic faith leads to young people's engagement with secular culture, making youth agents of ministry in their own right, not simply passive recipients of ministry practiced by others.

One ministry surveyed—a mid-size congregation that makes lavish and artful use of extremely sophisticated technology in worship—bears mention because we chose *not* to include it in this report. In many ways, this congregation took globalization more seriously, and it certainly was more intentional about addressing the technological dimensions of globalization than any other youth ministry we studied. The young people in this church help lead worship through the artistry of technology and find this experience extremely valuable both for their personal faith in Jesus Christ and their ability to function in a technological age.

However, one of the striking features of this congregation was how few teenagers were actively engaged in the church's intergenerational worship hour, which middle-aged adults seemed to value enormously. Although this project was not designed to ascertain why this might be the case, it was striking to us that this congregation paid the least attention to developing purposeful relationships between teenagers and caring adults; rather, these relationships seemed to emerge sporadically, not as a result of an intentional emphasis by the church's ministry with youth. The absence of a significant number of youth from the worship of this community suggests that technology may not be the whole answer in transforming young people who are "growing up global" into faithful believers in Jesus Christ.

Now for the three ministries:

HOPE THROUGH PRAYER, DISCERNMENT, AND MUTUAL CARE: THE "SURROGATE FAMILY" OF ST. JAMES UNITED METHODIST CHURCH

"Right hand down, left hand up." At 10 o'clock on Saturday morning, 60 African American young people close their hour of discussion, prayer, and praise at St. James United Methodist Church by circling around the table and praying for each other. According to one teenager, the symbolism of the clasped hands pointing upward and downward in the circle means "We see ourselves like a family. The right hand pointing down is a sign of giving, and the left hand pointing up is a symbol of receiving. The giving and receiving of God's love means a lot in this community. That's why we call it a family." The researcher assigned to St. James, Gregory C. Ellison II, remarked: "In an era when *broken home* has in many ways become synonymous with black households, I found it significant that this group referred to itself as an extension of the family unit."[2]

Located in a metropolitan Midwest city, St. James Church gives young people adrift in global culture "a place to belong." The surrogate family of the congregation is intended to serve as a source of hope. In 30 years, Rev. Emmanuel Cleaver II grew St. James from 127 congregants to more than 2,500, managing to simultaneously serve as his city's first African American mayor in the early 1990s. Cleaver, an avid activist in the Civil Rights Movement of the 1960s, integrates the ministries of St. James with the needs of the city, with services to children and youth prominent. In addition to programs designed to care for the children of incarcerated parents, food and clothing ministries, a welfare-to-work program, and political lobbying to entice corporate jobs to the metro area, Cleaver established Mayor's Night Hoops (to provide safe recreational alternatives and social development for teenagers) and built the Forty Acres and a Mule Activities Campus (the title itself invites notice!)—a wooded campus 15 minutes from the church that includes a competition-sized swimming pool, gymnasium, baseball diamond, driving range, and air-conditioned dining facility. As mayor, Cleaver's political agenda sought to offer support and stability for a community with scores of at-risk youth.

Given the size of St. James, the youth group is rather small—60 young people in a congregation of 2,500 represents less than three percent of the congregation. (Other ministry profiles for this project turned up youth group attendance equal to up to 10 percent.) However, the youth ministry at St. James extends beyond the youth group that meets on Saturday mornings. It permeates the congregation's consciousness and figures prominently in the congregation's outreach. Cleaver's own example of charismatic, hands-on leadership sets the tone for the adults who mentor youth at St. James. These adults intentionally serve as surrogate parents, grandparents, and aunts and uncles for teenagers whose own families have been fractured many times over.

The youth minister, "Mr. Bill" (a term of endearment that the youth bestowed upon Bill Johnson, which was borrowed from the iconic *Saturday Night Live* segment[3]), seeks a ministry that will provide young people with a sense of safety, support, and stability; and he cultivates advisors who view their role as a calling from God. One of the striking characteristics of these advisors is their unswerving commitment to this ministry, aware that they are called upon at different points to serve as ministers, parents, and counselors.

St. James youth share an immersion in the chaos of a society where borders of time and place are fading. Nothing has a clear beginning or an end: schedules, neighborhoods, and adolescence itself. In this setting the weekly rhythm of the youth group provides a welcome and rare form of boundaries and predictability. As one advisor put it, "Mr. Bill's continuity in returning every week is supportive for the youth because many of them have people constantly in and out of their lives. They gravitate to stability."[4]

Significantly, the advisors aren't the only ones who feel called to help provide stability for young people. The youth at St. James prize hospitality and engage openly in ministries of welcome to their peers, including those they don't know; and a high priority is placed on inviting newcomers to become "insiders" to the "family." Scattered across the city in different schools, youth and adults alike are deliberate in maintaining and strengthening relationships through email, retreats, worship, and prayer venues that allow them to grapple with difficult "life issues" and support one another in times of crisis. At the weekly gatherings, advisors act as consultants while young people make decisions regarding budgetary concerns, outreach, and upcoming activities in the group. After the business session, youth move into informal pastoral roles; some lead discussions of current events, while others lead prayers and praise, and still others function as informal peer counselors.

Every youth group meeting ends with prayer. The 60 youth and 10 advisors stand as a family interlocked, hand in hand, before God. The teenagers admit their vulnerability in prayer and freely share their broken spirits as they embrace one another in tears or distress. These prayer sessions also include joyous praise reports and testimonials; students hold one another accountable and offer encouragement to their brothers and sisters in Christ as they leave the altar to go into the world—until this time next week.

St. James is a self-consciously "African American community" meaning that, while persons of other ethnic backgrounds are welcome, African American identity is celebrated as a gift from God, and issues pertinent to African Americans are explicitly addressed by the congregation's ministries. Yet the ministry of St. James is anything but homogeneous. Like a family, its members bear an external resemblance to one another, but youth are keenly aware of their differences. The adults at St. James believe young people will be better able to confront "otherness" and pluralism if they have a secure, stable sense of their own sense of belonging to a church community. Adults take it upon themselves to model ways to confront risk in ways that are direct and unapologetically Christian.

As globalization accelerates forces that threaten the stability of families and local communities, St. James' "surrogate family" gives young people a place to belong, a family identity, stability, spiritual confidence, and moral courage. Secure families of origin demonstrate what it means to be faithful to one another (even to relatives we may not like) in a culture in which the one constant is change. Such steadfastness amidst flux offers a secure platform from which young people can begin to risk on behalf of others. Belonging to such a family, in fact, makes the culture of "risk" less threatening all around, as youth learn life skills that confront risk through the example of trusted adults. For African American teenagers growing up global, St. James' youth group offers a place to call home, a harbor of hope, and still waters in a global sea of change.

HUMILITY THROUGH SACRIFICE, DISCERNMENT, AND COMMUNITY-BUILDING: THE "NEIGHBORS" OF MISSION YEAR

The college students and young adults in Mission Year spend up to a year living and volunteering in an inner-city neighborhood. Humility pervades the Mission Year ethos, and that's new to many young people; as virtues go, humility is not high on the list of values prized by a global economy. When researcher Michael Baughman asked these young people what they preferred to be called, the enthusiastic reply was: *Neighbor*.[5] The goal of Mission Year participants, proclaims their Web site, is "to become the very best, most helpful, most openly loving neighbors they can possibly be, and to help advance the Kingdom of God throughout their neighborhoods."[6]

There is, of course, more to it than that. If St. James' youth group gives young people a place to belong, Mission Year gives them a way to live. They intentionally work to unlearn secular socialization in favor of a way of life grounded in Christian love and enacted as neighborli-ness. The intended outcome is a transformed worldview that leads to lasting skills for living as a Christian neighbor in a global society. Very quickly into their time in Mission Year, young people's perspectives begin to change. In one student's first letter home, she wrote: "We are beginning to meet our neighbors and to discover that, though we have come to serve them, they have just as much to offer us." This is no small discovery. Mission Year houses are located in inner city Philadelphia, in a part of town known for drugs and violence. Those who participate in Mission Year undergo a seismic shift in how they view social issues as they relate to the poor and the inner city. Part of the philosophy behind Mission Year, notes recruiter Dave Krueger, is "planting the seeds [in these youth] to function in a global community."[7] They learn how to navigate the mul-ticultural world and to develop relationships with people who are clearly "other," especially economically. Mission Year youth tend to be "haves" from middle-class or upper middle-class households. As Mission Year participants, they serve people who are "have nots" from areas of extreme poverty in an effort to transform the world "one street corner at a time."[8]

> **They intentionally work to unlearn secular social-ization in favor of a way of life grounded in Christian love and enacted as neighborliness. The intended outcome is a transformed worldview that leads to lasting skills for living as a Christian neighbor in a global society.**

For Mission Year youth, the substance of one's identity as a Chris-tian neighbor is spiritual discernment to work with the poor. One's way of being in the world is intended to be governed by discernment of what more can be done for the neighbor. Unlike congregation-ally based ministries, parachurch ministries like Mission Year lack a natural constituency; they recruit volunteers, generally without the benefit of family connections (or, often, family support).

The most obvious part of Mission Year's success stems from the fact that participants sacrifice material comfort to be a part of their program. A high level of sacrifice inevitably yields high investment in the program; no one wants such a commitment to return void. Participants each agree to what amounts to a vow of poverty; they each raise $9,600 for their mission year and live on a monthly allowance of $70 (plus a food allowance)—subsistence living in the United States. But the cultural and social sacrifices are even more substantial, designed to strip young people of the consumer orientation they have absorbed from global culture. As such, Mission Year youth not only move to an environment very different from the white suburban culture that most of them call home, but they also live in intentional Christian households with their peers where "un-Christian" behavior is forbidden (defined as sexual contact and use of cigarettes, alcohol, and drugs), television and Internet access isn't permitted, and computers may be used for word processing only (no video games). Phone time with family and friends is also strictly limited.

Despite the lack of technological access, Mission Year participants claim a deeper connection to the world, now defined in local terms of their neighborhood relationships. They self-consciously identify with the "have nots" in the global culture: people unable to communicate through mass media, unable to travel, unable to participate in the consumerism that constitutes much of American identity. The radical nature of the Mission Year commitment sometimes strains relationships between participants and their families. "[My] non-Christian family doesn't understand not getting paid," said one social work major from Indiana. "They're big into corporate America." Another team member added that her family "says it's okay to be a Christian, but don't make any weird decisions that might be radical."

It is, of course, the radical nature of the Mission Year decision that accounts for most of its appeal. Claiming humility, participants downplay their countercultural lifestyle. "They think we're doing some radical Christianity," said one youth from Michigan. "But we're not. We're just doing what Jesus Christ asks." When pressed, he admitted, "Well, it is radical, but it shouldn't be!" Many youth are so transformed by their experience that they decide to live in the inner city following the program. "I don't want to be bound by money," said one Mission Year alumnus, "I want to do unexpected things and make sure my children are exposed to different things . . . I don't want to be bound by what the U.S. tells me I need [in order] to live."[9]

Sacrifice is underscored by large doses of spiritual reflection used to discern how to be a good neighbor. Each Mission Year house— four to six young men or women—commits to a regimen of spiritual practices, participation in Bible study and a Mission Year curriculum, and training aimed at team members' faith development. Baughman observed, "The intentionality (a word used so often in Mission Year circles that it has taken on buzzword status) functions as a bridge between the Christian faith, spirituality, and how these youth live in our increasingly global culture."[10] This intentionality leads young people into relationships with their neighbors, who are almost always vastly different culturally from the Mission Year youth. These relationships grow out of such small activities as taking out the trash for someone or playing basketball with the local drug dealers. The majority of their time is spent building relationships with people in the neighborhood.

For safety, as well as for the advantage of an additional perspective, most relationship building takes place with other team members. Every decision made during the Mission Year on behalf of one's neighbors is designed to be the self-conscious outcome of spiritual reflection that takes place in community. This intentional use of Christian community is intended to be a ray of hope for the neighborhood, but its primary beneficiaries are the youth who must learn what Christian humility looks like when practiced at close range. Besides working together to build relationships with their neighbors, Mission Year households prepare meals, eat, clean, talk, and play together. They are well acquainted with the scriptural basis for their communal lifestyle, and quick to quote passages from Matthew 18 and 1 Corinthians that provide exhortations for community living. Because these youth work with as many as four social service agencies over the course of a year, they develop important networks with coworkers in the inner city. The assurance that they are not alone in their efforts to change the world convinces them that their sacrifice is not in vain. Community building is stressed—not just for the neighborhood, but also for the sake of the young people themselves.

The most obvious beneficiaries of Mission Year are the young people who undergo a reshaping of their identities as they substitute one set of cultural influences for another. Perhaps, in ways unacknowledged even by Mission Year, this is Mission Year's most important contribution to young people who are growing up global: *Inculcating the virtue of humility in youth who are on the affluent end of globalization's economic poles.* As globalization polarizes the world economically, Mission Year bridges these differences with Christian humility, calling for a way of life rooted in sacrifice and intentional acts of kindness on behalf of the other. Far from "denying" self in the psychological sense, the self-denial required of young people by Mission Year actually helps them "find" themselves and establish their identities in a context of radical giving, denial of excess, intentional spiritual praxis, and intentional community formation.

Sometimes the "humility" voiced by Mission Year participants admittedly rings hollow. After all, these young people are "trying on" a virtue that American can-do pragmatism (not to mention many American churches) has made virtually irrelevant, and it doesn't yet "fit" comfortably. Yet given the American arrogance that has often accompanied globalization in the past century, the importance of reclaiming Christian humility for ministry in a global age cannot be overstated. Because youth ministry traffics unabashedly in interpersonal relationships, youth ministry has a great deal to offer the church in this regard. Christian humility is the necessary virtue for the authentic relationships we are created to seek with God and with others.

While every ministry we profiled stressed the value of human relationships in helping young people address the issues that accompany globalization, only Mission Year *self-consciously* taught humility as a necessary component of Christian identity.

RISK THROUGH RELATIONSHIP, LEADERSHIP, AND MISSION: THE "DEEP FRIENDSHIPS" OF THE EDGE AT UNIVERSITY PRESBYTERIAN CHURCH

University Presbyterian Church (UPC), located in an upper west coast city, is a "mega" congregation to which 4,500 people commute from all over the area for worship each week. Its most well-known ministry is a thriving outreach to university students, in which a thousand college students gather weekly for worship and communion in the church's carpeted gym. However, for this project we profiled UPC's high school ministry, "The Edge," which is composed of approximately 200 active students (ages 14 to 18) from 33 different high schools, as well as 30 adult sponsors, who meet following one of UPC's Sunday evening "contemporary" worship services. "The commuter nature of UPC ensures that students know few [if any] of their peers at The Edge from school," observed researcher Dan Cravy. "This in turn means that the staff must be strategic about creating opportunities to develop a sense of 'neighborhood' [in other words, community] among them."[11]

As a result, although The Edge's focal gathering is the Sunday night large group event, the energy for its ministries comes from relationships developed in small groups with both students and adult sponsors: co-ed weekly prayer and conversation groups, same-sex Wednesday night Bible studies, Sunday morning classes, student leadership gatherings, monthly sponsor suppers, weekend retreats, camps, and both local and international mission opportunities for service and witness. Even the Sunday night meetings break down into small groups for discussion and sharing.

Like the youth program at St. James United Methodist Church, The Edge is part of the congregation pastored by a dynamic, well-known, and extremely supportive senior pastor, Earl Palmer. Like Emmanuel Cleaver at St. James, the extroverted Palmer is the quintessential relationally driven leader. Unlike the economically diverse congregation of St. James, however, the people who worship at University Presbyterian Church are overwhelmingly affluent, and they give generously to the youth ministries of UPC. In addition to a full-time associate pastor of youth mission and ministry (whose title speaks volumes), The Edge is also served by a professional administrator and three young adult interns, not to mention three 15-passenger vans, a basketball gym, ample meeting space, and a budget that—combined with the junior high program budget—exceeds $500,000 annually.

The Edge was unique among the youth ministries we profiled for its consuming interest in teaching young people the foundational elements of a relationship with Jesus Christ. They teach young people that a condition for growing in relationship with Christ is to have "a place to belong"; discovering "a way to live" is the natural outcome of this relationship. At UPC, faith is more than an experience of belonging or a social outreach. Christian faith has a definite content in the person of Jesus Christ, and students are encouraged to think about this content, ask hard questions, and wrestle with the Bible. The content level of Sunday evening talks is calibrated for 16-year-olds, forcing 14- and 15-year-olds to "think . . . *up.*" The goal of this instruction is for young people to discover or deepen their relationships with God. Every activity challenges them one step beyond their comfort zones. Relationships, servant leadership, and cross-cultural mission opportunities are all considered practice fields for faith in which our dependence on God is dramatized by the experience of vulnerability before the "other."

If *intentionality* is the buzzword of Mission Year, *relationship* is the buzzword of The Edge. Associate Pastor Jeff Towne says, "It's about being in relationship. It's about proclaiming the relationship we have—that we're privileged to have—with the God of the universe, but then living that out in relationship to one another!"[12] Adult volunteers are called "sponsors" instead of "leaders" to signify their commitment to walk alongside students in the faith. The sponsor recruitment packet states that the "goal is to reach adolescents with the gospel of Jesus Christ through a community of Christ-centered people committed to building relationships . . . with [them]." Cravy noted: "Nearly every promotional piece distributed by the youth ministry staff . . . trumpets this twofold goal of building friendships of depth with others (both students and adults) and discovering or deepening one's relationship with God." Towne and his staff are theologically explicit: "Our approach to Christian ministry must mirror God's approach in drawing us to him through becoming incarnate in Jesus Christ." Because God came to us in the flesh, Towne and his staff go to high school students "where they are." Much of The Edge's ministry, therefore, happens in unscheduled "contact work" in which sponsors go to high schools to share lunch, attend student sporting events and extracurricular activities, call students on the phone, or keep in touch through email. Even fundraising is considered an opportunity for relationship building between youth and adults. For a silent auction to raise money to build houses for the homeless in Mexico, youth are required to make more than 3,000 calls to gather donated items from the entire membership of the church. They raised more than $95,000—but in the process, they engaged in 3,000 conversations in which students and adults had to interact.

Yet these "contacts" aim for relationships of deeper significance: a community of trusted friends that allows them to be themselves. The Edge leadership considers such relationships risky for young people, and therefore "risk" assumes a prominent place in The Edge curriculum. On the first retreat for students transitioning from the junior high ministry (called "The Rock") into the senior high ministry of The Edge, students go rock climbing. At the end of the first day (climbing), leaders give a "Rock talk"—emphasizing that Jesus Christ is a solid, trustworthy Rock upon whom youth can depend. At the end of the second day (rappelling), leaders give an "Edge talk"—emphasizing that, because youth know the Rock of Jesus Christ who will not let them fall, they can risk stepping out in faith onto the often-fearsome "Edge" of God's purpose for their lives. Cravy describes the implicit philosophy—and theology of the metaphor:

> Most students have never experienced rock climbing before. What they find is that in order to make progress, they must trust that the rope will hold them in spite of their fear. The cheering crowd of adults and students below encourages them to risk falling in order to reach out for the next height. And when they fall, they find that the rope—secured fast to the rock—does indeed save them from death.

Students speak of The Edge as a place where they can be "real," a "safe" place in the sense that there is "no judgment." One student called the "glue" of The Edge "deep friendship"; others described it as generating a "contagious" excitement, a place where "everyone's on fire," a community of acceptance where students can discover new friends—especially through mission opportunities—and where "nobody cares that you're dirty or what you look like."

The Edge also places an emphasis on youth mission. This emphasis is underscored organizationally—the youth pastor's title is "Pastor of Youth Mission and Ministry"; the office space is designated "Youth Mission and Ministry Office"; and elders, youth ministry staff, and former staff proudly wear black vests embroidered with the letters YMM. The Edge sponsors local outreach in a number of ways, including teams of students to work in soup kitchens, feed and shelter street youth in the city, and tutor elementary school children who have few academic resources. But The Edge also emphasizes international mission in various forms as a way to heighten the "risk" of confronting "otherness": investing in the lives of youth in Scotland and Ireland, participating in social justice efforts in Guatemala, raising money to build homes for unsheltered families in Mexico.

If The Edge has a highlight event, it's the spring break mission trip to Mexico, a traditional building project accompanied—predictably—by liberal doses of Christian catechetical instruction. In the midst of shocking and discomforting poverty in Tijuana, youth observe that "the world has gotten smaller, and they ask questions aloud about who they are and about their responsibility as Americans and followers of Christ."[13]

Youth speak with conviction that the welcoming community of The Edge is the work of God. It is also the work of the adult sponsors who intentionally work to develop "deep friendships" among themselves that will be "contagious" to the youth. Sponsors meet monthly in a home as a "smaller church within the larger UPC family."[14] This is something of an understatement: the UPC "family" is the size of a small village, and small groups are necessary to avoid rampant anonymity in the congregation. Consequently, the sponsors have a parallel ministry to one another that strives for many of the same goals they seek with students. They gather for dinner, biblical teaching, and fellowship—as well as for a chance to brag about the youth they work with, and for the opportunity to pray for one another and for the students of The Edge.

Youth bask in the attention of their adult sponsors. One night, after a Bible study at the home of a sponsor named Mike, the boys noticed a pile of old clothing Mike had set out to take to Goodwill. They decided to recycle it themselves, and now all the boys proudly wear some of Mike's clothing—not unlike the way they try on Mike's faith, borrowing it long enough to learn how to live with and apply their own.

The most explicit way The Edge confronts globalization, of course, is the exposure to cultural "others" provided by the annual mission trip to Mexico. But The Edge helps young people address global culture in more subtle ways that bear notice. The Edge's unabashed emphasis on relationships yields a matrix in which "otherness" can he confronted and received as a gift, not a threat—including the "Otherness" of God. The Edge offers young people a similar advantage when it comes to the culture of risk that characterizes a global era; at UPC, students are given overt skills for living with risk: relationships, servant leadership, and positive encounters with people from very different backgrounds. Consequently, students at The Edge learn to embrace risk as a vehicle for growing closer to God, rather than fear it as a dangerous by-product of global culture.

YOUTH MINISTRY IN A GLOBAL AGE

	ST. JAMES UNITED METHODIST CHURCH (KANSAS CITY, MO)	MISSION YEAR (PHILADELPHIA, PA)	"THE EDGE" OF UNIVERSITY PRESBYTERIAN CHURCH (SEATTLE, WA)
COTRIBUTION TO ADOLESCENT IDENTITY	A place to belong	A way to live	A creed to believe
GOVERNING IMAGE	Surrogate family	Neighbor	Deep friendship
RADICAL COMMITMENT	Weekly accountability	Material/social sacrifice	"Think up"
ROUTE TO TRANSFORMATION	Prayer, ethical discernment, mutual care	Material sacrifice, spiritual discernment, community building	Teaching through risk (encountering God, encountering the other)
FORM OF COMMUNITY	Peer-led congregation	Intential community	Small groups
ALTERNATIVE CONSCIOUSNESS	Technology does not bring us together; the Holy Spirit brings us together	Stuff does lead to stress; sacrifice leads to joy	"Whatever" is not the norm; Jesus is the norm
THEOLOGICAL CONTRIBUTION TO "GROWING UP GLOBAL"	Hope	Humility	Love

CONCLUSION

Youth who are "growing up global"—like youth who have grown up in every era—hope for a place to belong, a way to live, and a creed to believe in. They hope for someone who knows and understands them and the culture in which they live; they crave an authentic community of friends, a cadre of trusted adults, a holy and noble sense of purpose, and a God who is big enough to hold together all the contradictions of their daily experiences in a global world.

If the church's dialogue with technological, economic, or cultural features of global culture is to make any difference to adolescents, this dialogue must take place in the context of significant face-to-face relationships. Christian identity seems most likely to emerge amid the recognition that *God* is global, just as our human communities of faith are inevitably local—while acknowledging that there is more to God's will than may be apparent from our limited geographic, economic, or cultural perspective.

So, sure, an iPod is nice; it may even make globalization and its multinational economic roots a little more obvious. But the resources for "growing up global"—not to mention the boldness required for changing such a world—still are found in young lives transformed by faith, empowered by hope, and energized by the sacrificial love of Jesus Christ.

DISCUSSION QUESTIONS

1. What finding from this research is most surprising to you?
2. To which of these three models or case studies are you most drawn? Why?
3. Kenda writes, "Christ calls the church to gather people around a common table to alleviate suffering, expand our concept of *neighbor*, and embrace the "other." Who are the "others" for us (make a broad list)? In what ways may you and I need to make new steps to initiate that embrace?
4. How have you seen globalization accelerate forces that threaten the stability of families in your local community?
5. What is the role of sacrifice in global youth ministry? Does the global need require a sacrificial response from us?

CHAPTER FIFTEEN

YOUTH, CULTURE, AND THEOLOGY IN PLURAL

PRESENTING THE WORK OF THE IASYM

DR. BERT ROEBBEN

Since the beginning of the 1990s, the International Association for the Study of Youth Ministry (IASYM) has been growing more important in regard to articulating youth ministry issues in academic settings. The biannual international conferences have been held in the United Kingdom since 1995.[1] The creation of the scholarly journal, *The Journal of Youth and Theology*, in 2002 was an important milestone for the process of building an internationally credible academic institution 'around' the work of youth ministers.

The word *plural* in the title of this chapter refers to the radical diversity of contexts, cultures, approaches, ministries, and theologies in the field of Christian youth ministry. This diversity not only is enriching for the exchange of ideas between youth ministry representatives internationally, but also refers to the deeply creative and innovative power of young people and their leaders. On further reflection, this deep diversity is also theologically relevant, as Elie Wiesel anecdotally declares: 'God created humankind, because he loves stories.' In the storytelling of adolescents, young adults and their ministers, the multifaceted Presence of the Holy in our world is 'reflected.'

A SHORT HISTORY OF THE IASYM

Pete Ward worked as the youth adviser of the Archbishop of Canterbury in the early 1990s. He discussed topics of Christian faith and culture with youth and young adults in different scenes in the United Kingdom, played in their bands, and was part of the popular culture surrounding them. But he felt the need for a thorough reflection on his work with youth as the theological convictions beneath youth ministry all puzzled him.[2] Not only the ministerial patterns, but he wanted to think about church organization issues and missionary methods—the spiritual ways of 'doing theology.' He began to gather both reflective practitioners and practical theologians on these topics from within and without the United Kingdom to help answer the pressing problems.

The first international conference on youth ministry grew out of the discussion of a small group of friends (Dean Borgman, Christine Cook, and Ward). They invited people from around the world to meet together in Oxford in 1995, to read their latest works to each other and to discuss those thoughts and be an encouragement to one another. Eight years later, as the gatherings grew and grew from that first meeting, an official constitution was accepted in the general assembly in Oxford. This was the official start of the IASYM.[3]

FUTURE DIRECTIONS FOR YOUTH MINISTRY RESEARCH

As the chair of the organization (and a Catholic theologian), I have the privilege of seeing the vastness and the unity-in-diversity of IASYM around the globe. The different confessions within the Christian community are represented, but there are also broad horizons of possibilities within these confessions. The perspectives of evangelical, Pentecostal, and mainstream Christians, all situated within the two great traditions of Catholics and Protestants, provide an excellent forum for systematic-theological and practical-theological discussions on youth ministry.

As I look out over the field of youth ministry, six directions for youth ministry research seem to set an agenda for the coming years, a short list of foci around which scholars, practitioners, and graduate students can focus their research and writing.

1. Empirical Research That Captures the "Voices" of Youth

Since our work and research with youth is ultimately a response to God, our research should help young people find 'life in abundance.' (John 10:10) To do this, we must first listen carefully and empathetically to their longings and daily needs. As we do research, write articles, and teach about youth ministry, we need to listen carefully to youth so that we can understand their world. We can learn much from large quantitative studies, but if you ask one qualitative question of students, you get very different answers. Therefore, we need both large-scale quantitative studies and focused qualitative work. We need to understand the dreams and expectations of young people. How do they react to the global challenges in their vulnerable lives? How does religion play a role in their quest? And how do churches and faith communities respond to this? Are current youth ministry responses truly effective? This is the first agenda for our future youth ministry leadership—that we truly capture their voices.

2. Models of Youth Ministry in the Church

In order to be helpful in reading the signs of the times and attractive to the next generations, churches should reflect on how they can open up their traditions, institutions, and buildings for young people. The ecclesiological dimension of working with youth in the church is one of the 'modern' problems facing churches in 'postmodern' contemporary culture. Youth ministry has flourished when there have been prominent models of youth ministry to study. This needs to continue. We need to discuss different models of presence of youth—and their ministers!—inside and outside the church.[4] Partial membership, believing without belonging, and vicarious religion[5] are postmodern outcomes of the 'old' modern question of the relationship between faith and culture that we see in Europe. The agenda here is to help youth ministry leaders shape the church as it prepares for the future.

3. Fresh Expressions of Church and Youth Ministry

In line with developing models for youth ministry, the specific phenomenon of youth and church needs further attention. Youth churches, liturgical renewal, 'alternative worship,' 'emerging churches,' and 'fresh expressions' are surprising local phenomena but differ on the global scale. The common factor is that young people and their leaders construct their own religious and ritual 'regimes' and often build their own (factual or virtual) congregations. With their explorations, they invent and reinvent the church.

What is the role of new media in the lives and faith of young people? How do youth understand their religious community? This is a challenge for research, to hear young people's voices and understand this new melting pot of faith, community, church, and new media.

4. Thoughtful Church Work with Youth

Young people are listening to the voices of passion and responsibility, they are searching for good reasons to ground their hope for a better world, and therefore they are desperately looking for 'soul food'. Churches cannot and should not leave them behind. Religious traditions and communities should be aware of their quests. What churches and youth ministries often want is fast growth. But fast answers aren't helpful to get to the heart of these slower, healthier questions.

When you're looking for 'soul food,' where do you go? Our contemporary culture looks for fast-food, which affects our 'soul food,' and we need to ask ourselves, "What are we offering?" We don't want fast-food answers. Jesus' story of the sower and seed illustrates the result of fast-food—the seed scattered on the shallow soil sprang up quickly, but then it quickly withered because it had no root (Matthew 13:3-9). Elements of liberation theology can help youth ministry to teach young people the tools to interpret their own precarious situations and act faithfully and correspondingly.[6]

5. Developing Theology for Youth Ministry

When theological constructions are debated in the discourse community of Christian youth ministers, it benefits youth ministry by providing an opportunity to develop and refine our theological language. One could say that every kind of theological position has been tested in youth work. Different perspectives in Christology, soteriology, and eschatology are dealt with in regard to teenagers' lives. Pastoral options are considered in the framework of practical theology, moral aspects are discussed in theological ethics. Congregational studies are used to describe and to improve youth churches and their relationship with the broader community. In this connection with the lives of adolescents and young adults, theology becomes refreshed and vital again.[7]

6. Youth Theology and Its Impact on Theology

The next logical step is the emergence of a specific, original youth theology. Young people not only devise their own churches, rituals, and morals, but they can also create their own theologies. Theology is in itself a way of living, a way of vision and discernment. In my mind, there is a huge resource of fresh theological thinking to be 'dis-covered' in regard to the way young people creatively deal with their ambivalent questions about God, the world, the other, and the self.[8]

CONCLUSION

A good research agenda should continuously be open for new developments and challenges. The international, ecumenical, and scholarly dimensions of IASYM remind its members of the work that still needs to be done. How is church reshaped when youth are in the picture? What happens with the church's 'intra' experience when youth are interacting with its 'extra' experience? How do they reveal the new meanings and intentions in the 'development of doctrine' (John Henry Newman)? How can young people help us to meet the deeper layer in education and youth work in a society which has another default—a market ideology? How can the vulnerability of young people open our eyes for the future of humankind?

These questions are open for further reflection. The presence of youth necessarily stimulates 'furthering the research, study, and teaching' of youth ministry. Hopefully this stimulus of IASYM as a global association can be expanded to you as a reader of this book as you work to reach the plural world of youth full of richness and opportunity. (You can learn more about IASYM at www.iasym.net.)

CHAPTER SIXTEEN

GETTING INVOLVED IN CROSS-CULTURAL YOUTH MINISTRY

AARON ARNOLD, RUSS CLINE, MEL ELLENWOOD

Leading youth ministry for the long term is difficult enough in your own culture—it can be even more treacherous in another. As part of this book project, we asked three North American leaders who have spent over 10 years leading youth in a particular country to share their insights for others who may have an interest.[1] Their advice is diverse and will provide a contrast for discussion.

SHOULD NORTH AMERICANS GO TO OTHER COUNTRIES TO LEAD YOUTH MINISTRY?

Aaron Arnold

In spite of my 13 years in international youth ministry leadership, I have wrestled with this question. I still don't have the perfect answer, but I know that if we are going to do cross-cultural youth ministry as North Americans, we need to be very intentional about the way we interact with youth ministry in a different culture.

Don't assume that no youth ministry exists before you get there. A first step upon arrival is to look for historic and current forms of youth ministry activity. I've seen the "no one is reaching out to youth in this region" attitude in people who came to Chile, and that arrogance immediately devalued any work being done by God's people who knew the language and culture well. It's important to recognize and respect previous efforts and to learn from and share your experiences with others in youth ministry as partners. Only through interdependent relationships can we hope to have any success in ministering to youth of a different culture.

As North Americans, we need to admit and believe that we can't always do it better. Too many times we go into a country with a "god-complex"[2] and believe that others aren't able to do youth ministry without us or as well as we can do it. We must repent of that ethnocentric superiority complex and trust that God has equipped them equally as he has us. I can attest to the incredible ability of non-North Americans to do youth ministry. We found that 70 percent of Chilean Christian adolescents felt as though the church responded to the majority of their needs, and 72 percent believed that their youth pastor or youth worker was prepared to help them in their life.[3]

Sustainable youth ministry rarely happens without partnering with the local church. God has chosen the church as the collective representative for kingdom work.[4] Not only is it viewed as disrespectful to circumvent the sacred institution that God ordained, but also doing so isn't practical. One of the consistent problems we've had to deal with in global youth ministry (and missions) is a lack of sustainability. Many global efforts have disappeared the moment both external funding and human resources ceased. The local church's long-term presence is the key to youth ministry with a lasting effect on the community where the young people live.[5]

Enter with an exit strategy. A missionary mentor of mine once told me, "I'm leaving someday, whether on a plane or in a coffin." If we're going to do youth ministry in another culture, we must have an end goal of working ourselves out of a job by equipping and empowering indigenous leadership. That can only happen if we let go of ministry and allow others to lead. Letting go of something that you created and in which you invested time and resources is not easy. However, it's a great way to foster effective long-term ministry.[6]

Effective global youth ministry has to be holistic. Many of the world's young people face serious issues such as poverty, HIV/AIDS, violence, and lack of education. Global youth ministry must understand that *all needs are spiritual*. When we become holistic, we'll see a transformation within the community where they live.

There are so many opportunities to reach out to youth and adolescents around the world. It is my desire that many accept God's call to go into all the world to minister alongside young people. However, we must be wise and cautious as we obey this calling. It is not our ability, experience, or country of residence that gives us the right to help; it's only our love for God and our desire to share with youth about how Jesus came so that they (and we) might have abundant life.

THE GROWING INFLUENCE OF YOUTH LEADER TRAINING IN LATIN AMERICA

Russ Cline

My first experience in youth leader training came just two months into my vocational ministry career. I attended a large North American youth ministry conference, took in every seminar, and purchased every resource that I could. I left encouraged, pumped up, and ready. Years later we moved to Ecuador to provide training, encouragement, and support to people doing youth ministry there.

As we connected with Ecuadorian youth workers, we became discouraged. The youth leaders, all volunteers, had received no training in youth ministry, received little support from their senior pastors, and were very discouraged. We learned that these were common realities at the time for youth workers throughout Latin America. The need was to a point of desperation. The youth ministry movement seemed stalled, and many youth leaders were leaving youth ministry.

Volunteer leaders had been placed in youth ministry leadership positions but never taught how to lead. Within a few short weeks or months, they quit . . . burned out and disillusioned.

But a revolution was beginning in Latin and South America. In the early '90s, various movements began throughout the region as organizations responded to the evident need for youth leader training. From Mexico to Argentina, Colombia and Costa Rica to Bolivia and Ecuador, a new wave of trained youth leaders rose up and swept across various churches and communities.

As we've discussed the various needs of those in global youth ministry, we've noticed that four basic needs seem to be coming up among leaders. [7]

Strategic Training

The loudest cry from youth leaders was for "applicable" training that fit their cultural context, was clearly useful (not outdated), and that would help them develop long-term ministry to young people.

Quality Resources

In Latin America there has been a surge of effective, indigenous resources in recent years. However, in many places resources that are culturally adapted, available, and affordable are difficult to find for global youth workers, if not impossible. North American publishing companies don't usually produce such resources, and not many volunteer youth workers have had the means to develop effective resources.

Relationship and Community

Youth leaders around the world want to know there are others with the same desire to impact young people. They desire to connect to the global youth ministry movement, to know they aren't alone.[8]

Mentoring and Coaching

Youth leaders want long-term relationships with people who will come alongside them for years, helping them to grow and develop over the long haul. They want to be a part of a movement with others who genuinely care about them and their development, not just those who use them for the benefit of a program or ministry.

Today, there are books written in Spanish, training seminars and conferences, youth ministry degree programs, online training and resources, and organizations and denominational leaders committed to reaching more than 270 million young people throughout Latin America. Things have obviously changed. The wave continues to move, and we're more convinced today than ever before that the key to reaching young people throughout Ecuador and Latin America lies first in the church and their effectiveness to teach the Word and impact their community, and second, in our ability to effectively identify, train, and equip leaders who will then pour into other leaders and young people.

OVERCOMING THE SILENT BARRIERS

Mel Ellenwood

Over the last decade, I've worked with many North Americans who've come to Central Europe to do cross-cultural youth ministry. Hundreds of youth workers try to be successful in their mission, but they often face three silent barriers: self-centeredness, an unwillingness to learn, and inauthentic community. All three are interconnected, and they can all be overcome by following Christ's incarnational approach.

Ethan came here from North America for an internship and with an open heart toward God's plan for his future. Ethan started each morning by consciously choosing to turn his rights and expectations over to God. His attitude resembled Christ's as he looked for ways to serve, and he was content to serve in ways that drew no attention to himself. **The silent barriers that Ethan had overcome were pride and self-centered expectations**.

Effectively cross-cultural ministry demands humility and a self-emptying process. Our model is found in the *kenosis* of Jesus Christ. (Philippians 2:3-8) If we are to be open to our new culture and learn and grow, we need to be open. I could tell Ethan had made a difference when he returned to the Czech Republic 10 years later and the people still remembered conversations they'd had with him and sought him out to spend time with him.

On the other hand, Samantha (another North American intern) was fun-loving and the life of the party. Initially the Czech students were drawn to her infectious personality. However, she constantly compared her host culture with her home culture, making sure everyone knew how much better it was at home. When she started to build deeper interpersonal relationships, she began to flounder. It was easy to talk about herself and be up front where she could "perform," but she struggled to engage with students who couldn't speak English well and who weren't part of the "outgoing and fun" group. Although she tried to be humble, the students saw right through it. She saw learning the language as a means to impress.

The second silent barrier is an unwillingness to learn from others. Cody is another North American who came to the field with a well-established philosophy of ministry and a lot of head knowledge about cross-cultural youth ministry. However, something about Cody's posture when engaging missionaries and Hungarian leaders made his "expertise" unpalatable. He assumed he had intercultural competency because of his education, and he was unwilling to admit he didn't know how to apply this knowledge practically. Because of his lack of cultural sensitivity, he appeared arrogant and unwilling to learn. His knowledge was of greater value to him than simply serving.

In contrast, Abigail joined her intern team with a zest for learning. She regularly asked cultural questions and listened respectfully to the answers. She wanted to learn everything she could. Her posture said, "I realize that everyone has something to teach me." It's no wonder her leaders found her a joy to work with because she was humble enough to receive correction. Abigail willingly allowed them to challenge her regarding areas of weakness in her life. She pushed past the fear of letting others discover her faults and allowed her teammates and leaders to openly engage those areas and call her to maturity.

This leads to the third silent barrier—an inability to live life with others in authentic community. Megan entered into her new culture unmotivated and indifferent. She built up a bubble of self-protection from anything and everyone that pressed into her comfort zone. Megan was fearful and saw every barrier as a wall to deter her, rather than a springboard to launch her into a new opportunity for growth.

She waited for everything to be perfect, unwilling to commit herself unless she could be guaranteed success.

But Alex immersed himself in the culture and worked hard to identify with the people around him. He entered into the lives of his students in order to fully experience the culture of their families, homes, schools, and social circles. He went *to* the people, meeting them where they were; and in turn, students wanted to come to the activities he'd planned for them. He simply embraced the differences between his home culture and his missional culture, knowing they would make him richer.

The Gospels are rife with examples of Christ's immersion in the communities of those around him—so much so that the Pharisees noticed his comfort in eating with tax collectors and "sinners" (Matthew 9:11-12).

Is God calling you to the "ends of the earth"? If so, empty yourself, be a learner, and enter into authentic community with others.

DISCUSSION QUESTIONS

1. What contrasts and similarities did you note among the three authors? What themes are important to them?
2. Who, from your experience, has entered a different culture in a way that overcame its barriers? How?
3. Youth leaders and students are moving in and out of different cultures all the time—whether through missions experiences abroad or simply reaching out to different groups at school or across the city. What are practical steps a ministry can take to disciple youth to overcome these barriers as they cross cultures?
4. What are some other ways that North Americans can show respect and trust in the ability of the indigenous people to do youth ministry?
5. What would another leader want to add? It would be a good exercise to locate a seasoned global youth ministry leader and ask him or her to share advice regarding crossing cultures and serving in global youth ministry.

ENDNOTES

INTRODUCTION

1. For more on Youth Ministry International, visit their Web site at http://www.ymionline.com.

CHAPTER ONE: THE YOUTH OF THE WORLD

1. Thanks to Dr. Dave Rahn, vice president of Youth for Christ USA, for championing these biblical values for youth ministry.

2. Herrera, L. (2006). What's new about youth? *Development and Change*, 37 (6), 1426.

3. Ashford, L., Clifton, D., & Kaneda, T. *The world's youth 2006*. Washington, DC: Population Reference Bureau.

4. Dr. Thomas Bergler at Huntington University (USA) has been instrumental in researching the economic power of American youth.

5. For simplicity's sake, *North America* is used in this book to designate the United States and Canada, though the term technically includes portions of Latin America and the Caribbean as well. We don't mean to ignore these other two important regions; indeed we acknowledge the great need to also hear the voices from Central America and the Caribbean. There simply aren't enough pages to include all that's going on in global youth ministry!

6. Curtain, R. (2004). Youth in Extreme Poverty: Dimensions and policy implications with particular focus on South East Asia. Paper for the National Institute for Governance. Melbourne, Australia. http://www.un.org/esa/socdev/unyin/workshops/curtain.pdf (accessed November 18, 2010).

7. Nilan, P., & Feixa, C. (2006). *Global youth?: Hybrid identities, plural worlds*. London: Routledge, p. ix.

8. Hurrelmann, K. (1994). *International handbook of adolescence*. Westport, CT: Greenwood Press, p. iv.

9. Miles, S. (2003). Young people in a globalizing world. *World Youth Report 2003: The Global Situation of Young People* (p. 291). Retrieved April 8, 2004, from http://www.un.org/esa/socdev/unyin/wyr03.htm.

10. Lartey, E. Y. Globalization, youth and the church: Views from Ghana. In Osmer, R. R. & Dean, K. C. (eds.). (2007). *Youth, religion and globalization*. Münster, Germany: LIT Verlag.

11. Erricker, C. (2008). In fifty years, who will be here?: Reflections on globalisation, migration and spiritual identity. *International Journal of Children's Spirituality, 13* (1), 15–26.

12. In particular, we note Andy Crouch's *Culture Making: Recovering Our Creative Calling* (InterVarsity Press 2008) and Alan Hirsch's *The Forgotten Ways: Reactivating the Missional Church* (Brazos Press, 2006).

13. Acts 10:43; Romans 10:9-10; Ephesians 2:8-9

14. Nsamenang, A. Bame. (2002). Adolescence in Sub-Saharan Africa. In Brown, B. Bradford, Larson, Reed W., & Saraswathi, T. S. (Eds.), *The world's youth: Adolescence in eight regions of the globe* (pp. 61-104). Cambridge, UK: Cambridge University Press, p. 63.

15. Luke 10:25-37

16. Various denominational and youth organizations, in coordination with Youth Specialties Canada and the Muskoka Woods Leadership Studio, recently completed a nationwide research project on the state of youth ministry in Canada (http://www.whatshappeningcanada.com/index.html).

17. To learn more about Amity Printing Company, visit http://www.amityprinting.com.

18. See David Livermore's *Serving With Eyes Wide Open: Doing Short-Term Missions with Cultural Intelligence* (Baker Books, 2006); Kara Powell, Terry Linhart, David Livermore, and Brad Griffin's article called "If We Send Them, They Will Grow . . . Maybe" in *The Journal of Student Ministries, 1* (6) (March/April 2007), 24–28; David Livermore's article called "Leave Your Baggage at Home: An Open Letter to Youth Workers Planning Short-Term Missions" in *YouthWorker Journal, 23* (2) (January/February 2007); Terry Linhart's article called "They Were So Alive!: The Spectacle Self and Youth Group Short-Term Mission Trips" in *Missiology, 4*, (2006), 451–462; and Terry Linhart's "Planting Seeds: The Curricular Hope for Short-Term Mission Experience in Youth Ministry" in *Christian Education Journal*, Series 3, 2 (2) (2005), 256–272.

CHAPTER TWO: YOUTH MINISTRY CHANGES MORE THAN YOU KNOW

1. For a description of this model, see Pete Ward's *Youthwork and the Mission of God* (SPCK, 1997). (*God at the Mall* is its American title.) He refers to it as "Inside-Out" youth ministry.

2. Davie, G. (1994). *Religion in Britain Since 1945: Believing Without Belonging.* Oxford, UK: Wiley-Blackwell, p. 53.

3. This statistic came from Peter Brierly of the Christian Research Association in his book *Reaching and Keeping Teenagers.*

4. For an example, see Pete Ward's *Youth Culture and the Gospel* (Zondervan, 1993).

5. Ward, P. (1997). *Youthwork and the mission of god.* London: Society for Promoting Christian Knowledge, chapter 2.

6. Warner, R. (1999). *21st century church: Why radical change cannot wait.* Eastbourne, UK: Kingsway Publications.

7. It is common for books describing the cultural shift to have lists that map the contours of modernity and postmodernity, contrasting the two. But the nuances of the lists can be quite different. See for example, *The Condition of Postmodernity: An Enquiry into the Origins of Cultural Change* (Blackwell Publishers, 1990) by David Harvey, *Threshold of the Future: Reforming the Church in the Post-Christian West* (SPCK, 1998) by Michael Riddell, and *Truth Is Stranger Than It Used to Be: Biblical Faith in a Postmodern Age* (IVP Academic, 1995) by Brian J. Walsh and J. Richard Middleton.

8. For a good development of this, see *Jesus in Disneyland: Religion in Postmodern Times* (Polity, 2000) by David Lyon.

9. Truth tends to be the postmodern theme that grabs most Christians' attention, as it's perceived to be the biggest threat. In *Texts Under Negotiation: The Bible and Postmodern Imagination* (SCM Press, 1993), Walter Brueggemann points out that it needn't be a threat—there are still limited options around the table.

10. In *Postmodern Culture and Youth Discipleship: Commitment or Looking Cool?* (Grove Books Ltd., 1998), Graham Cray says it's clear that consumerism is still alive and well. What *has* shifted is that identity is formed around consumption and taste, whereas in modernity it was tied up with production.

11. See, for example, Marshall McLuhan's *The Medium Is the Massage* (Gingko Press, 2001).

12. A good introduction to some of the themes of the new technological world is *Here Comes Everybody: The Power of Organizing Without Organizations* (Allen Lane, 2008) by Clay Shirky.

13. It's hard to pinpoint exactly where this surfaced. Pete Ward drew on it in *Youth Culture and the Gospel*. It was also a feature of papers being presented in the

early days of the International Association for the Study of Youth Ministry, such as Fuzz Kitto's "Shifting Paradigms of Youth Ministry" in the collection *The Church and Youth Ministry*.

14. Donovan, V. J. (1978). *Christianity rediscovered*. London: SCM Press, 1982.

15. Donovan, V.J., p. 30.

16. Roy Shelley made this poignant observation to me during a meal at one of the International Association for the Study of Youth Ministry (IASYM) gatherings.

17. Richard blogs at www.sundaypapers.org. If you select the category "Mission," you can read about his reflections on the journey so far.

18. See http.oxygen-online.org.

19. See www.saintlaurencereading.com.

20. This is the Anglican and Methodist term. (See www.freshexpressions.org.uk)

21. This term was used by Archbishop Rowan Williams in the introduction to the Church of England report *The Mission-Shaped Church*.

22. The designation "Ordained Pioneer Minister" is now recognized in the Church of England.

23. Newbigin, L. (1989). *The gospel in a pluralist society*. Grand Rapids, MI: Wm. B. Eerdmans, p. 141.

CHAPTER THREE: A WORLD OF IRISH YOUTH MINISTRY

1. See http://www.174trust.org.

2. Philip Orr is author of *Field of Bones* (2006 Dublin: Lilliput Press) and *The Road to the Somme*, (2008, Belfast: Blackstaff Press Ltd.). This summary is original to this book.

3. Graeme Thompson, youth development officer for the Presbyterian Church in Ireland, unpublished Ph.D. dissertation.

4. Central Statistics Office in Ireland, www.cso.ie/statistics.

5. Psalm 78:1-7

6. Hickford, A. (1998). *Essential youth: Why the church needs young people*. Eastbourne, UK: Kingsway Publications, p. 15.

7. It is helpful to note that Northern Ireland suffers from many forms of segregation, one of which is large-scale residential segregation. This continues to compound the problem of division between Protestants and Catholics. And as Ireland—North and South—in the new millennium "welcome" migrant workers from the former communist countries of Eastern Europe, a further layer of residential segregation is emerging. Former doctors, nurses, farm laborers, and shop workers huddle together in below-standard government or privately rented accommodations, often alienated and intimidated by locals.

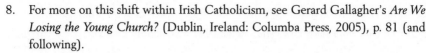
8. For more on this shift within Irish Catholicism, see Gerard Gallagher's *Are We Losing the Young Church?* (Dublin, Ireland: Columba Press, 2005), p. 81 (and following).

9. Borgman, D. (1998). *When kumbaya is not enough*. Peabody, MA: Hendrickson Publishers, p. 37.

10. This comes from a personal conversation with Michael Wylie, youth pastor of Carnmoney Presbyterian Church, Northern Ireland.

11. Beard, S. (2001). Foreword. In S. Stockman, *Walk on: The spiritual journey of U2* (p. vi). Peabody, MA: Relevant Books.

12. Mark 2:22

13. Jones, T. (2008). *The new Christians: Dispatches from the emergent frontier*. San Francisco: Jossey-Bass.

14. Gallagher, G. (2005), p. 55.

15. Minutes of the General Assembly of the Presbyterian Church in Ireland, June 2009, www.presbyterianireland.org/resources/assembly_archive.html.

16. Volf, M. (1996). *Exclusion and embrace: A theological exploration of identity, otherness, and reconciliation*. Nashville, TN: Abingdon Press.

17. Matthew 5:43ff

18. www.youthlink.org.uk

19. This phrase is my own construction and refers to the considerable impact of the prolific writings and media presence—in both Britain and Ireland—of Richard Dawkins, former professor of public understanding of science at Oxford University in England. His very popular book *The God Delusion* (2006) contends that a supernatural creator almost certainly does not exist. This book has made its way into UK schools and has given a new and bold confidence to those who wish to discredit Christianity (or any faith-based worldview).

20. Kenny, M. (2000). *Goodbye to Catholic Ireland*. Dublin, Ireland: New Island Books.

21. Report by Macauley Associates, June 2006, for Youthnet (www.youthnetni.org.uk).

CHAPTER FOUR: FROM APARTHEID TO SAAMHEID

1. Livermore, David. (2009). *Cultural Intelligence*. Grand Rapids, MI: Baker Academic, p. 12.

2. Yancey, G. E. (2003). *One body, one spirit: Principles of successful multiracial churches*. Downers Grove, IL: InterVarsity Press, p. 160.

CHAPTER FIVE: AFRICAN REALITIES FOR YOUTH MINISTRY

1. Scripture Union Africa, Report on Big Issues Research, 2008–2009.

2. From Faith to Action, report by Firelight Foundation, September 2009.

3. The First International Conference in Africa on Family Based Care for Children (held in Nairobi, Kenya Sept. 28–30, 2009) www.crin.org/docs/Draft%20 Programme%20text%5B1%5D.pdf.

4. Mutebe, J. (August 2007) "Making ministry to young people effective and meaningful." A research paper in partial fulfillment of the requirements for LEAD 670 – Field Research Project for the M.A. in Christian Leadership. Mukono, Uganda: Uganda Christian University.

5. Report on the Global AIDS Epidemic, UNAIDS (2008).

6. Nakakande, S. (2010, April 8) "It Is High Time You Got off the Network." *Daily Monitor*, 27 http://www.monitor.co.ug/Magazines/Health%20&%20Living/- /689846/894502/-/3c85uez/-/index.html.

7. Zakumumpa Henry. (2010, March 14). Africa is new battleground for global investors. Saturday Monitor. http://www.monitor.co.ug/OpEd/Commentary/ -/689364/884568/-/ah14lcz/-/index.html (accessed November 20, 2010).

8. You can find the 1996 report at http://www.see-educoop.net/education_in/ pdf/15_62.pdf.

CHAPTER SEVEN: THE NEW LATIN AMERICA

1. For more, see Heaney, S. E. (2008). *Contextual theology for Latin America: Liberation themes in evangelical perspective*. Eugene, OR: Wipf & Stock Publishers.

2. Patterson, Malco. Las diez puertas al éxito, edición adolescentes. Revista Continente Nuevo. Asociación Evangelística Luis Palau. Guatemala. pp. 22-25, 2004.

3. Sweet, L. (1999). *AquaChurch: Essential leadership arts for piloting your church in today's fluid culture*. Loveland, CO: Group Publishing, p. 167.

SIDEBAR: LATIN AMERICAN YOUTH MINISTRY

4. Internet World Stats, Miniwatts Marketing Group, December 2009.

5. Internet World Stats, Miniwatts Marketing Group, June 2010, http://www. internetworldstats.com/stats10.htm.

6. As of 2005, 15-to-24-year-olds made up 16.9 percent of the population in Latin America and the Caribbean (http://www.un.org/esa/socdev/unyin/qanda. htm), slightly more than Africa (16.4 percent).

CHAPTER EIGHT: WE LIVE IN A PERIOD WHERE YOUNG PEOPLE ACTIVELY SEEK SPIRITUAL TRUTH—YEAH RIGHT . . .

1. The great majority (more than 80 percent) of citizens in the Nordic countries of Denmark, Sweden, Norway, and Finland belong to the Lutheran Church, which is supported by the government (although the models differ from

country to country). The "free churches" consist of Baptists, Methodists, Pentecostals, and Catholics.

SPOTLIGHT: NORWAY: A CHURCH OF MANY MEMBERS BUT WITH EMPTY PEWS

2. Church of Norway, Basics and statistics, http://www.kirken.no/english/engelsk. cfm?artid=5276 (accessed September 24, 2009).

3. Davie, G. (2007). Vicarious religion: A methodological challenge. In Nancy T. Ammerman, *Everyday religion: Observing modern religious lives* (pp. 21–36). New York: Oxford University Press, p. 22.

4. All the quotations are from Morten Holmqvist's research published in the book *Jeg tror jeg er lykkelig . . . Ung tro og hverdag* (Kloster Forlag, 2007). They are my translations into English.

CHAPTER NINE: CONFESSIONS FROM A TRANSITIONAL COUNTRY

1. http://en.wikipedia.org/wiki/Heraclitus (accessed September 17, 2009).

2. Bosch, D. J. (2005). *Transforming mission: Paradigm shifts in theology of mission*. Maryknoll, NY: Orbis Books, p. 4.

CHAPTER TEN: MINISTRY TO THE DEAF: YOUTH MINISTRY IN AUSTRALIA IN THE NEW MILLENNIUM

1. See Acts 17:22ff where Paul equates the God of Christianity to the statue of the "unknown god" in Athens.

2. Matthew 28:16-20.

3. McBrien, R.P. (1988). *Ministry: A theological, pastoral handbook*. San Francisco: Harper & Row, p. 12.

4. See Dominian, J. (2004). *Living love*. London: Darton, Longman and Todd, pp. 1-4; Smith, A. B. (2004). *The God shift*. Dublin, Ireland: Liffey Press.

5. McBrien, R. (1981). *Catholicism*. San Francisco: Harper, p. 1057.

6. McQuillan, P. (2004). Youth spirituality, a reality in search of expression. *Journal of Youth and Theology, 3* (2).

7. Stolz, J. (2008) A silent battle: Theorising the effects of competition between churches and secular institutions. *Working Papers, Observatoire des religions en Suisse (ORS)*, Universite de Lausanne.

8. Hendry, J. (2003). *Understanding Japanese society*, (3rd ed.), New York: Routledge.

9. Hay, D. (2006). *Something there: The biology of the human spirit*. London: Darton, Longman and Todd.

10. Rankin, P. (2006). *Buried spirituality*. Wiltshire, U.K.: Sarum College Press.

11. See Tacey, D. (2003). *The spirituality revolution*. Sydney: Harper Collins.

12. Bouma, G. (2006). *Australian soul: Religion and spirituality in the twenty-first century*. Port Melbourne, Vic, Australia: Cambridge University Press, pp. 1–30.

13. Our two-semester course has been developed to provide an understanding of the spirituality of young people for those ministering to (or training to minister to) youth. It assists students to understand that, despite the marginalisation of religious institutions in mainstream Australian society—particularly among youth—the spiritual search is still a reality. It assists students to understand the challenges facing both young people and those who minister to them because of their relationship with this secular culture and their relationship with the self through their hopes and aspirations. In this way the course assists potential and active youth ministers to reflect on their professional practices and how they can walk beside young people.

14. McQuillan, P. (2009). Children of the deaf: the challenge of expressing spirituality in western society. In P. McQuillan (Ed.), *Encountering the mystery: Discovering God with young people in a secular world*. Haverhill, Essex, UK: YTC Press.

15. Mason, M., Webber, R., Singleton, A., & Hughes, P. (2006). Spirit of Generation Y: Final report of a three year study. Christian Research Association, www.cra.org.au.

16. Hay, D. (2007). Why is religion so difficult for westerners? In D. Hay, *Something there: The biology of the human spirit* (chapter 9). Philadelphia, PA: Templeton Foundation Press.

17. Hay, D., & Nye, R. (1998). *The spirit of the child*. London: Harper Collins Religious.

18. See Dev Mukherjee, *Socio-economic status and school system enrollments*. Erskineville, NSW: Australian Centre for Equity through Education. July 1999. http://www.aeufederal.org.au/Publications/DMukherjeepaper.pdf (accessed September 25, 2009).

19. Bouma, G. (2006).

20. Berger P.L. (1999) *The desecularisation of the world: A global overview.* In P. Berger (Ed.), *The desecularisation of the world: resurgent religion and world politics* (pp. 1-18).

21. Bouma, G. (2006), p. 5.

22. Bouma, G. (2006), p. 2.

23. There are numerous examples of this. They range from the Australian government and general public's response to the December 2004 tsunami that devastated the coasts of Sumatra, India, Burma, and parts of Malaysia to local

disasters such as the Victorian Bushfires of early 2009. The Australian government committed $1 billion to reconstruction in the wake of the tsunami, with public funds through various agencies raising a further $500 million. The Victorian Bushfire appeal raised $375 million through the Red Cross alone, with numerous additional appeals adding to these funds.

24. Tacey, D. (2003).

25. This opinion is also shared by Ronald Rolheiser. See Rolheiser, R. (1998). *Seeking spirituality*. London: Hodder & Stoughton (especially chapter 3, The non-negotiable essentials).

26. Hughes, P. (2007). *Putting life together: Findings from Australian youth spirituality research*. Melbourne, Australia: Fairfield Press, p. 70.

27. This question was the researchers' way of seeking a response to the traditional Christian theology of humanity being both body and soul, a concept derived from a Greek rather than Hebrew view of the world.

28. Hughes, P. (2007), p. 166ff.

29. McQuillan, P. & Marx, E. (2007) From original vision to world vision: A comparison of the level of recognition and reporting of religious experience of two groups of catholic high schools students. *Journal of Youth and Theology*, 6(2).

30. Hay, D. (1987). *Exploring inner space: Is God still possible in the twentieth century?* Oxford, UK: A.R. Mowbray.

31. McQuillan, P. (2009).

32. Rankin, P. (2006).

33. Bentley, P., Hughes, P. J. (1998). *Australian life and the Christian faith*. Kew, Vic: Christian Research Association.

34. In late 2009, youth unemployment in Australia was 9.7 percent compared to an overall rate of 6 percent, according to www.smartcompany.com.au and www.abs.gov.au (accessed September 24, 2009).

35. Inayatullah, S. (2002). Youth dissent: Multiple perspectives on youth futures. In J. Gidley & S. Inayatullah (Eds.), *Youth futures: Comparative research and transformative visions* (pp. 19-30). Westport, CT: Praeger Publishers.

36. In 1961, 40 percent of Australians claimed to attend church at least monthly; in 1980, it was down to 24 percent; by 1999, down to 20 percent. New Zealand figures are similar. In Britain church attendance declined from 18 to 7.5 percent, and in Canada from 55 to 22 percent. Even in the United States, often seen as being immune from these trends, it has fallen from 49 percent in 1958 to 40 percent in 2000. (See Rowland Crowcher et al. Does the Australian church have a future? (posted January 5, 2003), http://jmm.aaa.net.au/articles/8517.htm (accessed September 25, 2009).)

37. Mason, et al. (2006).

38. See Francis, L. J. & Kaldor, P. (March 2002). The relationship between psychological well-being and Christian faith and practice in an Australian population sample. *Journal for the Scientific Study of Religion, 41*(1), 179–184.

39. Mason, et al. (2006).

40. Hughes, P. (2007).

41. Dixon, R. (October 2002). Mass attendance trends among Australian Catholics: A significant challenge for the Catholic Church, *South Pacific Journal of Mission Studies*.

42. Australian Bureau of Statistics. (2006, January 20). Chapter 12—Culture and recreation: Religious affiliation. Year book Australia, 2006. http://www.abs.gov.au/AUSSTATS/abs@.nsf/bb8db737e2af84b8ca2571780015701e/bfdda1ca50 6d6cfaca2570de0014496e!OpenDocument (accessed September 25, 2009).

43. National Catholic Education Commission. National Catholic Education Commission annual report 2007. Canberra City ACT, Australia, 28. http://www.ncec.catholic.edu.au/index.php?option=com_docman&task=cat_view&gid=46&Itemid=53 (accessed November 21, 2010).

44. McQuillan, P. (November 2004). Youth spirituality: A reality in search of expression. *Journal of Youth and Theology*.

45. Berger, P., Davie. G, & Fokes. F. (2008). *Religious America, secular Europe?: A theme and variations.* Aldershot, Hampshire, England: Ashgate Publishing.

46. Stolz, J. (2008).

47. Berger, P. L. (1999).

48. Hay, D. (1987).

49. McQuillan, P. (2004).

50. Frost, M. & Hirsch, A. (2003). *The shaping of things to come: Innovation and mission for the 21st-century church.* Erina, NSW, Australia: Strand Publishing.

51. Smith, A. B. (2004). *The God shift.* Dublin, Ireland: Liffey Press, p. 224ff.

52. Spong, J. S. (1999). *Why Christianity must change or die: A bishop speaks to believers in exile.* Grand Rapids, MI: HarperCollins, p. 226ff.

53. Radcliffe, T. (2005). *What is the point of being a Christian?* London: Burns & Oats, p. 208ff.

54. Smith, A. B. (2004), p. 3.

55. In 2009, the contribution made to population growth by net overseas migration (63.4 percent) was higher than that of natural increase (36.6 percent). Although all states and territories recorded positive population growth over the 12 months ending March 31, 2009, there were significant variations among states showing a great deal of interstate migration as well. Western Australia recorded the fastest growth rate (3.1 percent) followed by Queensland (2.6 percent), the Northern Territory (2.2 percent), Victoria (2.1 percent), the Australian Capital

Territory (1.8 percent), New South Wales (1.6 percent), South Australia (1.2 percent), and Tasmania (1.0 percent).

56. Bouma, G. (2006).

SIDEBAR: AUSTRALIA—SCHOOL CHAPLAINCY: TAKING YOUTH MINISTRY OUTSIDE THE CHURCH

57. The scheme was to assist in the initial establishment of school chaplains, providing A$165 million over three years. Grants of up to a $20,000 per annum for three years were available to government and non-government schools to fund a two-days-per-week position of a chaplain employed through a non-government religious organisation (Australian Government National School Chaplaincy Program: www.deewr.gov.au/Schooling/NationalSchoolChaplaincy Program/Pages/nscp_frequently_asked.aspx).

58. In 2007 alone, 2,630 schools (primary and secondary government and non-government) successfully applied for funding grants for new appointments. In 2008, chaplains were employed in almost 2,000 of the 5,905 government schools nationally (primary and secondary). That represents 34 percent of schools in total, although 65 percent are still without an official chaplain.

59. A September 2009 Edith Cowan University report on "The Effectiveness of Chaplaincy" (by Philip Hughes and Margaret Sims) concluded: "According to the principals, 97 percent of chaplains have been effective in performing the major role of providing pastoral care for students. . . . The surveys and case studies have shown that chaplaincy is having a positive impact on students, staff, families, and schools, by providing pastoral care, support and guidance. Further, it is having a positive impact on the development of young people's interpersonal relationships and on the moral foundations of these, and on the development of moral values and, to a lesser extent, a commitment to social justice." The report recommended continuation of the original 2006 scheme, and the newly elected federal government did so.

60. Hughes, P. (2007). *Putting life together*. Christian Research Association. Australia: Fairfield Press, p. 151.

61. Australian Government Web site (www.abs.gov.au).

62. In Australia the separation of church and state is interpreted less narrowly than it is in the United States and other countries.

63. Involvement of adults in supporting students' voluntary Christian activities outside of class time—as well as groups for Bible study, outreach, and prayer—has always been assured.

64. Smith, C. (2005). *Soul searching: The religious and spiritual lives of American teenagers*; and The Australian spirit of Generation Y study (March 2006) reported in *Pointers, The Journal of Christian Research Association of Australia*.

65. *Pointers, The Journal of Christian Research Association of Australia*, March 2006.

66. Matthew 9:10-13; Luke 15:1-2

67. Joseph in serving Pharaoh in Egypt and Daniel serving under successive kings in Babylon are biblical models of leading through influence. Their demonstrated character and competence resulted in delegated authority, opportunity, and trust.

68. Bellamy, J., Mou, S., & Castle, K. (2004). Social influences on faith development. NCLS Research Occasional Paper 5, 30.

69. Hughes, P. (2007), p. 66.

70. Hughes, P. (2007). About 49 percent said they would 'definitely' try to work it out themselves, 31 percent would go to friends, 26 percent would go to parents (or family), 16 percent would go to prayer, 8 percent would go to an adult friend, 2 percent would go to a teacher, 2 percent a school counselor, and 2 percent to a chaplain.

CHAPTER ELEVEN: THE TEMPORARILY PARENTLESS GENERATION

1. My thanks to the following Southeast Asian and Filipino youth ministry leaders and OFWs for their participation and assistance: Ronald Astillero, Rudolph John Babar, Marvin Vincent Cayabyab, Satkhokai Chongloi, Bopha Pen Cobarrubias, Preciosio James Deposa, Jeanil Espina, Jean Gerard Galang, Sheree Go, Arnel Guinto, Mary Perpetua Bernadette Herradura, Dened Ili, Paul Kelly, Wirot Khwanthong, Irene Jocelyn Lardizabal, Alvin Lim, Margery Maderse, Ronald Molmisa, Laurence Mumar, Maribel Nebab, Rigel Oro, Dorothy Reyes, Hazel Hontiveros Russell, Samuel Sinkiat, Edwin Siva, Jr., Michelle Que, Joel Tardo, Lal Pan Thar, Aimee Tolentino, Randolph Velasquez, and Maria Zarla Yap.

2. *Pagtutuli* (or circumcision) is an important rite of passage for Filipino boys, usually done between the ages of 10 and 13. In many towns and rural areas (even among the urban poor), *pagtutuli* is a community event where preteen boys are gathered together in a common area and circumcised by a community elder or medicine man.

3. Since then Filipinos have been working all over the world as household service workers, waiters and bartenders, chair workers and cleaners, professional nurses, laborers, general helpers, electrical wiremen, welders, flame-cutters, building caretakers, caregivers, performing artists, IT-related workers, administrators and managers, clerical workers, agricultural workers, professional workers, sales workers, production workers, and service workers (POEA, 2008).

4. Aquino (2002) states that "one out of every four families is handicapped by the absence of one (17%) or both (8%) parents." (115)

5. Divorce is illegal in the Philippines, the only country in the world (other than Vatican City) with such a law.

6. "The continent of Asia is home to two-thirds of the world's people—and almost two-thirds of the world's poor." Retrieved October 1, 2010, from Poverty in underdeveloped countries—The poorest of the poor—Asia: The largest and most populous continent (http://www.libraryindex.com/pages/2669/Poverty-in-Underdeveloped-Countries-Poorest-Poor-ASIA-LARGEST-MOST-POPULOUS-CONTINENT.html#ixzz11PLLmXif).

7. The dispersion of the Filipinos.

8. Collas-Monsod, S. (2002). Poverty and its distortion of youth development. In *The changing face of the Filipino: A Salesian tribute to the youth of the Philippines* (pp. 198–207). Makati City, Philippines: Salesian Socity of Don Bosco.

9. $16.4 billion in 2008, as reported on the ABS-CBN News Web site (http://www.abs-cbnnews.com/business/02/16/09/ofw-remittances-hit-164-b-2008).

10. In many courts around the country, infidelity is becoming the number-one grounds for annulment and legal separation.

11. Sto. Tomas (2002). Overseas employment and its social impact on the youth. In *The changing face of the Filipino: A Salesian tribute to the youth of the Philippines* (pp. 165-175). Makati City, Philippines: Salesian Society of Don Bosco.

12. Coronel, F. K. and Unterreiner, F. (2007). *Increasing the impact of remittances on children's rights: Philippines paper*, p. 15. Retrieved on April 19, 2010 from http://www.unicef.org/policyanalysis/files/increasing_the_impact_of_remittances_on_childrens_rights_pdf.

13. Including that of gender identity. (See Belen T. G. Medina, *The Filipino family*. Quezon City, Philippines: University of the Philippines Press, 2001.)

14. This is not an exaggeration. Filipinos are very sentimental toward holidays and special events in one's life; they are to be celebrated by the entire family. Missing such events is seen almost as a mortal sin.

15. See Coronel, F. K. & Unterreiner, F. (2007), p. 14.

16. Dr. Len Kageler, Nyack (New York) College, conducted a global survey and asked me to conduct the survey of Filipino youth workers.

17. One of the fastest-growing campus youth ministries—if not the fastest—is Victory Christian Fellowship. It started as a ministry among students in Manila's university belt and has evolved into a denomination: Every Nation.

18. Some of our youth studies alumni at Alliance Graduate School, as well as other youth workers, have been tapped by Christian publishers to write church and Christian school curricula, devotionals, and other materials.

19. A tall grass that burns quickly and brightly—but just as quickly burns out.

20. Spanish for *tomorrow*. This trait is one of the residual effects of 300-plus years under Spanish rule.

21. Population Reference Bureau. (2006). *The World's Youth 2006 Data Sheet*. Washington, D.C.: Population Reference Bureau. http://www.prb.org/pdf06/WorldsYouth2006DataSheet.pdf (accessed November 22, 2010).

22. Roman Catholics make up 81 to 85 percent of the Philippine population.

23. Due to American movies and songs, many Asian youth are "coconut" or "banana" kids, even in their own countries: Brown or yellow on the outside, white on the inside. They look Asian, but they think like Westerners.

24. Thanks to Japanese manga and anime, Asian youth are adopting the hairstyles of their comic (or animated cartoon) heroes and heroines. Trend-setting Japan is also on the forefront of extreme youth fashion.

25. Korean's telenovelas or TV series (koreanovelas) and popular songs have invaded popular youth culture. Asian youth are learning and speaking Korean as a third language. (Their own national language and English are their first and second languages.)

26. China's one-child policy has led to this "six-pocket syndrome" where Chinese kids have financial resources from their parents and both sets of grandparents.

27. The majority of Filipino households don't have computers or Internet access, so youth frequent Internet cafes.

28. Asian Institute of Journalism and Communication. (2009). *Survey on Internet access and use by Filipino schoolchildren: Final report (summary of nationwide findings)*, p. 18. Commissioned by UNICEF. Retrieved October 9, 2010, from http://www.aijc.com.ph/survey_internet_access.pdf.

29. Young boys may perform sexual favors for homosexuals for money. (See "Kara David investigates online gaming addiction among Filipinos on I-Witness." (February 15, 2010). Retrieved October 9, 2010, from http://www.starmometer.com/2010/02/15/kara-david-investigates-online-gaming-addiction-among-filipinos-on-i-witness.

30. A Filipino colloquial term for *cosmetics bag*, although *kikay* itself means a girl who is "cute," "sassy," or particular about her appearance.

31. A man who is particular about his appearance and fashion (a trait sometimes attributed to homosexuals) but is not a homosexual.

32. Martin, Phillip. Why white skin is all the rage in Asia: From pills to lasers to cream, what's fueling the boom in skin-whitening procedures across the continent? *Global Post*. (November 25, 2009). Retrieved October 10, 2010, from http://www.globalpost.com/dispatch/china-and-its-neighbors/091123/asia-white-skin-treatments-risks.

33. There are approximately 11.6 million out-of-school youths in the Philippines. (See *The reporter: News, events, celebrities and information*. 11.6 M Filipinos are out of school (OSY rate in the Philippines). Posted June 15, 2008. Retrieved October 8, 2010, from http://www.jessie-simbulan.com/philippines/116m-filipinos-are-out-of-school-osy-rate-in-the-philippines.

34. Filipinos (especially youth) send 18 million text messages in a day. (See Philippines: SMS! SMS! Filipino mobile 'texting' culture—Zpryme. Posted April 16, 2008. Retrieved October 10, 2010, from http://zpryme.com/news-room/philippines-sms-sms-filipino-mobile-texting-culture-zpryme.html.

35. Asian Institute of Journalism and Communication. (2009).

36. Rizal, J. (1962). *Rizal's poems (centennial edition)*. Manila: Jose Rizal National Centennial Commission, p. 15.

CHAPTER TWELVE: WHAT DOES YOUTH MINISTRY LOOK LIKE IN ASIA?

1. Population Reference Bureau. (2006). *The World's Youth 2006 Data Sheet*. Washington, D.C.: Population Reference Bureau. http://www.prb.org/pdf06/WorldsYouth2006DataSheet.pdf (accessed November 22, 2010).

2. Population data from Central Intelligence Agency's *The World Factbook*. https://www.cia.gov/library/publications/the-world-factbook/.

3. Some say the origin of this proverb is Chinese (血浓于水), but it first appeared in print in Germany in the 12th century.

SPOTLIGHT: JAPANESE YOUTH ARE THE CHURCH

4. See Kageyama, T. et al. "Mental health research on the ways of youth suicide prevention." Institute of Mental Health Suicide Prevention Research Centers for Health Research. http://ikiru.ncnp.go.jp/ikiru-hp/english.html.

5. Word of Life Publishing Company Journal of Business (2007, Dec. 17). "Almost half of the church has 'a sense of stagnation': See the truth of the Church of contemporary Japan." http://jpnews.org/pc/modules/xfsection/article.php?articleid=1449 (accessed December 17, 2007).

6. "Cram school, also referred as supplementary education or tutorials, is a kind of private school that provides highly organized lessons conducted after regular school hours and on weekends." (http://wik.ed.uiuc.edu/index.php/Cram_school)

7. A pseudonym.

SIDEBAR: KOREAN YOUTH MINISTRY

8.   Lee, K. (1984). *A new history of Korea*. (E. W. Wagner, Trans.). Cambridge, MA: Harvard University Press.

9.   Tokunaga, P. (1998). Pressure, perfectionism and performance. In Yep, J., Cha, P., Cho Van Riesen, S., Jao, G., & Tokunaga, P. (Eds), *Following Jesus without dishonoring your parents: Asian American discipleship*. Downers Grove, IL: InterVarsity Press.

10. Weinberg, M. (1997). *Asian-American education: Historical background and current realities*. Mahwah, NJ: Lawrence Erlbaum Associates.

CHAPTER THIRTEEN: BACK TO THE FUTURE: LOOKING AHEAD AND BEYOND

1.   This chapter was presented as a paper on youth ministry at the All-India Congress on Churches in Mission (AICOCIM) held at Hyderabad in October 2009.

2.   UNICEF. (March 2010) India: Statistics. http://www.unicef.org/infobycountry/india_statistics.html (accessed March 24, 2010).

3.   The World Bank. EdStats (2007). Country Snapshot: India. http://web.worldbank.org/WBSITE/EXTERNAL/TOPICS/EXTEDUCATION/EXTDATASTATISTICS/EXTEDSTATS/0,,menuPK:3232818~pagePK:64168427~piPK:64168435~theSitePK:3232764,00.html (accessed March 24, 2010).

4.   Ganguly, S., (2008, October 15). Tide of intolerance. *Newsweek*, http://www.newsweek.com/id/164081 (accessed March 24, 2010).

5.   To learn more about this group, see http://www.hindutva.org.

6.   For more on this BAM model, see C. Neal Johnson and Steve Rundle, *Business as mission: A comprehensive guide to theory and practice*. Downers Grove, IL: InterVarsity Press, 2010. Also, the Lausanne Movement's Web page at http://www.lausanne.org/issue-business-as-mission/overview.html). Or J. Maxwell, The mission of business. *Christianity Today*, *51*(11), (2007), http://www.christianitytoday.com/ct/2007/november/24.24.html (accessed March 26, 2010).

7.   Along the lines of the National Network of Youth Ministries (NNYM) model, U.S.A. (http://www.nnym.net).

8.   Adapted from George Barna's *4/14 Window* document.

CHAPTER FOURTEEN: GOD VERSUS GLITZ: GLOBALIZATION, YOUTH, AND THE CHURCH IN THE UNITED STATES

1.   This chapter is an adapted version from a previously published chapter, "God Versus Glitz: Globalization Youth and the Church in the United States," (pp.

87–123) in Osmer, R. R., and K. C. Dean. eds. *Youth, Religion and Globalization.* Münster, Germany: LIT Verlag, 2007.

2. Ellison II, G. C. (2001, December 21). A broken home? St. James United Methodist Church Youth Family and the impact of globalization. Technical paper, 1.

3. The *Saturday Night Live* character, notes researcher Greg Ellison, provides a more-than-accidental analogy to the ministry Bill Johnson undertakes as the unordained youth pastor at St. James. On the TV show, Mr. Bill would get smashed, run over, dropped, or meet some other unfortunate end. And just before the disaster, someone would yell, "Oh no, Mr. Bill!" Even though Mr. Bill was annihilated, he endured the pain and always came back for more in the following weeks. "So, too" the youth pastor.

4. Cited by Ellison II, G. C. (2001), p. 5.

5. Baughman, M. L. (2001, December 20). Mission year: Making neighbors in a global society: A case study of mission year. Technical paper, 1.

6. http://www.missionyear.org

7. Cited by Baughman, M. L. (2001), 11.

8. Baughman, M. (2001), 11.

9. Cited by Baughman, M. L. (2001), 7–8.

10. Baughman, M. L. (2001), 6.

11. Cravy, D. (2000, May 1). Walking the edge: A profile of high school youth ministry at University Presbyterian Church, Seattle. Technical paper, 2.

12. Cited by Cravy, D. (2000), 3.

13. Cravy, D. (2000), II, 56.

14. Cravy, D. (2000), 5.

CHAPTER FIFTEEN: YOUTH, CULTURE, AND THEOLOGY IN PLURAL: PRESENTING THE WORK OF THE IASYM

1. There have been regional conferences in Asia, Africa, and Europe. More intensive cooperation with the North American Association for Youth Ministry Educators (http://www.aymeducators.org) has been realized since the Louisville conference in 2009.

2. Ward, P. (2008). *Participation and Mediation: A Practical Theology for the Liquid Church.* London: SCM Press.

3. The association has grown under the leadership of Dr. Pete Ward (King's College, London, UK), Dr. Malan Nel (University of Pretoria, South Africa), Dr. Steve Griffiths (Centre for Youth Ministry, Cambridge, UK), and Dr. Bert Roebben (Dortmund University, Germany), who have all served as chairs of the organization.

4. Roebben, B. (2009). *Seeking sense in the city: European perspectives on religious education*. Münster/Hamburg/London: LIT Verlag, pp. 187–200.

5. Davie, G. (2007). Vicarious religion: A methodological challenge. In Nancy T. Ammerman (Ed.), *Everyday religion: Observing modern religious lives*. New York: Oxford University Press, pp. 21–36.

6. White, D. (2005). *Practicing discernment with youth: A transformative youth ministry approach*. Cleveland, OH: Pilgrim Press.

7. Dean, K.C. (2004). *Practicing passion: Youth and the quest for a passionate church*. Grand Rapids, MI: Wm. B. Eerdmans.

8. Roebben, B. (2009), pp. 201–231.

CHAPTER SIXTEEN: GETTING INVOLVED IN CROSS-CULTURAL YOUTH MINISTRY

1. Numerous organizations (e.g. Global Youth Ministry, Greater Europe Mission, International Teams and Youth With a Mission) provide support for interested individuals while others (e.g. Global Youth Initiative, Josiah Venture, Youth Ministry International, and Youthworld) have specific global youth ministry programs. Add in the many denominationally-tied initiatives and the new and growing organizations (e.g. Global Youth Ministry Network and YouthHope), and you can readily see the growth in global youth ministry.

2. Corbett, S., & Fikkert, B. (2009). *When helping hurts: How to alleviate poverty without hurting the poor . . . and yourself*. Chicago: Moody Publishers.

3. Arnold, A. (2008). *Inside the lives of Chilean Christian adolescents: Beliefs, practices and perceptions*. Thesis. Huntington (IN) University.

4. Ephesians 3:10, "His intent was that now, through the church, the manifold wisdom of God should be made known to the rulers and authorities in the heavenly realms."

5. Boyd, S. *In the thick of it*. Report by Tearfund. (Posted July 19, 2009) http://www.tearfund.org/News/Press+releases/In+the+Thick+of+It.htm (accessed September 24, 2009).

6. This is also reflective of Paul's apostolic strategy.

7. Cline, R. (2002). *Four needs of the global youth worker*. Quito, Ecuador: Leader Mundial.

8. This would be a great focus for graduate-level research on global youth ministry: *What role does this "global connectivity" play in the lives of local youth workers in various contexts?*

Share Your Thoughts

With the Author: Your comments will be forwarded to
the author when you send them to *zauthor@zondervan.com*.

With Zondervan: Submit your review of this book
by writing to *zreview@zondervan.com*.

Free Online Resources at

www.zondervan.com

Zondervan AuthorTracker: Be notified whenever your favorite
authors publish new books, go on tour, or post an update
about what's happening in their lives at www.zondervan.com/
authortracker.

Daily Bible Verses and Devotions: Enrich your life with daily
Bible verses or devotions that help you start every morning
focused on God. Visit www.zondervan.com/newsletters.

Free Email Publications: Sign up for newsletters on Christian
living, academic resources, church ministry, fiction, children's
resources, and more. Visit www.zondervan.com/newsletters.

Zondervan Bible Search: Find and compare Bible passages in
a variety of translations at www.zondervanbiblesearch.com.

Other Benefits: Register yourself to receive online benefits
like coupons and special offers, or to participate in research.

ZONDERVAN®

ZONDERVAN.com/
AUTHORTRACKER
follow your favorite authors

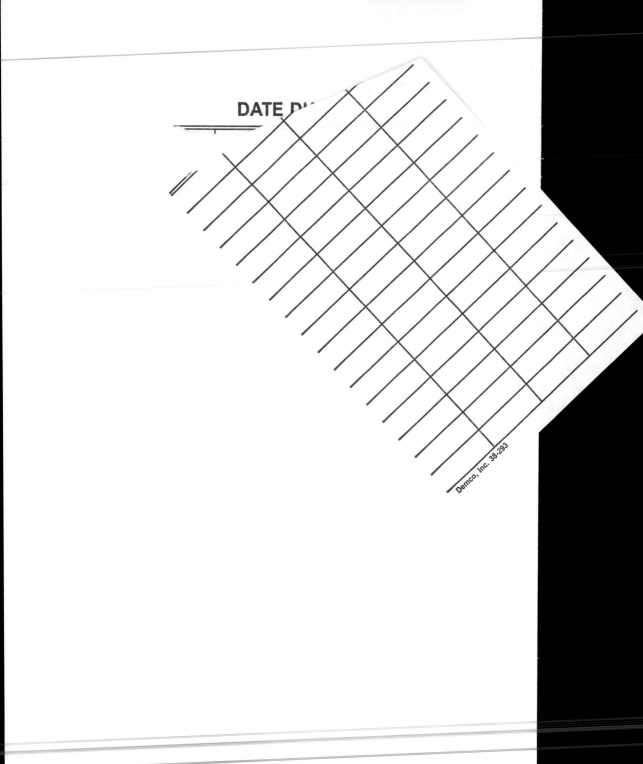

DATE DUE

Demco, Inc. 38-293